Sixty Million Acres

Sixty Million Acres

American Veterans and the Public Lands before the Civil War

James W. Oberly

THE KENT STATE UNIVERSITY PRESS
Kent, Ohio, and London, England

Library of Congress Catalog Card Number 90–4482
ISBN 0–87338–421–0
Manufactured in the United States of America

Library of Congress Cataloging-in-Publication Data

Oberly, James Warren, 1954–
Sixty million acres : American veterans and the public lands before the Civil War / James W. Oberly.
p. cm.
Includes bibliographical references (p.).
ISBN 0–87338–421–0 (alk. paper) ∞
1. United States—Public lands—History—19th century.
2. Bounties, Military—United States—History—19th century.
3. Land grants—United States—History—19th century. 4. Land titles—United States—History—19th century. 5. United States—Armed Forces—Recruiting, enlistment, etc.—War with Mexico, 1845–1848. 6. Veterans—United States—History—19th century.
I. Title.
HD240.024 1990 90–4482
333.1′6—dc20
CIP

Part of this work appeared in *Government Publications Review* 14 (1987): 287–94, and is reprinted with permission of Permagon Press, Inc.

British Library Cataloging-in-Publication data are available.

To Louise,
and to Nicholas
and William

Contents

Illustrations

Tables

Acknowledgments

This study has been many years in the making since it began in graduate seminars at the University of Rochester under Stanley Engerman and Mary Young. Those scholars have offered consistent encouragement and guidance as this book took shape. Many colleagues in economic history and in frontier history read all or portions of this work and offered helpful criticism and suggestions. From an early point in my research, Robert Swierenga gave support and advice, and he has gone out of his way to share his knowledge about this topic with me. I deeply appreciate the time that the following people spent in helping me improve my work: Allan Bogue, Stuart Bruchey, Henry Cohen, Margaret Cook, Virginius Dabney, Kay Domine, Mary Fay, Norman Forness, Paul Gates, Jackie Goggin, Claudia Goldin, Alice Goldstein, Susan Gray, Ben Harris, John Haskell, Larry Herbst, Roy Hoover, Reginald Horsman, Herbert Klein, Stanley Lebergott, Thomas LeDuc, Robert Margo, George and Alice Merriam, Rebecca Mitchell, Leslie Moch, John Munroe, Grace Paladino, Edwin Perkins, Malcolm Rohrbough, David Weiman, Donald Winters, and Martin Zanger. Four colleagues at the University of Wisconsin-Eau Claire have helped me think about the implications of my work, and I wish to thank Brady Foust, Bob Gough, Rick Pifer, and Ron Satz for their collegiality. Several student assistants, led by Barbara Wagner, Julie Liebl, and Bob Garrett, helped in the sometimes tedious and labor-intensive research tasks for this book.

As a former special collections archivist, I fully appreciate the time and effort spent on my behalf by archivists and curators at the repositories listed in the Sources Cited section of this book. I want to thank in particular Stanley Brown and Louis Smith of the National Archives' Washington National Records Center for their help in guiding me through the vast bounty land warrant files and preemption claim files of the General Land Office that are stored at their facility in Suitland, Maryland. Sean Hartnett and his students in the University of Wisconsin-Eau Claire Cartographic Laboratory helped draw the maps for this book. The Media Development Center at UW-Eau Claire helped with preparing the illustrative material. John Major, Donna Raleigh, Catharine Roraff, and David Skappel have assisted me with my frequent computing needs.

Several agencies have helped fund parts of the research for this book including the University of Rochester's Department of History, the University of Wisconsin-Eau Claire's Faculty Research and Creative Activities Grant program, the American Historical Association's Beveridge Grant program, and the National Endowment for the Humanities' Summer Stipend program. I wish to thank the editors of the *Journal of the Early Republic* for their permission to allow me to reprint part of a 1985 article of mine in chapter 2 of this book.

The staff at Kent State University Press has shown me every professional courtesy, a treatment quite gratifying to a first-time author. John Hubbell kept the reading and revising of the manuscript on a brisk pace, and Julia Morton has sure-handedly guided me through the production of the book. This book is dedicated to my wife and children. I hope this part of the history of the disposition of the public domain has not unduly disrupted our private domain.

Introduction

For more than two decades, Henry Clay and his followers debated and quarreled with the supporters of Andrew Jackson about the proper way to dispose of the federal government's land. Should the nation encourage emigration to the West by making federal land cheap? Or should the public lands be sold in limited quantities at a constant price, with the objective of using the public lands for the benefit of the older states? Clay and the Whig party advocated the latter policy and called it "distribution." Jacksonians, on the other hand, urged the adoption of a policy they called "graduation," that is, selling government land at reduced prices with the exact price determined by the length of time a tract stood unsold.[1]

Each viewpoint was entwined with other Democratic and Whig issues of economic development. Both parties favored economic growth but differed fervently on the means to that growth. Democrats championed a national policy of removing barriers to an individual's advancement or enjoyment of fortune, whether the stumbling block was a restrictive national bank, a tariff on imports, or too high a price on government land. Some Jacksonians believed that only labor gave value to land; therefore any price charged for public lands was too high. In contrast, Whigs sought economic growth through the building of a strong domestic market for agriculture and industry buttressed with protective tariffs, conservative national banking, and trade-promoting highways, canals, and, later, railroads. The Whigs looked at the rapid westward movement of Americans and saw many costs the Democrats did not acknowledge: a dishonorable Indian removal policy; higher transport and communications costs; beggar-thy-neighbor competition with the older states; and a casual attitude toward law and order among frontier settlers.[2]

How best to exploit the nation's treasure in land proved a durable issue from the 1820s through the Civil War. The Whigs got a distribution bill passed in 1841, and the Democrats ultimately enacted the Graduation Act in 1854, but then only as an alternative to a proposal to give away at no cost public lands parcels to settlers—the so-called homestead policy. As the two old parties crumbled and were recast after the Mexican War, the land issue, too, emerged in different form. The new Republican party attracted many northern followers of Clay, and yet it came to support the homestead idea. On the eve of the Civil War, the Democratic president and party spoke in opposition to free land. This reversed the direction in which the Democratic party had headed before the Mexican War. One explanation for this turn of affairs relates to the slavery question and its ramifications. Historians have maintained that the South fell behind the North in the westward movement, imperceptibly at first following the War of 1812, but more clearly after the Census of 1850 figures were published. Southerners, the argument continues, saw that a policy of promoting an even greater pell-mell rush West could only produce more free states and further tip the balance of power against southern interests. Using the same reasoning, the North and its spokesmen in the Republican party saw homestead as a method of guaranteeing a free-soil Great Plains and Rocky Mountains. As the Democratic party came to depend more heavily on southern states in national elections, it, too, came to adopt the southern outlook on the land issue.

Frederick Jackson Turner and his early twentieth-century students first put forth this explanation for the sea change in party positions on the land question. The Turner interpretation explains quite well the position of North and South in 1860 but not nearly so well as that in 1850 when free land had not seriously arisen as a party voting issue in Congress. In fact, a period of years passed between the start of the antislavery Wilmot Proviso, presumably the trigger for southern thinking, and the serious push in Congress for a policy of free land to settlers. What happened to public lands policy from 1846 to 1855? Is the answer solely to be found in the slavery extension issue? Or can it be connected to the workings of the land system itself? In other words, did the disappearance of the traditional framing of the land question contribute to the breakup of the two-party system and the coming of the Civil War? Or was it just

TABLE 1
Summary of Bounty Land Grants, 1847–1855

Act	40-acre Warrants	80-acre Warrants	120-acre Warrants	160-acre Warrants	Totals
1847	7,585	0	0	80,689	88,274
1850	103,978	57,717	0	27,450	189,145
1852	9,070	1,699	0	1,223	11,992
1855	542	49,491	97,096	115,783	262,912
Totals	121,175	108,907	97,096	225,145	552,323

SOURCE: Introduction, n. 8.

coincidence that both the land issue and the party system changed at the same time?[3]

This book will seek to explain the politics of the public lands at the end of the second-party system by pointing to the importance of a little-noticed Mexican War policy of military recruitment based on land grants. These soldiers' land bounties would have far-reaching effects on American land policy that few in 1847 could have foreseen. The decision to offer 160 acres of land to army volunteers in the fight against Mexico eventually helped lead both Democrats and Whigs to abandon in spirit the system of selling the public lands to private interests and helped to inaugurate a system of land give-aways that lasted until Franklin Roosevelt's New Deal. Soldiers' bounty land warrants served as the entering wedge for the new arrangement. Within a few years after Mexico's defeat, the United States extended its generosity to veterans and the widows of veterans of all the various American wars dating back to the Revolution. From 1847 through 1855, Congress passed four acts granting over sixty million acres of public lands to more than a half-million veterans, widows, and heirs (see table 1).[4] These vast grants had important consequences for the operations of the public land-system, both in Washington and on the frontier, and, as intended, they proved quite a boon to the old veterans. In fact, it is hard to think of any other antebellum federal transfer program that touched as many lives. And as the 1850s closed, the new land policy of large-scale grants did play a modest part in the North-South confrontation.

In addition to political history, this book will treat the history of the public lands between the Mexican War and the Civil War as part of the story of American economic growth. Economic historians of an earlier generation concentrated on the period between the Revolution and Civil War as the time when Americans transformed a static, agriculture-based economy into a dynamic, manufactures- and industry-based one. Economic historians no longer adhere so strictly to this description of the nation's past. Instead, wealth estimates suggest that the American colonies enjoyed the highest standard of living in the world as early as the 1770s, a standard based almost entirely on market-oriented agriculture. The productive colonial economy went hand in hand with a rapid rate of increase of the population in both the North and South. The economy of the early republic did suffer a period of retardation, but, to a great extent, continued prosperity after the Revolutionary War depended on making cheap land available to new producers in agriculture. More important, thinkers and leaders like Thomas Jefferson believed in the necessity of abundant, cheap land to the West for maintaining the republican virtue of the American people.[5]

A host of policies and actions flowed from the imperative of providing new land for a rapidly growing population: wars and Indian removal, explorations and surveys, transportation innovations and improvements, and, of course, the celebrated westward movement of people. The federal government could slow or speed, but it could not halt, this relocation of labor onto new land, by setting the price and terms for the land that it owned. The economic importance of the bounty land grants derived in part from lowering the cost of public lands to purchasers. This change came at about the time that the Upper Mississippi and Lower Missouri Valley prairies and plains were opened to extensive white settlement.[6]

In less than a decade, the United States gave more than 500,000 citizens an option on sixty million acres of public land. It is worth noting that contemporaries had no clear idea before each grant just how many people were eligible and how vast the giveaway might become. Before the largest grant, the Old Soldiers Act of 1855 that produced thirty-four million acres' worth of warrants, some legislators estimated that up to 300 million acres would be needed to satisfy all the claimants. In 1854, the Interior Department officially estimated that, if the Old Soldiers bill passed, the federal government would be obliged to give away eighty-three million acres.[7] The point here is not to belittle contemporary inflated and erroneous estimates. Instead, what deserves acknowledgment is that the men engaged in formulating and administering these bounty land grants knew that they were conferring an important benefit on the veterans and their heirs, that the acreage involved was far beyond any amount ever given in a similar program, and that such extensive land giveaways would alter the public lands system in important ways.

The intent of this book is to present the effects of the bounty land grants on both federal land policy and individual Americans. The people treated here include famous Washington politicians, not-so-famous state and local politicians, businessmen, and, of course, the old men, widows, and children who received the land grants. The first task is to explain why the bounty land grants between 1847 and 1855 came about when they did. This requires careful study of the political forces in and out of Washington that shaped federal land policy. After establishing bounty land-grant legislation for American veterans, Congress left the task of administration to the Pension Bureau and the General Land Office. Following the story of land warrants involves the study of how federal administrators responded to the needs of would-be recipients.

Upon receipt of the government's land bounty, what did the veterans do with their land warrants? This is another area investigated here. How many sold the warrants for cash, and how many located and received title to a tract of public lands with their warrants? Interested contemporaries suggested that most veterans unloaded the warrants for whatever prices they would fetch. How, if at all, did those who sold differ from those who located? For those veterans and heirs who sold their warrants, there is another story to pursue, that of the warrant's path to a distant western land office. A national network did form to seek warrants from veterans and to redistribute the valuable land paper to frontier areas. Several questions about the land warrant market deserve investigation. How did the national market operate? What factors influenced warrant prices? Who were the warrant brokers who mediated between buyers and sellers? Did those veterans who sold their warrants receive fair prices—or were they gouged, as many contemporaries believed? And finally, who were the users of land warrants? Were the warrants purchased outright for cash or were they bought on credit? In short, a consideration of the economics of the land warrant business requires an investigation into the public lands boom of the 1850s.

These are some of the questions this book will consider. The history of the Mexican War–era bounty land grants had three essential parts: the creation, issue, and disposition of land warrants. Understanding the politics of the four acts between 1847 and 1855 helps make clear the basic change in federal land policy from cash sales to free land. Investigation of the politics of the grants also helps explain the difficulties in administering the issuing and regulation of warrants. Finally, understanding the political, administrative, and economic aspects of land warrants helps make clear the working of the market for public land before the Civil War and how the warrants were used at western land offices on the frontier.

The three topics—creation, issue, and use—require different approaches with different sources. This book uses manuscripts, speeches, petitions, pamphlets, and newspapers to explain why land warrants were issued in such volume. The records of the federal offices charged with overseeing the bounty land program show the problems associated with running a benefits program in the nineteenth century. Explaining the behavior of the veterans and widows requires different sources since few of these people left written memoirs or letters. Instead, this book rests heavily upon four samples of warrantees, one drawn from the warrants created by each legislative act. Information tabulated and studied from 2,761 randomly selected warrant files, or 0.5 percent of the total, helps answer many of the questions posed in the following chapters. Together with the business records of firms engaged in warrant operations on the East Coast and on the Upper Mississippi frontier, the warrant files help explain the use people made of the government's bounty.[8]

This book is the first full-length monograph on the antebellum military bounty land grants, but it comes at the end of nearly a century of historical investigation of the West and the frontier. Those who work in the field of public lands and settlement history confront a rich and extensive historiography that in great part reflects the larger questions scholars have sought to ask about the American past. This historical writing falls into three phases, each rather closely identified with a leading historian, namely, Frederick Jackson Turner, Paul Gates, and Allan Bogue. I shall attempt here to engage some of their questions and hypotheses when applied to the story of the bounty land grants.

During the first part of his scholarly career, Turner and some of his students saw the importance of the West and the westward movement as having had a positive influence on the creation of an American democracy. Turner modified this position later in his career and instead came to see geographical sections rather than the western frontier as critical in shaping American history. Still, it is worth asking today how much and what kind of role the public lands issue played in the rough-and-tumble American democracy of the 1850s. The second school of writing on the public lands and westward movement is associated with Paul Gates, who in part agreed with Turner that the West and democracy should be a topic for study but disagreed about the conclusions. Gates's work in the 1930s and 1940s decried a federal land system that worked to promote land monopoly, corruption, and rural hierarchy. For Gates, the measure of our public lands history was whether it proved just and fair to the settler. Since the 1950s, Allan Bogue and scholars influenced by him have steered the history of the public lands and frontier settlement toward questions asked by social scientists, particularly economists and geographers. Above all, the focus of recent studies has been on the efficiency of the private market in operation on the western frontier.[9]

These are themes that I propose to take up in writing about the history of the Mexican War–era grants of land to American soldiers: democracy, fairness, and efficiency. Naturally, my answers may not be the same that the three historians named above might advance, but treating these three themes does run parallel to my narrative account of the creation, issue, and use of military bounty land warrants. In doing so, I hope to offer new information about the past while at the same time engaging in a dialogue with those who have led the interpretive way.

1

Bounty Land Grants of the Mexican War Era

Military land bounties did not originate with the Mexican War nor, if Roman precedent is acknowledged, with Americans. The practice of offering land as an incentive to enlist in wartime became quite common in North America, as several English colonies experimented with military bounty land grants in the colonial period. Indeed, many of the colonies used grants of land to achieve a number of policy goals beyond defense. Some colonies used land grants to promote the settlement of more people. The headright system, which originated with the Virginia Company in 1618 and was later copied by other colonies, encouraged emigration by granting fifty acres per new settler.

The United States, as a distinct entity, first offered bounty land grants to Hessian mercenaries, and though the invitation to leave the British for the American side failed, the attempt suggests that the land warrant as a technique of recruitment stood closer to the mercenary system than to the compulsory draft. Disenchantment with the volunteer militia of 1775 and 1776 forced the cash-strapped Continental Congress to build a regular army on the foundation of bounty lands. Veterans of the Revolutionary War, however, waited many years for the opportunity to acquire land with their warrants, largely because of congressional failure to create a national land system. Not until the mid-1780s did several seaboard states relinquish their claims to the Northwest Territory, the place the government envisioned for the use of its land bounties.[1]

Even as the United States established a military district in Ohio of more than 2.5 million acres, Virginia reserved four million acres in Ohio for its own state warrant holders. The Virginia Military District produced numerous legal wrangles over land title. In 1855, one congressman estimated that Congress had passed some forty-four acts dealing with the affairs of the Virginia Military District because, despite its origin as a state project, it soon became part of national public lands administration. Much of the problem stemmed from Virginia's refusal to survey the district adequately before settlement. As for the neighboring U.S. Military District in Ohio, few Revolutionary War veterans ever located warrants within its boundaries. The individual acreage allotted varied from one hundred acres for privates to five hundred acres for colonels. Most veterans grew tired of waiting, if they had ever intended to settle, and sold their warrants to speculators. One study estimates that just one hundred men controlled 1.4 million of the two million acres that passed from the United States to private individuals in the Military District.[2]

In preparing for war with Great Britain in 1811 and 1812, Congress again made use of land bounties to fight what soon became the War of 1812. At first, the bounty land law offered a quarter-section (160 acres) each to enlisted men and noncommissioned officers in the U.S. Army who agreed to enlist for five years. With the war going badly in 1814, Congress increased its offer to 320 acres but still restricted the grant to enlisted men. Government performance on its bounty promises after the War of 1812 was considerably better than that of the Revolutionary War, although there still remained considerable confusion in the Treasury Department's administration of the grants. Congress created three tracts of about two million acres each in Illinois, Michigan, and Arkansas. The tracts were designated as the only areas where holders of land warrants could obtain their bounty in land. The Michigan tract soon gained a poor reputation as an endless swamp, so Congress established additional tracts of 1.5 million acres in Illinois and 500,000 acres in Missouri.[3]

Land warrants from the War of 1812 were not assignable before the warrantee received his "patent" or title to the land. In other words, a veteran could not legally sell or transfer his warrant. He first had to select a parcel of land, register his claim at the land office (a process called "entering" or "locating"), and wait for his patent to be confirmed from Washington; only then could he sell the land. Partly because of the restrictiveness of the bounty, only a few more than 29,000 warrants were issued, extending almost five million acres to the veterans. A recent scholarly estimate places the total enlistment in the U.S. Army during the War of 1812 at over 60,000. Not all men in this estimate of the regular army fulfilled the requirements for bounty land, but even so, the actual number of warrantees points to the limited extent of bounty land benefits. About three-fifths of the 1812 warrantees located their land in the Illinois Military Tract. Ex-soldiers began their locations in 1817, but few made their homes there, and most sold their patents to buyers who intended to resell land in the tract to future settlers. Theodore Carlson, the historian of the Illinois Military Tract, has estimated that the average quarter-section sold by the veteran netted him about $115, or seventy cents an acre.[4]

Why did the government repeat its unhappy experience with districts or tracts instead of allowing the 1812 army veterans to locate their warrants anywhere on the public domain? The best explanation for this was offered over sixty years ago by agricultural economist and public lands historian Benjamin Hibbard. The reason for creating military reserves and requiring soldiers' bounty land to be located within their boundaries, Hibbard maintained, was to provide a screen of veterans between the older settlements and the Indians.[5]

Three decades after the federal government first issued War of 1812 warrants, Washington once again resorted to the granting of land warrants, this time as part of the Mexican War. Prosecution of the Mexican War suffered from the familiar problem of too few troops. Fighting on the three fronts of northern Mexico, California, and central Mexico required more troops than the war planners anticipated. The initial enthusiasm for Mr. Polk's War soon flagged, and the United States faced a serious shortage of men for its army. Congress solved the manpower deficiency by offering land as an enlistment lure. Nine months after war broke out, Congress passed the Ten Regiments Act of 1847 that granted 160-acre bounties to regulars and volunteers who served the war's duration or twelve months, whichever came first. Congress once again excluded officers from this benefit. In case of death, the bounty passed on to the next of kin, even if the deceased soldier had not served a full twelve months.[6]

Congressional debate on the Ten Regiments Bill centered on two questions: the minimum length of service for eligibility, and safeguards against the possibility of speculators' gaining possession of the land warrants. Congress decided with little rancor that one year's service, rather than the five years required in the War of 1812, was sufficient for eligibility. The debate over assigning land warrants, however, produced sharp disagreement. Senator Thomas Hart Benton of Missouri led one side, and he expressed such a strong fear of the land speculator's trail of "deserts" and wrecked communities that he sought to limit occupation of a patent based on a land warrant to blood descendants of the original veteran.

Opponents of Benton and his plan for an American version of entail clearly understood the uselessness to veterans of a warrant without the option to sell. Benton's adversaries argued that making the bounty less attractive would hurt the recruiting effort. This group, led by Pennsylvania's Simon Cameron, prevailed in 1847, with the result that warrant holders legally enjoyed the right to sell their land warrants. Moreover, the warrants issued under the Ten Regiments Act were not restricted to a remote military district as after 1815; instead, warrant owners could use the bounty anywhere on the vast public domain. Futhermore, Congress gave the veteran another option: he could choose to reject a land warrant in favor of $100 in Treasury scrip bearing 6 percent interest. After the act's passage and the president's signature, army recruiters busily signed up men on the basis of the new bounty. The army raised sufficient troops to finish the Mexican fighting, and after the war, by a ratio of thirty to one, the demobilized soldiers chose to take their rewards in bounty land warrants rather than the Treasury scrip. This choice may be explained by recalling that the warrants of 160 acres had a face value of $200 since the government charged would-be purchasers $1.25 an acre for its land.[7]

The practice of assigning land warrants received a bad name in 1848. Many veterans circumvented the regulation that required them to wait for receipt of the warrant before the land's sale. New Orleans served as the chief port of discharge for Mexican War veterans, and many land warrant brokers in that city offered returning soldiers a rewarding shortcut. Agents helped thousands of men fill out and mail off applications to Washington. They then had the soldiers sign over power of attorney rights that included the right to dispose of the land warrant when it arrived from Washington. The General Land Office, however, frowned on this practice because it specifically violated the provision in the act of 1847 prohibiting the sale of warrants before their issue. Although no one was hurt by the subterfuge, Benton's fears seemed confirmed that the entire bounty land program would work in practice to turn over the public domain to speculators. Land warrant agents soon learned to wait to make a purchase until after the Pension Bureau issued the veteran or heir the warrant. As one agent advised another, "In all our cases get an assignment after the warrant issues."[8]

The dispute over the use of land warrants by veterans tended to reflect earlier opinions about the government's proper role in disposing of the public lands. Benton made a career out of insisting that the federal government should deal directly with the settler, and not aid middlemen. The Missourian supported cheap prices for land as well as a policy of delaying the time of payment, an arrangement known as preemption or, more disparagingly, as "squatting." Granting land warrants to soldiers who intended to settle on the public domain did not trouble Benton, but he had an active fear that land warrants accumulating in the hands of middlemen and speculators could lead to "land monopoly"; this troubled him and other Democratic politicians in the 1840s. Whig politicians, on the other hand, insisted in 1847 and 1848 that the end use of land warrants should hold little interest for the government since the bounty had proved its use in raising the necessary forces. The warrants became private property upon receipt by veterans, and the disposal of this property did not concern Washington.[9]

Thanks to the Ten Regiments Act, over 88,000 Mexican War veterans or beneficiaries received a government land bounty. With rapid dispatch, these warrants passed from the soldiers to brokers, who in turn transferred the warrants to frontier land office towns where ultimately settlers bought them to use in acquiring land for new farms. As the army demobilized during the summer and fall of 1848, the ex-soldiers flooded the War Department's Bureau of Pensions with applications for bounty land warrants. Most of the 88,274 warrants were issued before the end of 1849, and many had entered into circulation by the end of that year. The effect on the land system may be seen in table 2. Warrant location entries at land offices exceeded two million acres in 1848 and rose another 50 percent the next year. Acreage sold for cash by the government had only just recovered to its 1840 level in 1846 after a long period of slow sales. The late 1840s also saw a rise in grain prices as a result of European demand, an occurrence that normally would have resulted in increased land sales to prospective farmers—possibly to the early 1830s level. Instead land sales were severely reduced because of the volume of land warrants let loose on the market.[10]

Ralph Waldo Emerson prophesied in 1847 that the Mexican War would "prove a form of arsenic to the United States," and he predicted that the poison itself would be the new land taken from the Mexicans. Indeed, the territory gained from Mexico led to immediate quarrels between the North and South over the question of slavery extension. Should slavery be prohibited from this captured territory, as Pennsylvania Congressman David Wilmot repeatedly urged, or should the new lands be open to slaveholders, as Senator John Calhoun insisted? The Compromise of 1850 only partly resolved this fundamental dispute. At the same time that Congress

TABLE 2
Public Land Entries by Cash Sale and Warrants, 1840–1860 (In Thousands of Acres)

Year	*Cash Sales*	*Warrant Entries*
1840	2,237	. . .
1841	1,165	. . .
1842	1,129	. . .
1843	1,605	. . .
1844	1,755	. . .
1845	1,844	. . .
1846	2,264	. . .
1847	2,521	240
1848	1,887	2,289
1849	1,330	3,406
1850	1,406	2,168
1851	1,847	2,454
1852	1,553	3,201
1853	1,083	6,142
1854	7,036*	3,403
1855	15,730	1,346
1856	9,228	8,382
1857	4,143	6,284
1858	3,805	5,802
1859	3,962	2,915
1860	3,461	2,783
Totals	70,991	50,815

SOURCE: Paul W. Gates, "Charts of Public Land Sales and Entries," p. 28.
*Includes Graduation Act sales after this date.

tied itself in knots over the slavery question in the former Mexican territories, the national legislature debated another issue more quietly: who should benefit from the newly acquired land?[11]

Giving away public lands through bounty land warrants did not end with the Mexican War. Instead, the practice continued during the next decade on a greatly expanded scale. The political impulse toward additional large bounty land grants after the Mexican War had several different sources. The momentum for more grants developed against the background of the spoils in land seized from Mexico. At the same time, changes in public finance freed the Treasury from its traditional reliance on revenue from public lands sales. Policymakers in Congress and the Executive came to believe that the federal government should rapidly divest itself of its holdings in land, and this gradually became the leading principle of public lands policy between the Mexican and Civil wars. As Missouri's Whig senator David Atchison said in 1850, "It is an object for the Government to convert the public lands into private property."[12] In the decade after the war, Congress adopted a number of different policies designed to rid the federal government of its wealth in land. Table 3 shows the great increase in public lands disposition, starting in 1848 with the implementation of the Ten Regiments Act, and continuing more dramatically after 1850. The chief explanation for this turn of events is that outright federal grants replaced sales as the main form of land transfer from public to private ownership. Bounty land grants to American veterans helped lead this change in federal land policy toward promoting land giveaways alongside land sales.

Beginning in 1848, and with increasing intensity during the following two years, veterans of the War of 1812 pressed Congress to grant public lands as a retroactive bounty. Here was a new idea: the federal government should give land away not simply as a recruiting device to attract young men to military service but rather to reward old men for service performed decades earlier. Such a proposal had little chance of acceptance before the Mexican War, though from time to time groups of officers who served in the War of 1812 did seek after-the-fact bounties. Congress had received petitions requesting bounty land grants for 1812 officer veterans not long after the war's end. For example, the New York City Committee of the Officers of the War of 1812 sent Congress a formal petition asking for bounty lands in 1826. Twelve years later, Pittsburgh's surviving officers sent a similar petition to Congress, complaining that "The undersigned have in vain sought for reasons which should deprive the officers of the second war of independence of the same munificence which was extended by the United States and by seven of the States, to the first."[13]

The protests of War of 1812 army officers continued after the Mexican War and were augmented in a decisive manner by similar demands from militiamen who had served in the war against Great Britain. The ex-officers represented a small group with limited political influence; however, the surviving militiamen and their families numbered in the hundreds of thousands of voters. The popular image today of the War of 1812 as a mistaken and bungled war has obscured the extent of citizen participation in that war. At least

TABLE 3
Public Land Disposition by Sales, Grants, and Warrants, 1833–1860
(In Millions of Acres)

Year	*Acreage*
1833	3.8
1834	4.7
1835	12.6
1836	20.1
1837	5.6
1838	3.4
1839	5.0
1840	2.2
1841	1.2
1842	1.3
1843	1.6
1844	1.8
1845	1.8
1846	2.3
1847	2.8
1848	5.2
1849	5.3
1850	14.7
1851	4.3
1852	12.7
1853	35.0
1854	21.6
1855	24.2
1856	36.1
1857	18.8
1858	11.0
1859	12.3
1860	7.1
Total	278.5

SOURCE: Thomas Donaldson, *The Public Domain*, pp. 196–258.

450,000 militiamen played some part in it—many more than the number who took up arms in the Revolution.[14] Only regulars in the U.S. Army had qualified for bounty lands on the basis of their 1812 service, and, for more than three decades, the ex-militiamen kept silent about asking for land bounties. Those militia veterans unrewarded and frequently reviled as fighting men during and after Mr. Madison's War came to life and expressed outrage that the army regulars, state volunteers, and militiamen of Mr. Polk's War should receive such generosity in bounty lands. In petitions and memorials to Congress, the old militiamen demanded parity in bounty lands with the Mexican War veterans.

The War of 1812 veterans reflected unhappily on the extensive bounty lands and cash pensions granted to Revolutionary veterans and the easy terms for Mexican War bounties. The initial protests of 1848 and 1849 came largely from veterans living in the Ohio Valley. Some Indiana veterans in 1849, for example, argued that the geographical setting of the western theater of the war made their claim especially meritorious:

> [We are] the only class of officers and soldiers who have not in one way or another secured some mark of remembrance from the Nation, and some bounty to compensate the perils and sufferings incident to service in the tented field. . . . To our services, rendered on the frontiers, and in the swamps and untrodden wilderness, more of privation and suffering was incident than to services rendered on or near the Atlantic seaboard in [the] time of the Revolution, or to services rendered in the cultivated country of Mexico; and we therefore confidently appeal to the magnanimity, and sense of justice of the Representatives of the States, and of the people to wipe away the reproach incident to the discrimination above alluded to, by granting to us, and our fellow compatriots such reasonable bounty taken from the National Domain.[15]

Other western veterans argued that the results of the War of 1812 secured the trans-Appalachian area and Mississippi Valley for the United States. In effect, they maintained that they had defended in battle what had only formally been acquired by the diplomacy of the Treaty of Paris and Jay's Treaty and so deserved land bounties as a simple matter of repayment. Thus, "in adding millions of acres to the public domain, which have brought also millions of dollars into the national treasury," as some Arkansas veterans argued, it would be "a small pittance in petitioning for an inconsiderable fraction of the unappropriated portion of the domain thus won by their valor and patriotism."[16]

Not all petitions and memorials came from western veterans, but Indiana and Kentucky did send in the greatest number in 1849 and 1850. At first, these Ohio Valley petitions proposed that Congress reward old veterans with bounty land in proportion to former military rank, along the lines of the basic bounty land laws of the Revolutionary War. For example, some Frankfort, Kentucky, veterans urged in January 1850 that "a part of the public domain to be appropriated to them according to their respective rank as a just reward for their services." A group of former officers living in the District of Columbia offered a more specific formula for retroactive bounty land: 960 acres for colonels, 800 acres for services as a major, 640 acres to captains, 480 acres to lieutenants, and 160 acres to all others.[17]

The suggestion that acreage be awarded according to rank ignored the policy that Congress had followed with the Ten Regiments Act of 1847: to exclude officers altogether, and to distinguish between men only on the basis of enlistment term. The 1847 law had awarded 160 acres each to those men who volunteered for twelve months or the war's duration, and forty acres for a special group of ninety-day volunteers. A few 1849 and 1850 petitions from Pennsylvania veterans did urge similar treatment for officers and enlisted men and showed a keener sense of political reality. When leaders drew up the legislation in the 31st Congress to reward War of 1812 veterans and soldiers from various Indian wars after the year 1790, they drafted a bill that provided for different treatment of veterans based on length of service and not on rank. Men who had served at least one month received a forty-acre land warrant, those whose active duty had lasted four months got an eighty-acre warrant, while those who had served longer than nine months won 160 acres in bounty land. The bounty land bill might have passed much earlier in the session had not the Congress devoted so much energy to debating and voting on the measures known as the Compromise of 1850. When at last the Compromise of 1850 passed the House and Senate, both chambers quickly took up and passed the bounty land bill, a bit of business that some saw as a healing measure because the proposed legislation honored both northern and southern veterans.

Study of a random sample of veterans benefiting under the 1850 act reveals the extent to which the War of 1812 was fought by militiamen. A sample of one-half of 1 percent of the 1850 act warrantees totals 945; of that number, 724 men or their heirs earned a land warrant under the act for service in the War of 1812. The balance of 221 warrantees earned a land bounty for federal service in a variety of Indian wars and Indian removal actions (see table 4). Among the subgroup of 724 War of 1812 recipients, 85 percent won a warrant as a result of militia service, 7 percent had served in state volunteer

TABLE 4
Distribution of Sample Land Warrants by War Service and Acreage, Act of 1850

War	*40 Acres*	*80 Acres*	*160 Acres*	*Total*
1812	402	84	238	724
Wayne's	0	1	2	3
Florida	53	36	27	116
Creek removal	17	1	2	20
Mexican	1	9	1	11
Black Hawk	24	1	5	30
Seminole	3	1	3	7
Tippecanoe	1	0	0	1
Missing/canceled	33	0	0	33
Totals	534	133	278	945

NOTE: Calculated from sample of act of 1850 warrants. See App. A.

regiments, and 8 percent served in either the U.S. Army or Marine Corps. The distinction between the types of veterans is that militiamen and the state unit volunteers tended to serve very short stretches of time, sometimes only a few days of service, while U.S. regulars served much longer fixed enlistment terms. The preponderance of ex-militiamen with short enlistments among War of 1812 veterans is reflected in the distribution of land bounties under the 1850 act: of those who received forty-acre warrants in the sample, 375, or 90 percent, were militiamen; among those in the sample receiving an eighty-acre warrant, 204, or 82 percent, served in the militia; while of those granted a full 160-acre land warrant for more than nine months of service in the War of 1812, only 26 in the sample, or 30 percent, were militiamen. The majority of 1812 veterans earning a 160-acre warrant under the act of 1850 were former U.S. Army regulars who had not served a complete five-year term or otherwise met the stringent requirements of the 1812 bounty land statute.[18]

Unlike the situation in 1847, Congress restricted the assignability of act of 1850 warrants ostensibly to protect the veteran or his heirs from fraud at the hands of warrant brokers. The memory of the practice of assignments under the Ten Regiments Act weighed heavily on some congressmen. One senator argued against making any new warrants assignable because, in 1848, "a set of land sharks, pirates and harpies arose in every portion of the country to defraud the soldier." In effect, this limit on the right to sell reduced the warrant's value, since few veterans sought to move to a public lands state solely to use their warrants. Contemporaries in 1847 might well have thought that young veterans would abandon their homes and move to Iowa or Arkansas or some other public lands state to use their 160-acre grants. Few in 1850 could seriously maintain that sixty-year-old veterans of the War of 1812 would actually use their warrants to start new homes and farms in the West. The 1850 grant rewarded the old veterans with a pension in land because there was not enough money in the Treasury to give them a cash grant. Congress might have done the next best thing, and given them assignable warrants that might be turned into cash, but nonassignable warrants constituted an asset without liquidity and could hardly help an old veteran or widow. In short, the congressional ban on the sale of warrants reduced the value of the bounty to the recipient.[19]

The decision to ban sales of warrants was actually made in the executive branch. Despite some last-minute confusion at the end of the session, Congress refused in September 1850 to specify whether the warrants could be assigned. The Senate rejected an amendment forbidding assignability, but neither house could pass an amendment authorizing the practice. In effect, Congress would not say what its policy was, so, in the absence of specific congressional authorization, the newly created and politically cautious Interior Department issued regulations prohibiting the assignment of land warrants. A coalition of unlikely allies acted in concert to assure this outcome: Bentonites opposed in principle to assignment joined congressional friends of warrant dealers who wished to protect their investment in 1847 warrants by making the new batch of 1850 paper worthless.[20]

The chief outcome of this congressional desire to protect veterans was a cry from those very veterans to end the restriction on assignment. The foes of assignability managed to frustrate any change during the short second session of the 31st Congress over the winter of 1850–51 but were completely routed when Congress convened again in December 1851. By that time, warrant dealers had disposed of most of their inventory of 1847 warrants, and the Benton opposition alone could not resist the demands for assignability. An act of March 22, 1852, much anticipated throughout the country as the

TABLE 5
Distribution of Sample Land Warrants by War Service and Acreage, Act of 1852

War	*40 Acres*	*80 Acres*	*160 Acres*	*Total*
1812	3	0	0	3
Aroostook	15	0	0	15
Cherokee removal	16	5	3	24
SW frontier disturbances	1	0	0	1
Black Hawk	1	1	1	3
Texas frontier disturbances	1	0	0	1
Patriot	3	0	1	4
"Indian"	5	0	4	9
Totals	45	6	9	60

NOTE: Calculated from sample of act of 1852 warrants. See App. A.

"Assignment Bill," explicitly made 1850 land warrants assignable. In addition, the act liberalized certain features of land warrant operation. Warrants now became eligible for use by preemptors in making their preemption payments. On lands selling at double minimum ($2.50 per acre, usually along railroad rights-of-way), a buyer could use warrants and cash in equal amounts. Also, militia veterans from sitzkriegs such as the Aroostook War and the Patriot's War of 1837–38 received bounty land for their services. In all, nearly 12,000 new warrants were issued under this act, representing almost 700,000 acres (see table 5).[21]

Not long after passage of the 1852 act, War of 1812 veterans began to clamor for another vast military bounty grant. All those men previously excluded now wanted to receive bounty lands. Proposed bills in Congress to enact such a grant failed in the second session of the 32d Congress and in the first session of the 33d. In each case, the bill was stifled in the Senate Committee on Public Lands. The issue could not be suppressed for long, however, and on March 3, 1855, sailors, marines, flotillamen, chaplains, teamsters, remarried widows, and others got their wish as Congress granted 160 acres of public lands to anyone previously unrewarded with bounty land who had served for more than two weeks in any American war since 1775. As in 1852, Congress made these new warrants assignable. In all, 263,285 persons claimed land warrants under the Act of 1855 covering more than thirty-four million acres, an area the size of Wisconsin. Those veterans who in the past had received less than 160 acres found themselves entitled to a new land warrant making up the difference. As in 1850, War of 1812 veterans emerged as the main beneficiaries of the new law (see table 6). Yet what is also striking about the recipients is the wide range of conflicts, skirmishes, and wars against various Indian tribes in which they had fought in every decade from the 1790s up to 1855. Indeed, several beneficiaries under the acts of 1852 and 1855 received warrants for service in unnamed "Indian Wars."[22]

A sample of 0.5 percent of the 1855 act warrantees, or 1,315 people, shows 545 warrantees receiving either 80-acre or 120-acre warrants to augment their earlier 1850 act warrants based on War of 1812 service. Out of this group of 545, all but 26 had served in wartime militia units. The 1855 act also created a new class of recipients, those who served less than one month but more than two weeks. The 1855 sample shows that 334 warrantees, all ex-militiamen of the War of 1812 or their survivors, earned 160-acre warrants in this manner.

Combining the sample warrantees under the two acts of Congress allows one to estimate the number of War of 1812 veterans or heirs who received a land warrant. A total of 1,604 warrants were issued under the two acts for 1812 service and divided by the sample size of 0.5 percent yields an estimate of 320,600. Of this number, 109,000 (or 545 in the sample) received two land warrants amounting to 160 acres; so subtracting the doubly counted 1855 warrantees results in an estimate that the number of War of 1812 beneficiaries totaled about 211,600. To put it another way: 144,800 first received a land warrant under the 1850 act for serving at least one month against the British, and 66,800 received their first warrants under the 1855 act for service during the War of 1812 of less than one month but at least two weeks.

This land giveaway to the older veterans of the War of 1812 overshadowed all earlier military bounty land grants. The four grants of the Mexican War era were about six times the size of the combined Revolutionary War and Act of 1812 grants. Why was Congress so generous after the Mexican War? The answer involves the disparity in the terms of the acts of 1812 and 1847; and, as one writer insists, the effects of the Ten Regiments Act "were inevitable in a democracy and swift in arriving."[23] The generosity of the bounty in land offered to volunteers in 1847 under the Ten Regiments Act far exceeded that offered to volunteers in the War of 1812 and must be

TABLE 6

Distribution of Sample Land Warrants by War Service and Acreage, Act of 1855

War	*80 Acres*	*120 Acres*	*160 Acres*	*Total*
1812	204	341	333	878
Aroostook	0	0	1	1
Southern frontier disturbances	0	0	1	1
Wayne's	0	0	2	2
Florida	18	29	27	74
Cherokee removal	2	13	5	20
Creek removal	3	35	19	57
Mexican	1	22	92	115
Sabine expedition	0	1	0	1
Southwest frontier disturbances	1	0	2	3
Northwest frontier disturbances	0	4	6	10
Black Hawk	0	28	10	38
Navajo	1	1	5	7
Seminole	1	3	7	11
Revolution	0	0	17	17
Qalla Battroo	0	0	1	1
Tripoli	0	0	2	2
California	0	0	1	1
Texas frontier disturbances	0	0	4	4
New Mexico	0	0	4	4
Rogue River	0	0	3	3
Cayuse	0	0	3	3
Apache	0	0	6	6
Utah	0	0	1	1
New York frontier disturbances	0	0	8	8
Northeast frontier disturbances	0	7	3	10
"Indian"	0	0	2	2
Missing/cancelled	0	0	35	35
Totals	231	484	600	1,315

NOTE: Calculated from sample of act of 1855 warrants. See App. A.

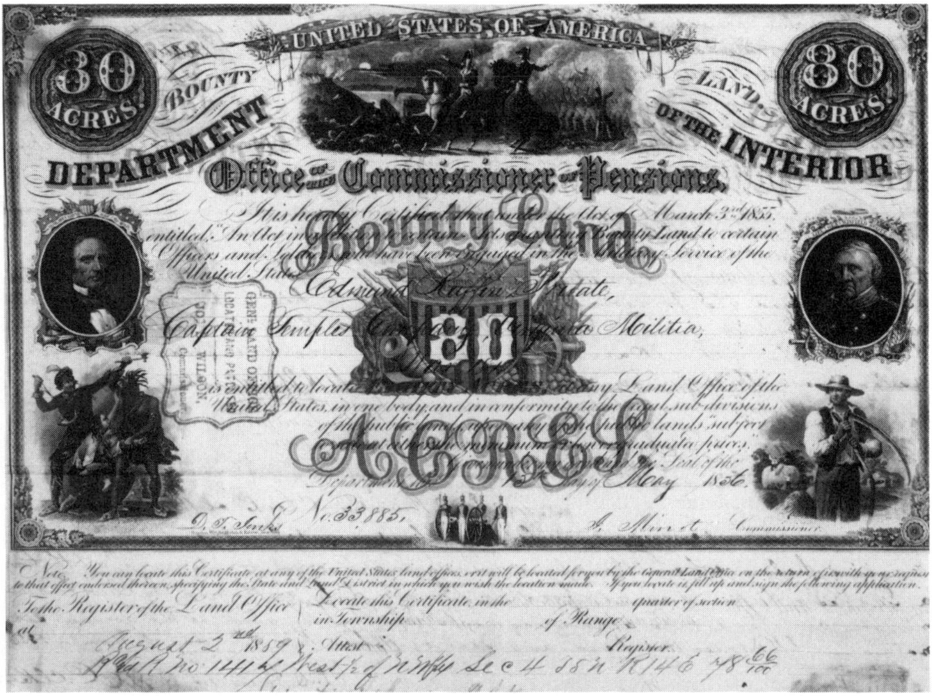

FIG. 1. ACT OF 1855 LAND WARRANT. Engraved eighty-acre warrant issued to Edmund Ruffin for service in the Virginia Militia in the War of 1812 under the act of 1855. Note the view of the War of 1812 including scenes from the Niagara campaign and frontier battles with the Indians (courtesy of the National Archives).

acknowledged as the cause of the subsequent bounty land acts of 1850, 1852, and 1855.

The timing of the retroactive grants requires more careful study. These were exciting years when the Congress and the voters discussed and debated how to organize the territory wrested from Mexico. The discussion of bounty land grants must therefore be placed within the context of the aftermath of the Mexican War and the breakup of the two-party system.

2

Acres for Old Men: The United Brethren of the War of 1812 and the Politics of Land Grants

The Mexican War effectively marks the informal end of the cash system of public lands disposal, although a law prohibiting further sales was not enacted until 1890. Starting in the 1840s, Americans followed a rather haphazard policy in giving away their public domain. The cash system, dating back to Robert Morris and Alexander Hamilton, reflected a belief that the U.S. government should profit from disposing of its land. Hamilton had instituted the policy of selling land only in large blocks and at high prices, with the intent of raising money for the government and of discouraging too active a flight westward. Though modified continually over the years in the direction of smaller minimum purchases, the land system was still unmistakably based on cash sales at the beginning of the Mexican War.[1]

Besides the cash sales system, the United States also followed a policy of endorsing preemption, sometimes known as "squatters' rights." Many people settled on the public lands in advance of scheduled auction sales and claimed the right to preempt, to exercise an exclusive right to obtain a parcel by promising to pay the government price when the General Land Office brought to auction the townships in which the parcel lay. During the early part of the century, Congress repeatedly forgave this unusual form of trespassing with special, limited preemption acts. Finally, in 1841, Congress legalized it with a general preemption law. Still, preempting merely put off the time when a buyer had to pay for his land but did not negate the necessity for payment.[2]

While the country remained tied to the idea of cash sales for land before the Mexican War, the true center of government finance was found in the various customhouses from Boston to New Orleans.

Since President Washington's time, customs receipts had provided the major part of federal revenue, and, in the history of American public finance, revenues from public lands sales exceeded 20 percent of total federal revenue in only four years, the "flush times" of 1834–37. Receipts from public lands sales stayed below 10 percent in most years. By the Mexican War, Democratic tariff reductions notwithstanding, Hamilton's policy of public lands disposal based on cash sales had become obsolete. A short war such as the Mexican War could be paid for in a few years by customs revenue. In issuing debt certificates during the war, the United States pledged its full faith and credit. Behind that credit stood the ultimate collateral of federal ownership of the public lands. Yet, in the changed atmosphere after the war, public officials knew how easy it would be to pay off the debt, and although all considered it an important matter, many thought the pledge of collateral behind the debt no longer essential.[3]

A combination of events worked to weaken the old connection between the public lands and the public debt. The experience of public finance after the Ten Regiments Act of 1847 showed that the nation could survive without significant revenue from public lands sales. Indeed, the vote to raise troops with land warrants represented a decision to give precedence to the war emergency over maintaining the collateral for the public debt.

The old belief that the public lands should be managed to pay the public debt did not fully disappear after the victory over Mexico. Senator Alpheus Felch of Michigan warned in 1850 against graduation (his party's stated policy), homesteads, and more bounty land grants: "however abundant may be the resources of the country, and however secure the payment of the indebtedness from other sources of income, it would seem to imply a want of good faith, without the consent of the creditor to give away the property specifically hypothecated for the payment." A decade later, the turmoil of the Civil War caused at least one Republican leader to reconsider the wisdom of giving away public lands with the nation's credit in jeopardy. The old Whig leader and later New York Republican boss, Thurlow Weed, urged in early 1864 that "the Homestead Act be repealed and the public lands be sacredly devoted to the payment of the national debt, [and the] national credit will be placed upon an impregnable basis."[4]

Before the Mexican War, congressmen could still argue for the cash sales policy on the grounds that the public domain and the Treasury were inseparable, that Congress could give neither land nor money away as special favors. This was fully consistent with Jacksonian laissez-faire principles. Prevailing constitutional theory held that Congress could not make cash or land grants for specific ends because such responsibility belonged to the states. This reasoning fell out of favor after the war, and, as one senator maintained in 1854, "the Federal Government administers the public land upon one principle, and the money in your Treasury upon another principle." The new constitutional doctrine for disposing of the public lands came to be known as the proprietorship argument. Adherents to this approach contended that Congress could properly act as proprietor of the public lands and dispose of acreage as it wished so long as the result did not cause any revenue loss to the Treasury. The structuring of the 1850 Chicago-Mobile railroad land grant shows the proprietorship view in operation. The General Land Office reserved land along the proposed right-of-way and, for every section of land given to the railroad, an alternate section was doubled in price. Thus, the government, acting as proprietor, received the same revenue from sales and promoted an intersectional railroad as well.[5]

The proprietorship argument moreover could be expanded to justify expenditures of public lands as a discharge of other federal obligations. It is precisely at this point that bounty land grants were employed to exploit the difference between a cash sales policy and a proprietorship policy. In 1850, and subsequently in 1852 and 1855, spokesmen for veterans of American wars antedating the Mexican conflict beseeched the Congress for aid. Veterans asked for such federal help outside the normal pension system because they claimed that the nation owed a long-overdue debt to the soldiers who had fought on the country's behalf. Congress concurred several times and paid the obligation in land.

It may be too strong an assertion to say that the land warrant grants alone represent a watershed between the cash sales policy and the homestead policy of free land. Instead, Congress adopted a series of land policies granting public lands for numerous purposes after the Mexican War, as shown in table 3. Indeed, in 1841, even before the Mexican War, Congress had begun to make indirect proprietor grants to new states for the purpose of having the states promote internal improvements. But clearly, after the Ten Regiments Act, Congress was willing to make large grants of public lands to promote specific goals like draining swamps or constructing railroads. To some extent, the public lands were available to those who could muster sufficient arguments to sway Congress. The change was gradual not immediate; the years between the Ten Regiments Act of 1847 and the Homestead Act's passage in 1862 may best be seen as a long divide in public lands history between cash sales pure and simple and free land for the asking.[6]

Sometimes the contradictory thinking about public lands policy could be seen in one individual, most notably President Franklin Pierce, who in 1854 vetoed a bill giving ten million acres of public land to aid the indigent insane. The plan was associated with Dorothea Dix, the noted prison and asylum reform advocate, and her call for federal land grants to help the afflicted enjoyed wide support. Pierce opposed the indigent insane land grant because it did not meet his idea of proprietorship or sound management in the older sense; that is, a grant of ten million acres (worth $12.5 million at the government's set price for land) would not shortly produce an equal amount of revenue for the nation. Nonetheless, a few months later he quietly signed legislation granting thirty-four million acres of public land to old veterans without pretense that the grant would produce revenue. As the federal government issued more grants of public lands in the 1850s, inevitably some grants conflicted with others. President Buchanan faced this difficulty in 1859 when he vetoed a homestead bill because it threatened to diminish the market value of already issued military bounty land warrants. In short, Buchanan maintained that one giveaway would work to make less valuable an earlier giveaway; hence, the homestead policy should be turned down as a matter of justice to the veterans who had not yet profited from the sale of their bounties.[7]

Some political leaders after the Mexican War did see that public lands disposition need not be restrained because of the new war debt. When the Ohio congressman Frederick Vinton opposed further bounty land grants in 1850 on the grounds that such grants broke a promise to fund the public debt, he drew this response from Mississippi's Albert Brown:

> But says the gentleman, these lands are pledged to the redemption of the war debt. The gentleman forgets his own vote to grant land in bounties after that pledge was given. He then, doubtless, thought, and thought correctly, that so long as the interest on the debt is paid, and the stock redeemed as it falls due, the holders of the public securities do not care a fig what you do with the public lands. The stock was never taken on any pledge of lands for its redemption, but on the good faith of the Government that the interest should be paid and the debt redeemed at maturity.[8]

The success of the war against Mexico emboldened special interests to ask for what, before the war, might have seemed unreasonably large land grants. Congressman Brown exemplified this new attitude in his reply to Vinton:

> The Government is rich in its landed possessions, and out of this abundance I would freely reward the soldiers' honest toils. I would give him a home, make him feel that he had served his country to some purpose. What if it takes ten millions of acres? I care not, sir, if it takes ten times ten millions. . . .[9]

After the Mexican War, the land issue became transformed from the traditional Democratic-Whig question of how much to charge for public lands to a new formulation of who would get grants of land from a generous federal government. The earlier struggle over the correct minimum price and quantity formed one of the issues of the two-party system. To be sure, Whigs in public lands states more resolutely favored easier terms than eastern Whigs, who sought high prices to produce revenue and to limit westward migration, but party policy on the land issue did generally mesh with Democratic and Whig views on national economic development. When the federal government began giving away land by the tens of millions of acres to American veterans, other interest groups began asking for similar gifts. Such a fragmented approach to the land question did not so easily fit into the two-party arrangement and, in a modest way, helps explain the demise of the party system of Democrats and Whigs.

Historian Michael Holt has argued that the second-party system self-destructed before 1854, in part over the slavery extension issue and especially the immigration question, but also in part because of exhaustion. The old issues of tariffs and banks, Holt contends, had played themselves out by 1852, and voters drifted away from the Whig party in particular because of the increasing irrelevance of its economic program. The land issue, too, as argued before the Mexican War, was less relevant to the situation after the war, and, for several years, a politics of expediency in giving land away to the loudest and most clamorous replaced the earlier politics of party positions on graduation and distribution.[10]

How was the winning of such extensive federal benefits accomplished? Who promoted the concept of a retroactive land grant to former soldiers? Further political demands by veterans seemed in order as soon as War of 1812 veterans compared their benefits with those of the Mexican War veterans and concluded that they had been unfairly treated in a material and political way. Had the 1847 Ten Regiments Act come as a response to a war with Britain over Oregon, the old veterans' complaints would not have had such a bitter edge. Since the act passed during a war on a fellow republic, the old soldiers decided that the Polk administration valued the contributions of the soldiers in Mexico more highly than those of the 1812 soldiers, a fact that angered the survivors of the earlier war. From the end of the Mexican War until the beginning of the Civil War, veterans of the War of 1812 formed a national lobby and combined a simple call for bounty land parity with a more complex effort to parade their ancient services and ideals before what they saw as an ignorant younger generation.

The immense booty in land taken from Mexico, the organizational strength of the veterans' lobby, and the justice and sentiment behind their cause proved a combination that Congress and two presidents could not resist. By 1855, after several years of lobbying, the War of 1812 veterans not previously granted 160 acres won land bounties equal to those awarded Mexican War soldiers. Accomplishing this feat also had the unforeseen effect of creating the prototype of veterans' fraternal organizations that are such a feature of the twentieth century.

The Mexican War itself came at an important time in the history of the lives of the 1812 veterans. As the men aged into their fifties and sixties, they faced a generational conflict as well as a political one, for the Mexican War with its unbroken series of American military victories contrasted clearly with the War of 1812's paucity of victories. Moreover, the two wars had been fought by different types of military units. Men who had served in the War of 1812 had belonged predominantly to the state militias and, by and large, convinced many professionals of their ineptitude in battle. The Mexican War, on the other hand, had an American force composed more of regular army troops and of state volunteer units outside the militia. The successes of the Mexican War forces signified the decline in the American military command of the state militias; indeed, during the Civil War, both Union and Confederacy relied on state volunteer units organized into national armies.[11]

In a peculiar way, the years surrounding the Mexican War prompted something of a national review of the history of the War of 1812. Andrew Jackson's death in 1845 caused many writers to recall his exploits in 1814 and 1815 against the Indians and British. The controversy over the Oregon Territory and its subsequent

FIG. 2. WAR OF 1812 MILITIAMEN. A jaundiced view of the militiamen of the War of 1812, drawn by D. C. Johnston (1832).

peaceful resolution brought back memories of earlier United States–British relations. Even the prosecution of the Mexican War gave occasion to remember the earlier war since Army General Winfield Scott had first won victories in the Niagara Frontier campaigns of 1813 and 1814. Just as the Mexican War began, the Philadelphia congressman Charles J. Ingersoll published a two-volume history of the War of 1812, a frankly revisionist work in which he argued for more American brilliance in arms in 1813 and 1814 than had earlier writers. Ingersoll's history represented a new, reliable, and scholarly account of the war and portrayed the struggle as both noble in intent and effective in prosecution. The Ingersoll volumes, soon followed by many others on the same topic, appeared at a time when 1812 veterans were seeking to convince the nation both of the importance of their earlier service and (a more difficult task) of a defense based on militiamen.[12]

The veterans of the War of 1812 were led by a collection of retired politicians who employed all the tools of the Jacksonian mass lobby: petition drives, local meetings, national conventions, and even a friendly march on the White House. The records of these political actions tell much about the leaders and something about their followers. The national conventions produced lengthy programs that reproduced the speeches of various delegates. A careful reading of these speeches, and of newspaper accounts of national and local War of 1812 veterans' meetings, reveals much about how leading veterans saw themselves, their war service, and the importance of land warrants. The records of the veterans' meetings also characteristically list those in attendance and their homes, so some idea may be gained of the geographical strength of the veterans as a lobbying force.

A petition drive in 1854 and 1855 was launched to pass a bounty land bill giving 160 acres of land to each veteran. The petitions to Congress for bounty lands are preserved in the National Archives committee files of both houses of Congress. The petitions are a measure of the strength of sentiment behind the veterans' cause, if only because signing a petition was an affirmative political action on the part of a citizen.[13] This effort to mobilize public opinion behind what observers termed the Old Soldiers bill surpassed petition drives undertaken in earlier congressional sessions. More than eleven thousand citizens signed petitions asking Congress to change the bounty land laws. They vary in size from the handwritten plea of four Maine "Officers of the Aroostook War" to a printed form signed by over six hundred citizens of Monroe County, New York. The latter group argued that considering "the privations and sufferings which that gallant Band of Patriots in the Second War of Independence endured, [we] believe that some relief extended to them by Government, at the present time, would, in the estimation of the citizens of this great Republic, be regarded as nothing more than an act of Justice."[14]

Most of the Pennsylvania and New York petitions came in printed forms with a statement of the grievance at the top and ample room for signatures on the balance of the sheet. Eleven states supplemented the lobbying drive and sent official resolutions to Congress favoring more liberal eligibility rules for bounty land applicants. Legislatures in Illinois, Iowa, Indiana, Wisconsin, Kentucky, Virginia, Tennessee, Pennsylvania, New Jersey, Rhode Island, and Massachusetts went on record as instructing their U.S. senators to support more bounty land grants.

Table 7 presents a breakdown of the geographical origins of the bounty land petitions sent to the 33d Congress. The figures show that the petition drive drew most of its support from the Northeast, an important change from the petitions that inspired the 1850 act. This in turn suggests the actual base of strength of the leaders of

TABLE 7
Geographical Distribution of Bounty Land Petitions to the 33d (1853–55) Congress

Origin	*Number of Petitions*	*Approximate Number of Signers*
Maine	13	365
Pennsylvania	24	2,500
Ohio	4	190
New York	47	7,100
Virginia	4	200
Connecticut	2	350
Kentucky	1	25
Massachusetts	5	150
New Hampshire	2	20
New Jersey	2	75
Missouri	1	1
Maryland	2	30
Indiana	1	5
Tennessee	2	8
Illinois	1	1
Oregon Territory	1	1
Totals	112	11,021

SOURCES: Petitions to the Senate, Record Group 46, National Archives; and Petitions to the House of Representatives, Record Group 233, National Archives.

the 1812 veterans. Although local groups of 1812 veterans had formed in some of the larger cities in the 1840s, funerals provided the chief excuse for a gathering. Decades after the 1812 veterans were dead, their descendants in New York, Philadelphia, and Baltimore quarreled over which city had formed the first corps of veterans. The champions of each city claimed priority, but it does seem that a group called the Defenders of Baltimore, who had fought at Fort McHenry in 1814, had organized a few years before the Mexican War.[15] In any event, the bounty land issue gave such fraternal organizations a cause to press. The politicking began at the time Congress considered the 1850 bounty land bill. The "Veterans Corps of the War of 1812" in New York City met in September of that year as the Senate debated bounty lands and urged New York's two senators to vote in favor of the bill already passed by the

House. The Veteran Corps also set up a board of trustees to receive donations of land warrants from more wealthy members of the corps on behalf of needy members. This philanthropic attempt had grown by 1855 into a Wall Street brokerage house that bought and sold land warrants.[16]

The restrictions of the 1850 bounty land law produced great unhappiness among veterans and led to more organizing. Philadelphia became the scene of much of the agitation to overturn the despised sections of the 1850 act. Veterans in that city heard the call to organize in January 1851, just a few months after passage of the law. Joel Sutherland, a physician in the War of 1812 and later boss of the Southwark Democrats, demanded "one hundred and sixty acres of land in lieu of the miserable pittance of forty or eighty acres granted under the Bounty Act of 1850." In 1852, the Philadelphia veterans organized themselves into a corps; by 1854, Sutherland had made Philadelphia the most powerful corps agitating for more bounty lands. Local veterans' corps also met in 1854 in Baltimore and Frederick, Maryland, Painesville, Ohio, and Portsmouth, New Hampshire, among other places.[17]

A January 1854 veterans' assembly at Poughkeepsie, New York, highlights many of the features of the local meeting. The gathering opened by offering a salute to fallen comrades; the balance of the meeting was devoted to considering how best to secure additional bounty lands. The featured speaker and leader of the Poughkeepsie veterans, General Leonard Maison, argued:

> It is very evident that forty acres of uncultivated land was totally insufficient for the support of any individual, and offered no inducement to make location and improvement; we were constrained to sell our land warrants for the best price that could be obtained for same; the avails of the sales being a very inadequate compensation for the privation, suffering and loss, which the most of us endured in the public service.[18]

The Poughkeepsie veterans demanded that their congressman vote in favor of the Old Soldiers bill to raise all veterans to a 160-acre grant, and the group appointed Maison to create a Committee of Correspondence that would work for bounty land parity with Mexican War veterans. As in New York, Philadelphia, and other cities, the leaders of the Poughkeepsie veterans' corps were high-ranking officers. Indeed, veterans' meetings at the local, state, and national levels followed a distinct military hierarchy, with nominal colonels and generals in charge. General Maison won his title, not during the War of 1812, but afterward in the peacetime New York State militia, a tribute as much to his political skills as his military prowess. Success in the militia reflected and reinforced success in business life, and Maison figured prominently among the Poughkeepsie bourgeoisie as an attorney and investor. He managed to acquire a modest fortune by allying himself with the powerful Vassar family brewing interest. In the 1830s, he invested with Matthew Vassar, Sr., in the Dutchess Whaling Company and served as attorney to Matthew Vassar, Jr., in the 1850s. In 1853 and 1854, Maison helped the younger Vassar buy over fifty bounty land warrants for use in Wisconsin and Michigan land speculations and aided Vassar in founding the town in Michigan that bears the family name. His public advocacy of the veterans' demand for land warrants complemented his open business interest as a land warrant broker.[19]

Men like Maison went on to represent their hometowns at state conventions like the one held in Syracuse in June 1854. The newly formed New York Central Railroad offered free passes to Syracuse for veterans making the journey. Eleven hundred New York veterans of the War of 1812 met to hear speeches about old battles and to issue a set of political demands. The leaders of the Syracuse convention, a collection of retired lawyers, merchants, and editors, consisted almost entirely of men bearing the title "colonel" or "general." Some won their ranks in the peacetime state militias, while others were appointed to them by the very veterans' corps who had sent them to Syracuse. "General" James Bogert of Geneva, New York, illustrates this type. He served as a junior officer in the War of 1812 and rose to colonel in the peacetime militia before resigning in 1830. Bogert had a long career as a Geneva newspaper editor and Finger Lakes politician, and as an honor the veterans' "Brigade of Northern New-York" made him their "brigadier-general" in the 1850s. In its activity, the state convention mirrored the local chapters. A Committee on Resolutions, composed of one member from each county, urged that "not less than 160 acres ought to be granted the Soldiers of 1812 for any term of service however brief" and decided to set up a central committee of New York State veterans' leaders to work with those from other states to secure the desired action. The goal of 160 acres of bounty land stands out as the main message of the Syracuse convention, and departing delegates were told to "carry its recollection with you to the Ballot Boxes, and justice will no longer be withheld."[20]

War of 1812 veterans staged two national conventions, one at Philadelphia in January 1854 and one a year later in Washington, D.C., each held on the anniversary of Andrew Jackson's victory at New Orleans. Although the Philadelphia convention drew delegates from twelve states and the District of Columbia, the great majority of conventioneers came from Pennsylvania, and in turn Philadelphia dominated the Keystone State delegation. Over one thousand delegates squeezed into Independence Hall, and they promptly elected Joel Sutherland as the convention's president. The convention then passed resolutions demanding that each veteran receive land warrants totaling 160 acres; in addition, they urged land warrants for those Americans captured and sold into slavery at Tripoli and those confined in "the loathesome Dartmoor and other foreign prisons during the war of 1812." The balance of the convention was given over to telling vivid stories of the War of 1812. One speaker after another recounted the injustice of impressment, the savagery of the British and their Indian allies, and the gallantry displayed at battles such as Plattsburgh and New Orleans. A committee of fifty was appointed to lobby Congress for bounty lands and to plan for future gatherings. Sutherland closed the convention by noting that the veterans had staged the "largest convention that was ever held in this country" and gave his oath never to rest until the bounty land grants sought by the veterans became fact.[21]

The group (now formally renamed the United Brethren of the War of 1812) that met the next year in Washington, D.C., on January 8–10, 1855, resembled more a national convention than the Philadelphia gathering, though Pennsylvania still brought the largest delegation (see table 8). At a time when most churches and other national organizations had divided on a regional basis, the veterans of 1812 managed to organize on an intersectional basis. Cooperation came from a shared interest in the glorious past, largely uncelebrated by the younger generation, as well as from the prospect of more land warrants. The delegates again elected Joel Sutherland president of the convention.

Colonel Sutherland led his troops on a march from convention headquarters at Washington's Presbyterian Church to the White House. Most newspaper reports commented on the thrilling sight made by the procession of grayheads as it marched slowly and with great dignity down Pennsylvania Avenue under the banner of "Free Trade and Sailors' Rights," the battle slogan of the summer of 1812. President Pierce greeted Sutherland and other representatives of the

TABLE 8
Delegates by Origin to the 1854 and 1855 National Veterans Conventions

Origin	*1854 Convention*	*1855 Convention*
Maine	0	3
New Hampshire	0	3
Vermont	0	7
Massachusetts	9	10
Rhode Island	0	5
Connecticut	0	2
New York	54	59
New Jersey	52	0
Pennsylvania	656	250
Delaware	23	5
Maryland	41	107
District of Columbia	13	37
Virginia	8	89
North Carolina	0	2
Kentucky	1	6
Louisiana	11	0
Missouri	1	0
Texas	1	1
Ohio	3	5
Indiana	0	2
Illinois	0	2
Iowa	0	1
Michigan	0	1
Wisconsin	0	1
Totals	873	598

SOURCES: Proceedings of the National Convention of the Soldiers of the War of 1812, 1854; Proceedings of the United Brethren of the War of 1812.

convention in the East Room of the White House and commended their services, but he would not openly commit himself to their cause of 160 acres of bounty land for each veteran.[22]

Once reassembled, the delegates passed the by now familiar resolutions demanding bounty land parity with the Mexican War soldiers. One delegate present wrote a friend, "I never saw such a sight as the convention exhibited—upwards of a thousand respectable looking gray headed men, assembled together in one body." Speakers repeatedly called on the old soldiers, as one old-timer thundered, "to go before Congress now and ask for justice, not charity, and if they refuse, we will meet them again at Philippi. They shall hear our voices at the polls, as loud as drums and trumpets, next election day, and in the presidential campaign of 1856." The veterans formed a permanent lobbying committee, headed by Colonel Sutherland, with instructions to stay in Washington and secure the desired bounty land legislation.[23]

By the opening of the 1855 convention, careful observers knew that Sutherland's four-year effort for more bounty lands was near success. The Old Soldiers bill had wide support in Congress. One indication of this was the large number of active politicians who attended the Washington convention; many were not veterans of the War of 1812 or, in some cases, had yet been born then. Senators Sam Houston, Lewis Cass, James Shields, James Jones, and James Cooper joined ten congressmen, seven ex-congressmen, and three former governors as delegates. Political operatives like New York's Thurlow Weed and Leslie Combs of Kentucky sat as delegates, along with Pennsylvania's Lewis Coryell. Three delegates to the Washington convention held positions on the central committee of the Pennsylvania Democratic party.[24]

Congressional passage in March 1855 of a bounty land bill, seven weeks after the Washington convention, is tribute to the political skill of the veterans' lobby leaders. Over 260,000 veterans, widows, and heirs, about 187,000 of them from the War of 1812, benefited from the new legislation. Of the veterans' leaders, Joel Sutherland stands out as the one most deserving credit for effective leadership. He had graduated from the University of Pennsylvania medical school just before war broke out in 1812, and after service as a battle surgeon, took up the law and fashioned a career for himself in politics, first in the Pennsylvania Assembly and, from 1827 to 1837, in the U.S. House of Representatives. He returned to Philadelphia to sit on the Court of Common Pleas and to oversee Democratic affairs in South Philadelphia. In the often strange world of Pennsylvania Democratic politics, he sided with the Dallas faction yet managed to remain on good terms with rival James Buchanan. After retiring from the court, Sutherland kept a private law practice in Philadelphia and did occasional lobbying for railroads.[25]

One of Sutherland's protégés in Philadelphia politics was Thomas Florence, a genuine artisan-intellectual involved in many different areas of city life. The son of a boatbuilder, Florence was

FIG. 3. JOEL B. SUTHERLAND. President of the United Brethren of the War of 1812 (courtesy of the Maryland Historical Society).

apprenticed to a hatter and set up his own hat shop at the age of twenty-one. He lasted in that business eight years only to go bankrupt in 1841. He moved next to a career in education, serving nine years as secretary of the city's Board of Controllers of Schools. In 1851 Philadelphia sent him to Congress, where he devoted himself to contracts for the navy yard and passage of bounty land and pension bills, earning the nickname "the widow's friend."[26]

Sutherland had a fellow veteran of Pennsylvania Democratic politics in James M. Porter, a United Brethren convention vice-president in 1855. Son of the Revolutionary War general Andrew Porter, James Porter rose from private to colonel during the War of 1812. He lived in Easton and, following Lafayette's 1824 visit to the town, persuaded his fellow citizens to found a college in honor of the marquis. He served as president of the board of trustees of Lafayette College for twenty-five years and spent a term in Congress, all the while maintaining a law practice in Northumberland County. Porter briefly served as acting secretary of war in the last part of the Tyler administration and crossed swords with Senator Benton over the conduct of the senator's son-in-law, John C. Frémont. Benton and Porter became bitter enemies; a decade later they would again find themselves on opposing sides over the land warrant issue.[27]

In 1836, Porter took into his office a young lawyer named Richard Brodhead, who within six years got himself elected to Congress. Brodhead loyally supported the Polk administration in its policies, except for its downward revision of tariff duties in 1846. In 1851, at age forty, Brodhead moved up to the Senate as a compromise choice among warring Pennsylvania Democrats. He soon antagonized many of his supporters in Pennsylvania by a clumsy attempt to sabotage James Buchanan's 1852 presidential aspirations. The young senator needed to mend fences at home, and from 1852 on he made the bounty land question his issue. At every session thereafter he worked for a bounty land bill granting 160 acres to each veteran, regardless of length of service. On the first day of the 1854–55 session, Brodhead once again introduced his bill; over the next four months he successfully guided it through the Senate, an accomplishment that pleased his old mentor Colonel Porter.[28]

Two ancient adversaries from Kentucky forgot their animosities long enough to work together lobbying for the bounty land cause. General Leslie Combs, Henry Clay's right-hand man in the Kentucky Whig party, had fought in the War of 1812 and two decades later in the Texas Revolution. He served one term per decade in the Kentucky legislature from the 1820s through the 1850s, and spent much of his time after Clay's last presidential run lobbying the Texas debt and bounty land issues. On the same platform at Philadelphia and Washington sat General John McCalla, a lifelong Kentucky adversary of Clay and Combs. President Polk had appointed McCalla second auditor in the Treasury, where he oversaw pension and Ten Regiments Act bounty land claims. After the Whig victory in 1848, McCalla remained in Washington to open a government claims agency specializing in bounty land and pension matters. Like others in the United Brethren, McCalla combined the business of securing warrants for claimants with the politics of agitating Congress for more land warrants on easier terms. He urged clients to write Congress and demand a more liberal bounty land law. He also served as Washington coordinator of the lobby, writing Sutherland in Philadelphia and other veterans' leaders in New York, Kentucky, Virginia, and Michigan about organizational details.[29]

Although forming a single-issue lobby, the veterans brought forward a heterogeneous and sometimes conflicting body of ideas in support of their demands for land warrants. Veterans' spokesmen presented three different arguments to Congress: the argument that bounties would be a suitable "republican" reward for service well done; second, the Jacksonian argument of "equal rights"; and finally, the blunter argument that a vote cast in favor of more land warrants would help a politician's career. These ideas reflected the political discourse common during the lives of the elderly men who convened in local, state, and national meetings. The republican ideas of the eighteenth century, though constantly revived up to the beginning of the twentieth century, were at their strongest in the early part of the nineteenth century. The equal rights doctrine meant more than the constitutional protection of equality before the law and reflected the laissez-faire beliefs of the 1830s that the government should not favor some over others. Finally, proponents of more bounty land grants used a combination of cajolery and threats to persuade their congressional representatives to vote as requested. It seems likely that some congressmen reacted favorably to this pressure. The House of Representatives, scholars have shown, was very much a place of turmoil from the close of the Mexican War through southern secession, and, as the 1850s unfolded, sectional and local loyalties competed with national, party-based allegiance. In this climate, fealty to the demands of constituents had appeal for some congressmen seeking to retain their seats.[30]

The very fact that the veterans coalesced when they did says much about how Americans had come to view the War of 1812. Veterans of the War of 1812 preferred in public to call it the Second War of American Independence, indicating their belief that what had begun at Lexington and Concord had ended forty years later at New Orleans. Nearly all veterans who spoke at assemblies exhibited a strong Anglophobia, best seen in the thanks one speaker offered the Czar of Russia for holding Great Britain's attention in the Crimea. The speaker insisted that, without the Crimean War, the British would surely have continued their active scheming to recapture the United States. Colonel Sutherland frequently proclaimed the importance of American victories in the War of 1812 because they "bound England over to keep the peace, which has already continued for forty years."[31] All speakers and petitioners agreed with New York's General James Nye, an intimate of Senator William H. Seward, in saying that "Our fathers fought to *obtain,* you to *retain* the principles of Republican liberty." The republican liberty dearest to all veterans was represented by the absence of a standing army and the virtue of a citizens' militia, the surest barrier to would-be tyrants. Nearly every veteran sought to explain the successes of the War of 1812 as the outcome of the superiority enjoyed by a citizens' army:

> It [the War of 1812] taught monarchies the salutary lesson, that though they may boast of their achievements in other lands, over a soldiery not free but hirelings, when they strike a blow against a nation that is free, against a soldiery that are Sovereigns, that in that conflict they must fall, that the banner on which is inscribed the magic word of Freedom will be found waving when the conflict is over.[32]

Veterans' leaders showed little embarrassment in moving from the celebration of sharpshooting militiamen to the demand for material rewards for such selfless service. Pennsylvania's Colonel Porter argued that "we come not as mendicants to seek this as a boon from the charity of our country; we come respectfully to claim the payment of a just debt, due to us from the country we served, now abundantly able to pay us." Invoking shame in his argument, General Nye contended that

> ours is the only country that does not provide well for its Soldiers. Even the semi-barbarous nations make ample provision for their Soldiers and their families. A republic like ours, should be the most ready to be generous. . . . It is a sad thing to see the old war torn Veteran an inmate of the Alms House. . . .[33]

The veterans sought to convince themselves and the public that they had upheld the ideals of the Revolutionary War generation. The 1855 Washington convention delegates made a solemn pilgrimage to Mount Vernon to make speeches about George Washington's genius and the way his spirit still guided the nation. The 1855 convention also passed a resolution urging completion of the planned Washington monument. Washington's adopted son, George Washington Parke Custis, attended the 1855 convention as living proof of republican continuity. The visit to Washington's grave also emphasized a different aspect of the republicanism they shared with him, namely, the willingness of the citizen in a republic selflessly to serve his country, especially in wartime. Land warrants, from this perspective, represented not so much a reward as an acknowledgment of thanks from the nation.

How consistent was the republicanism espoused by the veterans? Analysis of the speeches and writings of veterans' leaders shows that their republican ideas consisted largely of the fear of standing armies and monarchs—representing only a small part of the commonwealth or Whig ideology of revolutionary America. It is noteworthy that, amid all the special-interest legislation and place jobbing of the 1850s, the colonels and generals leading the 1812 veterans had nothing to say about political corruption. The veterans' spokesmen also were silent about the dangers of great riches and luxury in society. Men like Leslie Combs and John McCalla feared Catholic immigrants not only because of their alleged servility to a despotic Pope but also as competitors for public lands. This rather narrow, if sincere, republicanism suggests that veterans of the War of 1812 had come to interpret, in restricted fashion, the meaning of the revolution they claimed to have defended. This is one measure of how the concept of republicanism had been altered since the beginning of the federal system.[34]

Veterans also employed Jacksonian language against artificial "ranks" in society. Here they were careful to distinguish between military rank and ascribed rank in civil society. The United Brethren of the War of 1812 accused the 1850 bounty land act of promoting ranks in civil society because older veterans received different treatment than Mexican War veterans. Specifically, the veterans were determined to overturn the restrictive prohibition on sales of 1850 series warrants. Although the ban was intended to prevent speculators from buying large quantities of warrants, veterans saw it as restricting their right to dispose of private property, a right enjoyed by Mexican War soldiers. The argument eventually swayed Congress, and in March 1852 it reversed itself and made warrants assignable. In addition, the old veterans used the rhetoric of "equality" to attack the 1850 apportioning of acreage according to time served on active duty. Thousands of Pennsylvanians signed petitions containing the following sentence:

> Believing that Members of Congress unanimously desire to deal out equal and exact justice to the soldiers of the various wars of the Republic, the undersigned respectfully present this memorial, asking for the same amount of land, that was given by the Government to the soldiers, who were enlisted just before the close of the late Mexican War, and never marched to Mexico.[35]

The philosophical justification for a grant of 160 acres to all veterans rested on the assertion that a soldier or militiaman could be shot as easily in his first month of service as in his thirteenth month. Some citizens of Albany County, New York, took this thought and fused the equal rights doctrine with republicanism:

> . . . it would be more in accordance with the spirit of equality which pervades our republican institutions, that when the services of all the claimants are equally meritorious, because all equally obeyed the call of their country in its time of need, and remained in its service as long as they were required to do, therefore all should equally participate in the bounty which the government is pleased to voluntarily bestow.[36]

The logic of the equality doctrine required that no one with the slightest claim to a land warrant be excluded. Chaplains, teamsters, marines, flotillamen, sailors, and members of the Quartermaster's Corps all clamored for land warrants, and all were included in the Old Soldiers bill. Another group excluded by the 1850 act, widows who had remarried, had their champions to push their claim for benefits under the proposed new bounty land bill. The authors of the 1850 act reasoned that remarried widows did not need the material benefit of a land warrant. Such discrimination later brought rebuke from many quarters. John W. Stephens, a Washington land warrant broker, insisted in a letter to his congressman that remarried widows "think the law so amended will be more Republican, dispense justice and equal Rights." At times, the proponents of equality could lapse into buffoonery—as when one congressman urged eligibility for remarried widows lest Congress discriminate against beauty in favor of ugliness. Along similar lines, some Virginians claimed the 1850 law discriminated in favor of idleness and against industriousness:

> Those who attended in Company Service only are shown by the muster rolls to have served less than one month, while they were called out at different times for one, two, and three days and sometimes for only a half-day, but were considered Minute Men and subject to a call from the beat of a Drum or fire of a Cannon at any hour of the day or night; but the effect of this law is to include but few except those who served a monthly guard, which were usually selected from those having most leisure.[37]

A third type of appeal was directed to the self-interest of congressmen. When making their case for generous, nondiscriminatory bounty land grants, veterans rarely failed to point out the benefits to individual congressmen. The Baltimore Veterans Corps suggested that

> a grant to them [the old soldiers] will reach almost every family in the nation; that children and grandchildren will be interested in such a bounty of the government; that, consequently, such a provision could not fail to be popular with the whole country; and that therefore, the legislation herein indicated would be, but in strict truth, the reflex of the popular will.[38]

This is part of the language of the 1850s, the votes argument, and it was a popular demand with appeal for congressmen. Since veterans in many states stood to benefit, a general bounty land grant, in the words of one senator, "attracts to it voters and influential men in the country." The same appeal had worked in passing the 1850 act. One bounty land supporter in Congress admitted in 1850 that he favored warrants for 1812 veterans simply because they did vote but defended his decision because he "thought that to secure this right to vote was the very thing they had been fighting for."[39]

Threats of electoral retribution constituted the other side of the appeal to a congressman's self-interest. Kentucky's General Leslie Combs made this clear in his speech to the Washington convention:

> If the voices of the remnant of gray-headed veterans who now alone remain of the four hundred thousand gallant youths who fought in 1812–15 shall remain unheeded, we will muster millions of children and grand-children and come down like an avalanche upon our cold-hearted representatives.[40]

The very success of the bounty land issue hastened the demise of the United Brethren of the War of 1812 as a force in politics. The United Brethren never held another national meeting and dissolved back into state and city fraternal corps. Men like Colonel Porter turned their attention away from the politics of veterans' benefits to the price of English grass seed "and how thick it ought to be sown to the acre to make a good soil. Several persons and I wish to get it for their plots in the cemetery." Joel Sutherland sought to keep the veterans' lobby alive by agitating for a general cash pension to War of 1812 veterans. He wanted equality in treatment for his men and Revolutionary War veterans, the latter having received pensions under an act of Congress in 1832. It took fifteen years of trying before Sutherland's new efforts on behalf of the 1812 soldiers had any success, but by that time, the old colonel was no longer living—and neither were most of the contemplated beneficiaries.[41]

Also lost after 1855 was the interesting conservative unionist message preached by the leaders of the veterans' lobby. "It seems to me," reasoned New Yorker James Nye, "that notwithstanding the sectional jealousies of the time, your petition, when presented to Congress, must command attention. . . . So universal was the effort, that a lisp of Sectionalism would be hushed into silence. The blood of all sections flowed too freely to admit of any jealousies."[42]

In fact, soon after passage of the 1855 Old Soldiers Act, northern and southern members of the United Brethren openly debated the slavery issue and the role that the 1812 veterans should play in its resolution. The break came when upstate New York veterans invited Leslie Combs to speak at their Fourth of July meeting in Utica. He politely declined; and, in a public letter from his Lexington home to New York commander General John Van Renssalaer, he made it clear that southern veterans expected the New Yorkers to rebuke abolitionism and free-soilism as contrary to the legacy of the Revolution and the War of 1812. Combs knew that he invited conflict when he wrote this to the New York veterans; much of that state's leadership in the United Brethren was politically tied to the Republican presidential hopeful William H. Seward, especially the United Brethren secretary Thurlow Weed.[43]

Can one attribute the passage of the Old Soldiers Act of 1855 solely to the lobbying efforts of the United Brethren of the War of 1812? How much credit is due Joel Sutherland and his fellow graybeards? The speeches of interested participants point to the importance of the veterans' lobby, but the questions can also be answered by study of the voting in Congress on bounty land issues between 1853 and 1855, the years when Sutherland and others built a national movement.

The 33d Congress was elected in November 1852, in the last national election contested by Democrats and Whigs and effectively the close of the Jacksonian political era. The Democratic candidate for president was Franklin Pierce, who had been an ambitious but obscure New Hampshire politician until the Ten Regiments Act gave him the chance to show military leadership as a general in Mexico. In 1852, Pierce trounced his former military boss, the Whigs' General Winfield Scott, and brought a large Democratic majority with him to Washington.

Pierce and the Democrats ran on a platform with a public lands plank nearly identical with the 1836 platform, that is, support for preemptors and land for sale at modest prices. Pierce himself had no original ideas about what to do with the public domain. His first annual message offered the platitude, "It is believed that experience has verified the wisdom and justice of the present system with regard to the public domain in most essential particulars." The Whig platform that General Scott endorsed also offered no new initiative on the disposition of the public lands. While the two parties remained solid in their thinking about public lands policy, different groups of people pushed for alternative methods of giving away portions of the public domain. Railroad promoters and groups like the United Brethren, with its goal of rewarding earlier military service, sought land grants to accomplish certain tasks under the rubric of congressional proprietorship. At the same time, a group of self-styled land reformers advocated free land for those who would farm it. In just a few short years after the Mexican War, the two old political parties of Whigs and Democrats had become less relevant in shaping and leading the discussion of public lands policy. Yet, by the end of the decade, the two parties of Republicans and Democrats had coherent and opposing views about how best to make use of the nation's public lands. The two parties' platforms in 1860 show the difference: Republicans advocated a homestead policy, and Democrats opposed it.[44]

How did this realignment of positions come about? Earlier students of 1850s congressional voting on the public lands issue tended to emphasize the split between those favoring a free land, or homestead, policy and those opposed to such a policy. In 1917 George Stephenson, a student of Frederick Jackson Turner's, wrote one of the first complete accounts of the late antebellum wrangling over the public lands. Stephenson never identified homestead opponents, but he considered them wicked men who would use any means to stop the free land movement. Their dirtiest trick, in Stephenson's view, was the use of military bounty land warrants "by far the most odious to the West and to the friends of Homestead." He did not see warrants as a means of lowering the price of public lands; instead, Stephenson viewed the bounty land grants solely as an aid to speculation and as an encouragement to land monopoly and higher prices.[45]

The early Progressive approach, what was essentially a "frontier interpretation" that Stephenson described, provides one starting point for understanding the politics of the public lands in the 1850s. His was a frontier interpretation in the sense that he saw the basic conflict as a regional one: the democratic West struggling to overcome a hostile policy imposed by a distant East. Stephenson's *Political History of the Public Lands* remains a useful account of the maneuverings that led from the Preemption Act of 1841 all the way to the triumph of homestead in 1862. Stephenson based his history on a careful reading of the floor debates as reported in the *Congressional Globe* and of editors' accounts in newspapers of the day. An alternate explanation of the politics of the public lands in the 1850s also relies on geographical section. However, instead of seeing the conflict as Stephenson did, of East against West, later Progressive writers like Roy Robbins stressed a North-South split. In *Our Landed Heritage,* Robbins perceptively described some of the land giveaways of the early 1850s, such as railroad grants and bounty land grants, as a departure from the old cash sales policy; moreover, he attributed the change in policy to an alliance between the Northeast and Northwest. The older region got the use of public lands for corporate and other purposes, while the latter got cheaper and eventually free land. This agreement over land policy, Robbins argued, formed the basis of the coalition that elected Lincoln and then prosecuted the Civil War.[46]

Political parties are elements in American politics not fully understood or appreciated by the Progressives and, accordingly, slighted in favor of regional or sectional explanations of events. Post–World War II era historians, beginning with Roy Nichols (*Disruption of the American Democracy*), have come to recognize the important role that antebellum parties played in Congress and the electorate and the coming of the Civil War. The concentration on the breakup of the old two-party system and the emergence of antagonistic Republicans and Democrats has had the effect of pushing aside interest in the public lands issue; recent accounts have focused instead on ethnocultural issues and the slavery extension controversy.[47]

Study of roll call votes in the Senate and in the House can show the effects of various influences and constituencies on congressional voting on public lands issues in the 33d Congress, starting with the Senate and then going to the House. Three factors are tested here for their influence on congressional voting: (1) section represented; (2) constituency in a public lands state or not; and (3) party identification. The results of statistical testing in part confirm the Progressive view put forward earlier in the twentieth century but also point to some complexities that the dualistic outlook cannot explain. Indeed, many legislators did fit the Progressive pattern. For example, Iowa's two senators, George Jones and Augustus Caesar Dodge, had perfectly prohomestead voting records. On ten roll call votes in

1854 and 1855, each cast five votes for homestead measures and five against bounty lands. South Carolina's Josiah Evans and Senator John Clayton of Delaware compiled perfect pro–bounty land voting records on the same ten roll calls, the reverse of Jones and Dodge.[48]

Sectionalism, the factor given such prominence by Robbins, shows a curious pattern in the 33d Congress on homestead and bounty land votes. On three homestead roll calls, a senator's section (northern free states vs. southern slave states) proved a very strong indicator of how he would vote, while the same was true on only one of five bounty land votes (see App. C).

The explanation is that in 1854 southerners as a bloc stoutly fought homestead, but they split on bounty lands. Southerners opposed homestead for two reasons. First, some southerners had an old desire to see revenues from land sales form as large a part as possible of the government's total revenue. This southern policy would then work to lower the high tariff, a perennial cause of complaint for many southerners. In an earlier day, South Carolina's approach, led by John Calhoun, was to oppose any policy that lowered federal revenue from land sales. By the mid-1850s, this no longer received the backing of South Carolina's two senators; both voted solidly for bounty land grants and steadfastly against homestead. Senator Andrew Butler realized that the Calhoun policy had no chance in Congress, so Butler supported the more palatable option, a large bounty land grant: "I am inclined to vote for it because I believe it is the best form of distributing the public lands, because I believe it is better than the system which has heretofore been recommended, of giving them to every person who will go and settle upon them." A second southern reason for opposing homestead was the concern that aid to western migration would produce more free-soil states and thus tip the balance in the Senate against the South.[49]

The party in Congress, as described by historians of Jacksonian legislative politics, served as the chief organizational power and disciplinary device. However, this may have been less true in the 33d Congress, where party discipline was less relevant to the disappearing minority of Whigs. It was also quite costly to exercise, as the dominant Democrats learned in passing the Kansas-Nebraska Act during the first session. The parties in their 1852 conventions took no formal stand on bounty lands or free homesteads as a method of distributing the public lands, and so political party did not strongly influence the Senate voting; on only three of the ten roll calls did party represent a significant variable. What replaced the party as a guide to policy was the self-interest of legislators favoring their constituents. In this case, the split was more one of East versus West. The public lands issue between 1852 and 1855 does show how vulnerable a weakened partisan Congress was to single-interest groups.[50]

The strongest overall predictor of a senator's vote on the ten roll call votes was whether his state contained federally controlled public lands (or, like Ohio, had once been a public lands state). In six of the ten roll calls (and four of the five bounty land votes), this factor proved statistically significant. The voting worked as follows: men representing states with public lands tended to support homestead (whether they were northerners or southerners); men from the eastern, non–public lands states more often favored bounty land grants, whether they were from New England, the Mid-Atlantic states, or the South Atlantic states.

The potency of the veterans' lobby was a factor not described in previous writers' accounts of the congressional debate over the public lands in the 33d Congress. The presence or absence of public lands in a senator's state also serves as one proxy for the power of the veterans' lobby. Most of the 1812 veterans still lived in states east of the Appalachians. Thus, Atlantic seaboard senators who voted for what Stephenson called an "odious" land policy of granting military bounty land warrants actually voted to help their constituents and to pay tribute to a war that had a deep resonance in their states' memories. Those public lands states senators who opposed military bounties to veterans in 1855 did so in part because of the persistent fear that speculators would unfairly use the land warrants, but also (with the possible exceptions of Ohio and Alabama) because few of their constituents stood to benefit directly. If the goal of a legislator representing a public lands state was cheaper land, than homestead promised a more effective means than land warrants.[51]

The House, then as now, had about four times the number of members as the Senate. New York and Pennsylvania, the two states with the strongest veterans' corps, also had the largest delegations in the House. An analysis of roll call votes cast in the House in part substantiates much of George Stephenson's 1917 account; but again, additional factors that shaped attitudes must be acknowledged (see App. C). In the House, the South Carolina delegation more closely followed Calhoun's tradition and led the fight against any land giveaways. However, sectionalism, or a free state–slave state antagonism showed up only on homestead votes. This was particularly clear in the voting on a motion to limit homestead entries to whites only. Southerners voted overwhelmingly for such a restriction, while many northerners opposed it as irrelevant to the homestead measure. Study of the House voting statistics on the bounty land votes shows no significant North-South difference.

The East-West split that showed in the Senate also proved important in the House. On all three bounty land roll calls, representatives from non–public land states were more likely to support the Old Soldiers bill, while "westerners" from public lands states tended to oppose it. On homestead, however, this East-West split was statistically significant on two of the three votes. It should be noted here that Progressive writers tended to think of the West as more properly the Old Northwest, while the analysis given here points to a fuller notion of the West. The North-South split seems largely absent on bounty land votes, though not homestead ones; this nicely reflects the intersectional nature of the United Brethren of the War of 1812 and suggests that the veterans' lobby had the most influence in making bounty land grants as the favored method of public land disposal after 1850.

Political party shows up in the voting analysis as a more important factor in the House than the Senate. On all three homestead votes, the Whigs were more likely to oppose free land, while Democrats were more likely to support it. An observer in 1854 consequently could not easily predict the reversed positions that became apparent in the Buchanan years. Party was important, moreover, in distinguishing representatives on two of three bounty land votes; one such vote illustrates how this operated. Representative Benton moved once again in 1855 to make the new issue of warrants nonassignable. The Democrats in the House split on this issue, but to a man the Whigs opposed it.

Voting in the House and Senate on homestead and bounty lands presented congressmen with options about public lands policy and confronted many representatives with cross-pressures. George Stephenson, in his reading of debates, correctly identified a strong regional flavor to the disputes between legislators as one of the factors at work. In addition to the East-West distinction between public lands and non–public lands states was the basic free state–slave state sectionalism. The debate over whether to make homestead or bounty lands and other grants the basic land policy took place against a backdrop of party confusion and realignment. For some representatives, the various pressures of region, section, and party all pushed in one direction. To take the case of Iowa's Augustus Caesar Dodge again: his western and his northern regions favored homestead, and his Democratic membership in 1854 put him on the side of easier terms for settlers, in this case, homestead. Other representatives and senators saw matters differently. Some voted for both homestead and bounty lands as complementary land policies, not conflicting ones, thereby anticipating the postbellum pattern of an "incongruous" land system that Paul Gates identified in 1936. Others, and here the South Carolina representatives come to mind, opposed both homestead and bounty land grants as contrary to good constitutional practice and political interest.[52]

In retrospect, the decision to issue millions of acres in military bounty land grants, but not grants of free land to settlers, is inseparable from the larger politics of the late antebellum years and follows rather closely the twists and turns of the debates over slavery expansion and immigration restriction. The political history of bounty lands and homesteads divides into three overlapping phases: from 1847 through 1852, when the initial decisions were made about the territory conquered from Mexico; from 1853 through 1855, when the slavery expansion issue was reopened at the same time as anti-immigrant and anti-Catholic sentiment peaked; and after 1855, when the actual workings of popular sovereignty in the West became an issue.

In the first phase, during and after the Mexican War, Congress approved land warrants under the Ten Regiments Act as a wartime expediency. Once the Compromise of 1850 seemingly settled the question of how to administer the territories, Congress continued its public lands policy in the direction of giveaway grants under the doctrine of proprietorship, notably to War of 1812 veterans as part of the act of 1850 grant, and to the Mobile and Ohio railroad project. A public lands policy of free land to settlers was not then endorsed by either of the two main political parties. The Assignment Act of 1852 might best be seen as the close of this first phase of bounty land politics by making act of 1850 warrants more useful to the veteran recipients. During the years after 1852, Joel Sutherland and his fellow veterans built a lobby outside the weakened party system to demand ever larger bounty land grants. The United Brethren tried to influence a Congress now committed to rapid disposal of the public domain, and had to fight against a growing sentiment in public lands states for an outright homestead policy. The United Brethren managed to build a congressional coalition of those who supported additional bounty land grants and those who opposed homestead. Appeals to patriotism, what Lincoln would later call "the mystic chords of memory," combined with calls to exclude immigrants from federal generosity in land. Congress passed the Old

Soldiers Act in 1855 at the height of the nativist furor, and many found the awarding of large parts of the public domain to veterans an appropriate policy of rewarding American citizens first. As 1856 began, a two-party system of Republicans and Democrats emerged, and during the Buchanan administration Congress once again debated the homestead policy. By 1860, the Republican party had brought homestead into its constellation of free labor ideas; by contrast, military bounty land warrants after the panic of 1857 came to be associated with the worst of the Buchanan-led Democrats: speculation, corruption, and financial ruin to struggling settlers.[53]

Success spoiled the United Brethren, but as the sectional crisis worsened during the Buchanan administration, what might have been a respected voice of conciliation from the veterans was simply absent. When the war finally came in 1861, the War of 1812 veterans' corps in Pittsburgh promptly offered its services to President Lincoln to save once again the Republic on the battlefield from its enemies. So, too, did some southern veterans come forth in response to President Davis's call to defend the Confederacy in a new war for American independence.[54]

In the end, the veterans' efforts to combine a Northeast–South Atlantic alliance proved unfeasible. After passage of the Old Soldiers bill, the veterans' lobby leaders could not come forth with new workable ideas or suggestions either for their own members or the nation at large. As Leslie Combs's 1855 letter to New York's General Van Renssalaer showed, southern 1812 veterans saw the slavery issue and the "fanaticism" of northern antislavery men as more important than the shared heritage of blood shed against Great Britain. Many of the New Yorkers held the opposite view, as spelled out by their champion Senator Seward in the congressional debates over the Kansas-Nebraska bill and later. They agreed with Seward that the political leadership of the Revolutionary generation had created a system designed to contain and eventually eliminate slavery. This view necessarily gave a different interpretation to the meaning of the War of 1812.[55]

The formation of lobbies like the United Brethren, republican in name and motivation but also special interest in design, signals the beginning of the end of the old republic of Washington and forecasts the onset of the "Big Barbecue" of the Gilded Age and the "Organizational Society" of the twentieth century. The bounty land issue did not neatly fit into the old Democrat-Whig debate over the use of the public lands. Until the Mexican War, both Jacksonians and Clay men had agreed that the public lands had value and that the federal government should receive some of that value in cash; they disagreed over the price and terms of that value. Land give-aways represented a change in basic policy and forced both Democrats and Whigs to think again about the future of public lands distribution. The Democrats under Pierce and Buchanan found themselves unable to go much beyond a policy of scattered give-aways: bounty lands for veterans, grants for railroads, and so forth. The new Republicans, including the old Whig element, moved by 1856 to propose the homestead idea of free land to the settler as central to their party's philosophy of promoting a republic of small producers. The homestead issue in the end did become part of the North-South confrontation, in part because the terms of the older public lands debate had permanently changed after the bounty land grants had weakened the cash sales system.[56]

The lasting accomplishment of the United Brethren was to make veterans' fraternal organizations respectable and no longer perceived as subversive—the way Americans saw the old Society of the Cincinnati. The immediate accomplishment was winning tens of millions of acres in bounty land grants for its members. However, before the hundreds of thousands of veterans and widows could enjoy their bounty, they had to face a different Washington fight, a struggle with the federal Pension Bureau over obtaining the bounty at all.

3

"Best Evidence": Obtaining a Land Warrant from the Pension Bureau

The twentieth century has witnessed the growth of the large-scale federal benefits programs that make up the modern welfare state. By the more modest standards of nineteenth-century federal programs, the government's bounty land warrant grants in the 1840s and 1850s touched a sizable percentage of the nation's families. As shown in table 1, the federal government disbursed more than 552,000 warrants to over 405,000 veterans, widows, and heirs. Of this group of more than 400,000 recipients, about 225,000 received single warrants for full quarter-sections of 160 acres, mainly under the acts of 1847 and 1855. Another 147,000 benefited under the act of 1855 by receiving supplementary warrants to total 160 acres. Finally, just under 33,000 received warrants for less than 160 acres before the act of 1855, but, for whatever reason, failed to obtain second warrants under the Old Soldiers Act provisions raising them to the full 160 acres. Assuming the 400,000 plus came from different households (a reasonable assertion despite the chance that some Mexican War or Indian Removal veterans lived in the same household as 1812 veterans), a land warrant was thus given to about one in nine households.[1]

If one thinks of the warrants as an "entitlement" program, then the percentage of beneficiaries is comparable to twentieth-century entitlements in breadth. However, land warrants were not meant to be renewable after 1855; moreover, the grants were not at all based on need or income level. Much of the rhetoric of the United Brethren of the War of 1812 did stress the poverty, broken health, and old age of veterans, but the arguments advanced by the United Brethren for bounty lands also involved ideas of tradition, justice, and power.

This chapter considers the administration of the land warrant program, with particular attention given to how well veterans were served by federal officials in charge of disbursing land warrants. For many of the veterans and widows, the experience of obtaining and making use of land warrants proved quite frustrating. All prospective warrantees had to deal with two federal agencies, the Pension Bureau and then the General Land Office. The Pension Bureau administered the application and issue of land warrants, and it was charged with determining the eligibility and suitability of applicants. The General Land Office oversaw the use of land warrants in the actual acquisition of public land. In this regard, it dealt not only with the veterans receiving warrants but also the assignees of the veterans who sought to make use of the bounty land grant.

Congress set forth what it thought were clear eligibility standards on land warrant qualifications for all four acts between 1847 and 1855. The common requirement was that the applicant had to have served his country at the "seat of war." However, what constituted service and where the seat of war existed were two questions that vexed secretaries of the interior and attorneys general through the presidency of Chester A. Arthur. A man who drove an army wagon in Texas south of the Nueces River between 1846 and 1848 earned himself a land warrant, while at the same time, an army teamster driving a similar wagon at Leavenworth west of Missouri did not qualify. Men from Maine who rushed to the wilds of Aroostook County, ready to settle a border dispute with arms, received land warrants. More precisely, those men who served in the Maine militia and who were called into federal service earned bounty land from a generous Congress in 1852. The Aroostook War of 1838–39 had also involved Down Easters organized as a civil posse to chase off British "trespassers" from land claimed by Maine. When posse members applied for bounty land in the 1850s, the Pension Bureau ruled that Congress intended to reward only military service, not civil duty. In 1838 and 1839 Vermont militiamen, without the bidding of the federal government, also manned their border with Canada in case the British launched an invasion. The British did not, and the Vermonters never received land warrants because they had not served at the seat of war.[2]

Following the 1850 act granting bounty land to those who served in U.S. wars after 1790, several attorneys general began deciding what qualified as a bona fide war. Justice Department lawyers decided that the 1836 Creek Disturbances (part of Andrew Jackson's Indian removal) represented a war; the Texas Revolution did not because the United States did not become officially involved in the latter conflict. The Patriot War in Michigan (a border standoff similar to the Aroostook War) was first purged from, and then later rehabilitated to, the list of U.S. wars. One remarkable Tennessean disqualified himself by serving in one war too many, first by volunteering to fight with his state's forces under Jackson in the War of 1812 and then in a Confederate troop during the Civil War. For whatever reason, he did not manage to apply for his land warrant until 1867, at which time he ran afoul of the new laws attainting the claims of traitors to the Union.[3]

How did the veteran or heir apply for a land warrant? The prospective warrantee sent his or her application to the U.S. Pension Bureau, located, after 1849, in the newly created Interior Department. Before that date, the War and Navy Departments maintained separate pension offices. In February 1847, the Pension Bureau at the War Department was a rather small government office with about twenty-five employees. It directed three pension programs: payments to Revolutionary War veterans and dependents; a half-pay arrangement for some Virginia veterans of the Revolution; and disability allowances to veterans wounded in war. About 20,000 veterans or dependents collected monthly disbursements from the Pension Bureau. A nationwide network of part-time agents handled funds, complaints and questions. The pace quickened, however, at the Pension Bureau after the Ten Regiments Act of February 1847. The bureau processed over 700,000 applications for bounty land during the next fourteen years and, on at least one occasion, found itself the target of a hostile congressional probe. The agency never shrank again to its earlier size because the Civil War unleashed an unprecedented volume of new claims. In the twentieth century, the Pension Bureau has undergone several changes, in 1930 becoming the Veterans Administration, and in 1989, the Department of Veterans Affairs.[4]

Shortly after passage of the Ten Regiments Act, Commissioner of Pensions James L. Edwards set forth the procedure for warrant applications. The commissioner wrote a public letter instructing persons to

> send to, or deposit with, the Commissioner of Pensions, Washington city, evidence of enlistment, service, and honorable discharge, as required by law. The best evidence on these points is held to be the original discharge of the applicant, which must, in all cases, be produced if in existence, accompanied by the applicant's affidavit.[5]

The affidavit was a statement that the applicant was indeed who he claimed to be, sworn before two witnesses, and certified by either a notary public or a justice of the peace. What did the applicant do in case of a lost discharge? He had to provide more sworn oaths about his company and regiment, the dates and places of enlistment and discharge, and the testimony of a surviving officer that an honorable discharge had been granted. Most Mexican War veterans held onto their discharge papers, but the same cannot be said of veterans of the War of 1812. Here the problem was one of record keeping as well as of mislaid papers. The militias of the War of 1812 did not produce standard discharge forms for their demobilized troops. Rather, the discharge was often a note hastily scribbled on a handy scrap of paper. Not surprisingly, many men lost such papers over the course of forty years. Veterans who were themselves members of Congress received numerous entreaties for help from their former comrades-in-arms. Wisconsin Senator Henry Dodge, an officer in the territorial militia during the Black Hawk War, was informed by one correspondent that "most of your old soldiers have the idea that it is best to send their applications through you."[6]

For those without discharges, the Pension Bureau printed application forms that requested the following information: residence, date, name, age, rank, company, company commander, regiment, regimental commander, enlistment point, term of enlistment, discharge point, discharge date, signature or mark, signature or mark of two witnesses, and the seal of a notary public or justice of the peace. For widows or minors, the dates of marriage and birth, respectively, and the date of the veteran's death, had to be included. The applicant who was turned down by the Pension Bureau because of the lack of written evidence faced an additional challenge. He, or his widow or heirs, had to secure written affidavits from two fellow members of the militia company that he had indeed served at the specified time. One land warrant dealer who aided veterans in applying to the Pension Bureau advised a rejected claimant that "officers are preferred, but if you cannot get their testimony, the affidavits of soldiers in the ranks will answer." Applicants for bounty land under the act of 1855 were also asked to state whether they had ever received bounty land under an earlier act and, if so, the act and warrant number. This last requirement may have been too much to ask, and the Pension Bureau, to guard against fraud, soon began checking every applicant's name against a master index of all previous warrantees.[7]

To the twentieth-century reader accustomed to filling out forms, the Pension Bureau's form does not seem unduly demanding. There are many indications, however, that then prospective applicants found the paperwork overwhelming. In his annual report for 1853, Pensions Commissioner Loren P. Waldo mentioned, "I also found great embarrassment attending the examinations and final dispositions of these claims, in consequence of the difficulty in communicating with the claimants; their inability to state the facts connected with their services as explicitly as is desirable, and the want of muster rolls, known to be authentic to verify their statements."[8]

Commissioner Waldo's complaint about the applicants' limited capacity to communicate is borne out by examination of the writing ability of the men and women receiving land warrants. A striking feature of the warrant applications and warrant files is the number of applicants and warrant recipients unable to sign their names. Instead, such persons "made their marks," usually a ragged X somewhere in the vicinity of where a friend or clerk had written their names. Of the random sample of more than 2,700 land warrants under all four acts, some 680 recipients were unable to sign their names, a rate of 25 percent.[9]

The evidence of illiteracy and semiliteracy makes it plain why so many older veterans and their heirs had difficulty properly filling out the warrant application. In the 1830s the Pension Bureau had encountered such problems, when Revolutionary War veterans had applied for pensions. In the absence of reliable muster rolls, the Pension Bureau had required veterans in the 1830s to make sworn oral statements in local courts and have the transcripts sent to Washington. No such generous policy was followed for the bounty land grants of the 1850s. The Pension Bureau insisted throughout the first half of the decade on "record evidence" to sustain applicants' claims, that is, "a discharge, the muster or pay rolls in any public office in the State in which the service was rendered, a contemporaneous entry of any kind made by a person whose duty it was to notice and register the date, the records of any town, or any accredited history, etc." In the absence of record evidence, a claim was suspended, and only by going through a complex process of oath taking and affidavit registering could an applicant get a second examination of the claim. Unlike the complete land warrant files of the General Land Office, the Pension Bureau's land warrant application files have not survived intact. As a result, it is impossible to determine whether illiterate applicants were turned down at a greater rate than their literate comrades.[10]

It is possible to make a rough count of the extent to which surviving veterans did apply for land warrants both by refining contemporaries' estimates and by performing additional calculations. Before he became pensions commissioner in the Pierce administration, Loren P. Waldo served in Congress, where he acquired a reputation as an authority on veterans' affairs. He spoke during the debate on the 1850 bounty land bill about the number of surviving veterans of 1812 who might apply for land warrants. Waldo estimated that the regular army in the war had consisted of about 60,000 men, 40,000 who had qualified under the act of 1812 bounty grant and 20,000 who had not. Waldo also estimated that 165,000 militiamen had served the minimum time during the war to qualify for a land warrant. He proceeded to guess that only one-quarter of the regulars and militiamen still lived in 1850; consequently, he expected only about 5,000 regulars and 40,000 militiamen to apply for warrants.[11]

Waldo's estimate turned out to be quite good for the regulars but too low for the militiamen. The samples from the 1850 and 1855 warrant acts show that thirty-five regulars (projected to 7,000 by multiplying the sample size by 200) received land warrants for 1812 service. This is about one-quarter of those eligible: some of the 20,000 whom Waldo had counted as ineligible under the 1812 law were eligible, as were another 10,000 regulars whom he had overlooked who were actually eligible for an 1812 grant but had simply failed to apply for bounty land after the war's end in 1815.

On the militia side, about 144,800 War of 1812 veterans applied for and received land warrants in 1850. A separate group of 66,800 short-term 1812 militia veterans received warrants under the 1855 law. This estimate is derived from the sample of warrant files taken for the purposes of this study. The sample shows that 1,569 people received warrants under either the 1850 or 1855 act for militia service during the War of 1812. Of this group 1,104 were surviving veterans, 415 were widows, and 50 were minor heirs. A closer look at this sample figure of War of 1812 militia beneficiaries shows that many received supplementary warrants under the 1855 act. Subtracting the group that received two warrants to make the sum total of 160 acres leaves a core group of 1,058 militia beneficiaries in the sample. When this figure is multiplied by the sample size of 200, the estimate projects to 211,600 veterans or other beneficiaries.

Colonel Leslie Combs hinted at the toll that age had taken on the "remnant of gray-headed veterans who now alone remain of the four hundred thousand" in his 1855 speech to the United Brethren. Did the 211,600 separate recipients comprise the entire pool of eligible applicants in the 1850s? At first glance, that number seems modest compared to Combs's 400,000, or in contrast to a modern estimate that places the total number of militiamen who served in the War of 1812 at about 475,000. It is not possible to estimate how many of the 475,000 militia soldiers served less than the required fourteen days muster during the war. It is clear that short-term service was the rule throughout the war, and that the number of ineligible veterans was likely substantial, based upon evidence from different sources. Many thousands of veterans served only a few days as reflected in the muster rolls compiled by the adjutant generals of the various state militias. Under the act of 1855, 341 people in the sample (projected to 66,800 by the sample size) received 160-acre warrants for War of 1812 service, most for active duty of from fourteen days up to a month; as Congress made more liberal the threshold for wartime service in granting bounty land warrants, it greatly expanded the pool of recipients. The surviving veterans constituted better than two out of three of the 211,600 warrantees who qualified because of War of 1812 service, with widows receiving about 66,400 warrants—or about thirty percent—based on sample projections. Estimates of the mortality of the veteran population suggest that the widows may have been underrepresented, implying that perhaps they were less likely to apply for bounty land in the first place, and less likely to complete succesfully the requirements of the Pension Bureau's application forms.[12]

Shortly after the 1850 bill became law, Interior Secretary Alexander H. H. Stuart issued a circular with an interesting proposal:

> I beg leave respectfully to recommend to the proper authorities of each county and township to employ a suitable agent, at the expense of the county, to supervise the preparation of the applications and proofs of claimants. The ignorant and unwary would thus be protected from imposition, the poor soldiers from burdens they are not able to bear, and the Government from many embarrassments that may result from the awkwardness of incompetent agents.[13]

The idea met with no response, and the marketplace that Stuart mistrusted for this task was soon filled with private agents to help warrantees. The larger purpose of such agents was to buy and sell land warrants, but many sought to attract customers by promising help to bewildered applicants. The offer represented sound business strategy since an agent helping an applicant could usually expect the first opportunity to buy the land warrant.[14]

Every state and most cities of consequence had bounty land agents soliciting the applications of veterans. Advertisements in three New York newspapers, the *Herald, Tribune,* and *Times,* show thirty-four separate bounty land agents operating in New York City in the 1850s. Some specialized in aiding applicants to obtain their warrants, while others dealt chiefly in the purchase and sale of warrants. Most were one-man operations, but a few were partnerships, the most famous of which was the New York branch of the Philadelphia banking house of E. W. Clark, Dodge and Company, the firm where the soon-to-be famous banker Jay Cooke worked and through which he bought land warrants for Iowa land purchases. About half of the agents were notaries public or attorneys, men well suited to hearing sworn statements and affixing official seals.[15]

Many of the New York land warrant agents placed advertisements in the daily press calling attention to their skills at procuring land warrants from the Pension Bureau. In 1855, the firm of Pitkin and Dixey proclaimed, "Let the six thousand soldiers and sailors in and about New York, entitled to one hundred and sixty acres under the new law, apply at once at the Bounty Land Office." Some warrant brokerage firms sought to emphasize their particular expertise. Edward Bissell, a specialist in sailors' claims, routinely advertised "bounty land warrants obtained, bought and sold," claiming that his former position as purser in the U.S. Navy gave him a knowledge of government operation. Numerous agents advertised under an official-sounding name. P. T. Betts ran the "U.S. Bounty Land Office," and there were three different New York operations using the name "U.S. Bounty Land Agency." Other agencies played on the veterans' connection to draw business. The Bounty Land Agency of the Veterans Corps of the War of 1812 was an aspect of the outfit so important in the national veterans' lobby. The corps urged its members to use the agency for help in applying for warrants and as a party to which they could assign their land warrants. Epenetus Wheeler, yet another agent, sought business by proclaiming he had served as a regular in the U.S. Army's Forty-sixth Regiment in the War of 1812.[16]

New York and Washington were not the only homes to the antebellum version of the revolving door between business and government. Richmond agent Abel U. Mayo boasted of his past government experience: ". . . having been engaged as a clerk in the Pension and Bounty Land Department at Washington, for nearly three years, I have peculiar advantages for prosecuting these claims." Land warrant agents like Mayo had on hand blank application forms from the Pension Bureau. With the application completed and dispatched, the initial labors of both applicant and warrant agent (and prospective warrant buyer) ended.[17]

How long did the veteran have to wait before he was awarded his land warrant? The answer is the story of the performance of the Pension Bureau. On receipt of each application, the bureau mailed a form letter of acknowledgment. If application was made during a slack time, the Pension Bureau issued the warrant within one or two months. If the application came during the rush after passage of the 1850 or 1855 act, the wait might reach a year. When warrant applications poured in at over 3,000 a day, as happened in April 1855, the Pension Bureau struggled simply to keep up with the task of acknowledging receipt of applications and had to postpone actual processing.[18]

Although the federal government refused to embark on the type of publishing program that Secretary Stuart had envisioned, the Pension Bureau did find it useful to print a series of pamphlets and forms in order to speed the processing of applications. In 1855, the Pension Bureau published a pamphlet explaining the mechanics of land warrant applications. "Instructions and Forms to be Observed by Persons Applying to the Pension Office for Bounty Land under the Act of March 3, 1855" mainly benefited warrant agents. It was not routinely sent to those writing to Washington for a warrant application and had to be asked for by name. Another of the bureau's pamphlets, "Pension Laws Now in Force," appeared regularly in the 1840s and 1850s. It detailed current bounty land and pension procedures and was also directed mainly toward agents rather than recipients.

The Pension Bureau also produced several series of one-page circulars—form letters, actually—designed to be filled in by government clerks and sent to applicants throughout the nation. One series, started after the 1850 act, consisted of circulars numerically coded by the Pension Bureau to accord with specific application problems. For example, Circular 2 was sent to those who applied for bounty land on the basis of federal service of less than one month. Applicants who had not sent in their discharge slips along with their applications (or had not sent in affidavits of service) received Circular 4. Those who had neglected to have their applications notarized had their claims suspended and received notice of this action by Circular 6.[19]

The Pension Bureau produced a similar set of circulars after the 1855 act, although this time the circulars were lettered, not numbered. The most common circular issued by the Pension Bureau was Circular A, notification to applicants that their claim for bounty land had been denied because, for example, of an insufficient length of

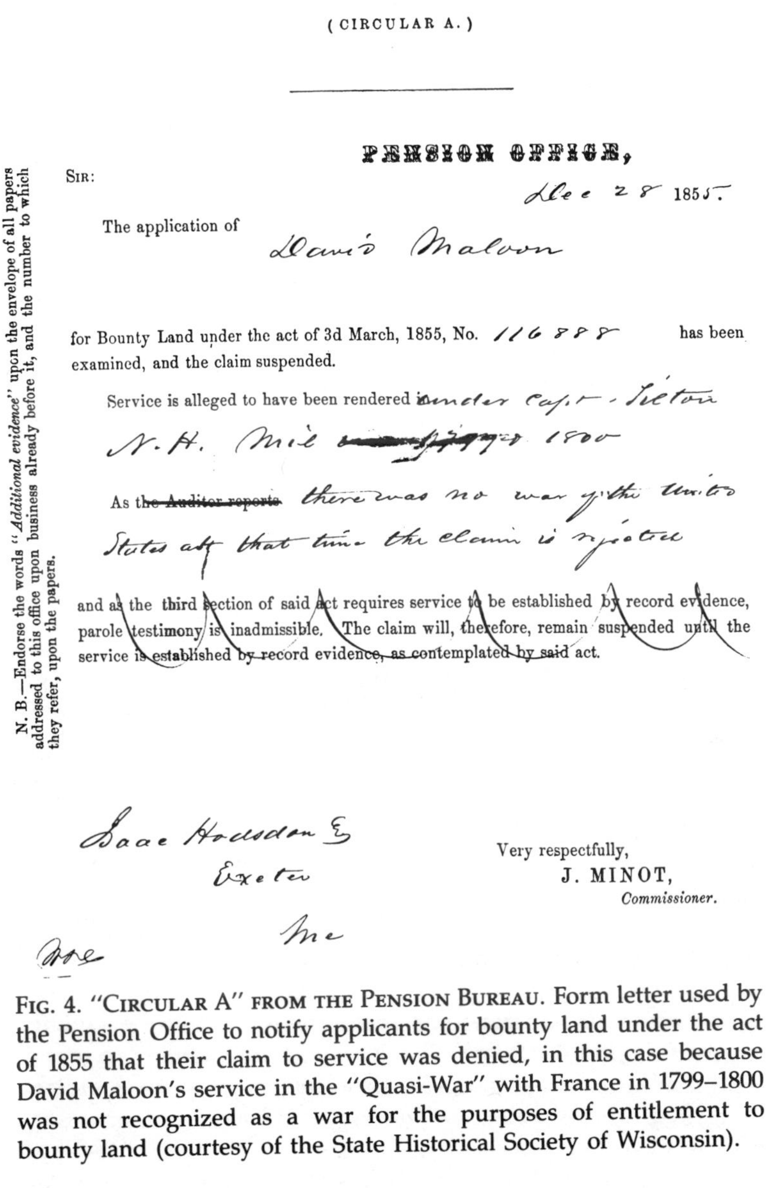

(CIRCULAR A.)

PENSION OFFICE,

Dec 28 1855.

SIR:

The application of David Maloon

for Bounty Land under the act of 3d March, 1855, No. 116888 has been examined, and the claim suspended.

Service is alleged to have been rendered under Capt. Tilton N. H. Mil 1800

As ~~the Auditor reports~~ there was no war of the United States at that time the claim is rejected

~~and as the third section of said act requires service to be established by record evidence, parole testimony is inadmissible. The claim will, therefore, remain suspended until the service is established by record evidence, as contemplated by said act.~~

N. B.—Endorse the words "*Additional evidence*" upon the envelope of all papers addressed to this office upon business already before it, and the number to which they refer, upon the papers.

Isaac Hodsdon Esq
Exeter
Me

Very respectfully,
J. MINOT,
Commissioner.

FIG. 4. "CIRCULAR A" FROM THE PENSION BUREAU. Form letter used by the Pension Office to notify applicants for bounty land under the act of 1855 that their claim to service was denied, in this case because David Maloon's service in the "Quasi-War" with France in 1799–1800 was not recognized as a war for the purposes of entitlement to bounty land (courtesy of the State Historical Society of Wisconsin).

wartime service. Circular A also went out to bounty land applicants who claimed a warrant based on wartime service in a conflict that the United States refused to accept as federally related. For example, men who participated in the 1799 "Quasi-War" with France applied and were denied because the conflict was never officially deemed a war. A related Pension Bureau mailing was Circular K, sent to applicants from Maine who claimed bounty land because of membership in a private posse on the Maine frontier in the 1830s. Men in the state's militia won bounty land for their services, but the posse members were deemed "private" and "civil" soldiers and thus not entitled to the federal government's reward. Other circulars addressed shortcomings in the veteran's application such as failure to specify the unit served in, the unit commander, or the dates of muster.[20]

The effect of all these Pension Bureau circulars was to inform applicants that their claims had been rejected, suspended, or delayed. Pension clerks usually were spare in providing detail in the circulars about how to correct the problem. The most frequent notation on a Circular A simply said "not on rolls of said Co." and so did not offer much hope to the applicant of ultimately qualifying for his bounty land.

Processing land warrant applications involved several steps. Commissioner Josiah Minot, new to the job in 1855, devoted much of his first annual report to explaining the procedure for bounty land administration. He noted that "Most persons have a very indefinite idea of the course of business under this [1855] act. To them, it seems a very easy and ready course to receive an application and issue a warrant; and few, indeed, have an accurate idea of the real difficulties and labors of that business."[21]

Commissioner Minot strongly advocated the division of labor among his clerks, and he wrote in his report that each warrant application passed through a series of different operations. The bureau first had to decide whether the applying veteran's military service qualified under the law. This involved presence at the seat of war. Next, the bureau had to check the applicant's reported military service against official records to determine or verify the necessary length of service. This was a time-consuming task, in part because of the sworn enemies of the old soldiers, the British whose forces, during the sack of Washington in 1814, had burned the War Department's records, including enlistment papers. Fortunately, the Treasury Department maintained a separate set of records. Treasury, however, would not surrender its files to the War Department. Instead, it worked out an arrangement whereby the Third Auditor's office in the Treasury did the actual searching through the records. This worked well when pension requests trickled in but broke down completely under the deluge of 1850 land warrant applications.[22]

A third task, necessary only for applicants under the 1855 act, was to check past warrantee files for previous grants to an applicant. The Pension Bureau provided two sets of application forms under the 1855 act, one for first-time applicants and the other for those who had benefited before without receiving the full 160 acres. As a matter of policy, however, the bureau treated *all* applicants as prospective frauds, checking each applicant against the old records. In the process, it wound up doing more paperwork. Scrutinizing the oaths, dates, and affixing signatures (or the X marks of illiterates) was the fourth and final chore before issuance.

Of the three major acts, 1847, 1850, and 1855, administration of the first was smoothest. Several factors help explain this. Even though the bureau was new at administering a large bounty land grant (or more accurately, rusty, having been out of practice since the years after 1815), the 1847 act provided the fewest technical problems. For instance, the applicant pool reached about 90,000, less than half the number for 1850 and little more than a third of the 1855 figure. Moreover, the bureau had accurate foreknowledge of how many applications to expect—all estimates were in the 90,000 range, so planning efforts paid off. Also, the bureau never became swamped with applications and never fell far behind schedule in processing incoming claims. This was because the Mexican War did not end until a year and a half after land warrant operations began. As individual volunteer units disbanded and their members made applications, the requests arrived steadily, with only a modest surge in the summer of 1848 at war's end. For the first ten months of 1847, the bureau received 18,360 applications, and somewhat less than three times that number in 1848. By the end of 1849, most of the work had been done: 83,000 applications received, 9,000 rejected, 70,000 warrants issued. At no time during the administration of this act did the spread between applications received and warrants issued exceed 15,000. With about thirty clerks, the office could issue about 200 warrants per day, or about 5,000 a month.[23]

The immediacy of the war helps explain the ease of administration in two more ways. The Pension Bureau was located in the War Department for most of the processing time of 1847 and 1848. It had access to War Department enlistment records for the Mexican War and did not have to deal with the Treasury Department's Third Auditor. Moreover, the applications themselves presented far fewer problems than those of 1850 or 1855. The applicants generally had discharge papers and knew the details of their recent war service. The relation between informed applicants and ease of administration was direct; the volume of correspondence related to land warrant applications was less than for the later acts, thus freeing more clerical staff for actual processing.[24]

Nearly all the elements that made for a happy administration of the 1847 statute were absent in 1850, and other complications arose as well. The bureau had the misfortune to be transferred to the newly created Interior Department and suffered congressional enmity from those who feared the potential tyranny of a British-style "Home Department." In addition, the office of commissioner of pensions became highly partisan in the fall of 1850: the average job tenure of a bureau head from 1851 until the Civil War was just eighteen months.[25]

The most obvious problem the Pension Bureau faced was the larger volume of warrant applications, which eventually reached a quarter of a million. Unlike the situation obtaining for the Mexican War grants, under the 1850 act no one was entirely sure of how many would seek a bounty. Outgoing Commissioner James Edwards noted in the fall of 1850 that "from the year 1790 up to the present time, more than half a million of militiamen have been called into the service of the United States." He went on to guess that only half that number would seek land warrants—a very good guess, as it turned out, but the fact remains that administrators had far less knowledge of the expected volume of 1850 applicants than of the Mexican War veterans. Land speculators, too, had no clear idea of how many warrants would be issued. The Wisconsin firm of Washburn and Woodman, with good Washington connections, told its clients that the bill would "give bounty lands to every body that has ever served in any war." Six months after the act of 1850 became law, Cyrus Woodman wrote, mistakenly, that the law granted bounty land to all "that ever shouldered a musket."[26]

Along with volume, the Pension Bureau faced a major problem of timing. In 1847, the bureau had enjoyed a breathing spell until the end of the war in which to organize its processing system. This did not hold true in 1850. For the first thirteen months after passage of the 1850 act, applications arrived at a monthly rate of 12,000. On especially heavy days, the Post Office delivered 1,500 applications.[27]

In 1847, the Pension Bureau issued the first warrant five weeks after President Polk signed the Ten Regiments bill; the first 1850 warrant did not leave the Pension Bureau until almost five months after passage of the enabling legislation. In December 1850, Congress began receiving letters from constituents concerning the whereabouts of the promised bounty land warrants. Wisconsin land warrant dealer Cyrus Woodman wrote in mid-December that the new 1850 act warrants "may be a good field of operations, if it will not take eternally to get the warrants after the papers are filed." Woodman helped Wisconsin veterans of the War of 1812 and the Black Hawk War make their applications in October 1850, but not until February 24, 1851, did one of his clients receive his warrant, "the first of the new ones that has yet been rec'd by any applicant here, so far as I know."[28]

In response to such complaints, the House set up a select committee to investigate the Pension Bureau. Chaired by Indiana Democrat John Robinson, the committee held hearings and interviewed clerks and bureau heads. Before the committee issued its report in early January 1851, it even took a field trip to the Tombs, the basement of the Treasury building where the Third Auditor kept old military papers. The Robinson committee heard four excuses offered by the Pension Bureau for its poor showing. First, the bureau argued that warrant issuing could not begin until plates arrived from the engraver. The committee report dismissed this out of hand but did not determine why the 1850 warrants were engraved at all. Ex-Commissioner Edwards, sacked in the general federal shakeup after the death of President Zachary Taylor, offered some relevant testimony on this point:

> The Secretary of the Interior caused the regulations for carrying into effect the act of 28th September, 1850, to be drawn up and printed before I saw them, or knew the purport of them. He also ordered plates to be engraved, upon which the location certificates are to be printed. These plates were not completed when I left the office [Dec. 1, 1850]. Had the usual course been pursued by writing these certificates on letterpress printed forms, the issue of warrants might have commenced as early as the 20th October last.[29]

Secretary Stuart, a Whig politician from Virginia's Shenandoah Valley, apparently did not like the plain letterpress format of the 1847 series warrants. Instead, the 1850 warrants feature patriotic art with dramatic scenes of past battles, stately portraits of American heroes, and pastoral scenes of American farmers at work. Secretary Stuart divided the 1850 engraving work among three contractors.

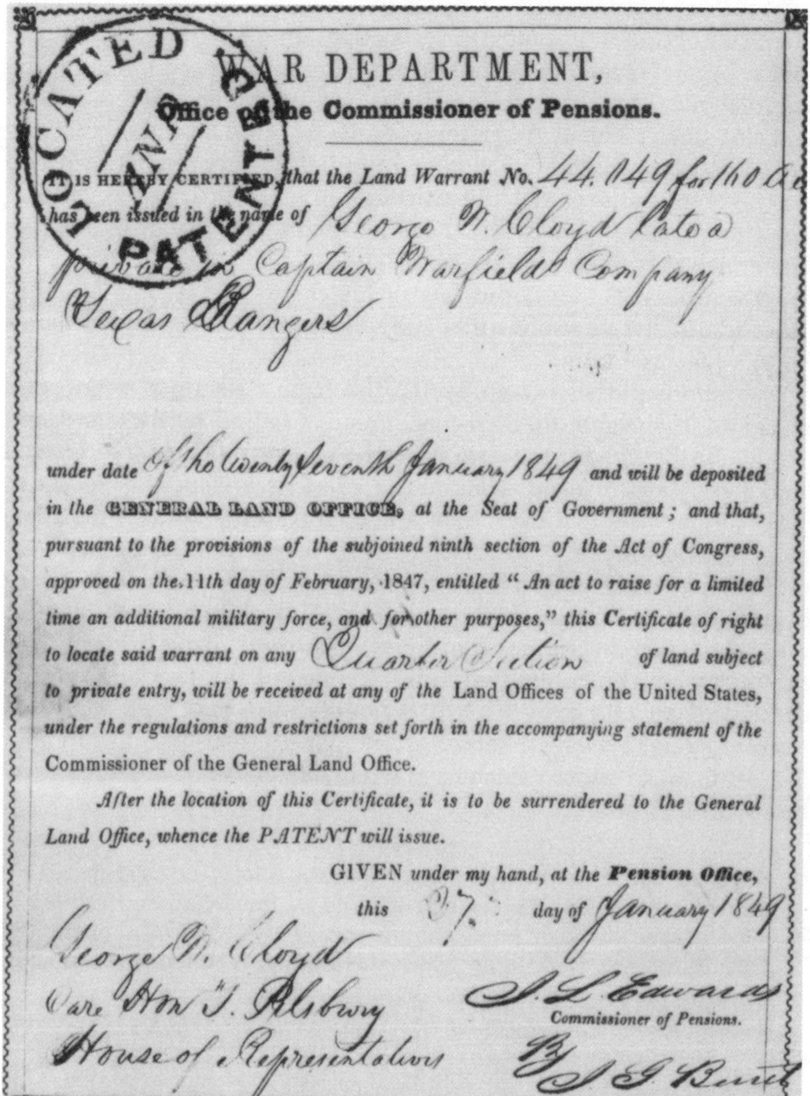

LOCATED PATENTED

WAR DEPARTMENT,

Office of the Commissioner of Pensions.

IT IS HEREBY CERTIFIED, that the Land Warrant No. 44.049 for 160 Ac has been issued in the name of George W. Cloyd late a private in Captain Warfield's Company Texas Rangers

under date of the twenty seventh January 1849 and will be deposited in the GENERAL LAND OFFICE, at the Seat of Government; and that, pursuant to the provisions of the subjoined ninth section of the Act of Congress, approved on the 11th day of February, 1847, entitled "An act to raise for a limited time an additional military force, and for other purposes," this Certificate of right to locate said warrant on any Quarter Section of land subject to private entry, will be received at any of the Land Offices of the United States, under the regulations and restrictions set forth in the accompanying statement of the Commissioner of the General Land Office.

After the location of this Certificate, it is to be surrendered to the General Land Office, whence the PATENT will issue.

GIVEN under my hand, at the Pension Office, this 27 day of January 1849

George W. Cloyd
Care Hon T. Pilsbury
House of Representatives

J. L. Edwards
Commissioner of Pensions.
By J. G. Burt

C. Alexander, Printer, Washington.

FIG. 5. ACT OF 1847 LAND WARRANT. Letterpress-produced 160-acre warrant issued to George W. Cloyd of the Texas Rangers for service in the Mexican War under the Ten Regiments Act of 1847 (courtesy of the National Archives).

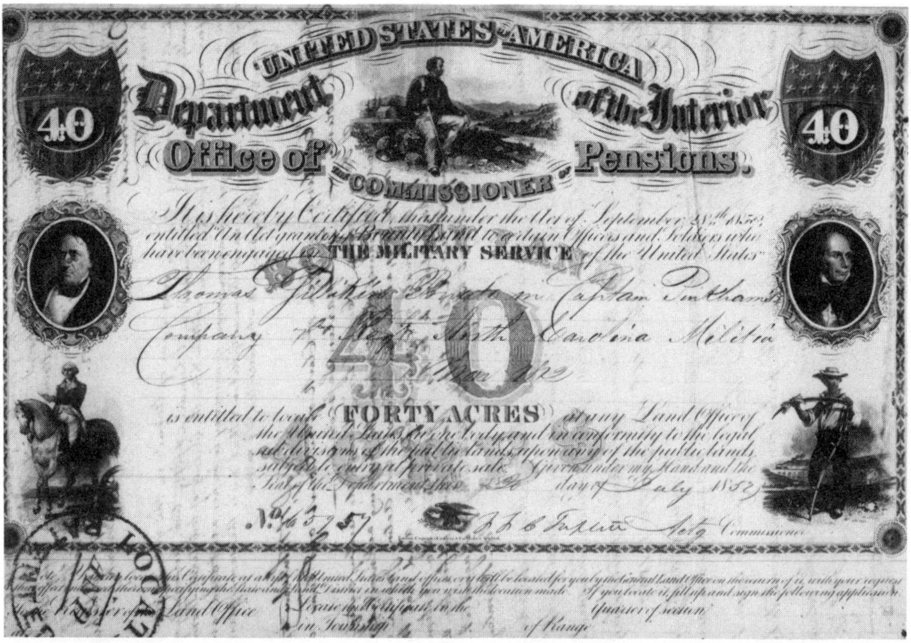

FIG. 6. ACT OF 1850 LAND WARRANT. Engraved forty-acre warrant issued to Thomas Gillikins of the North Carolina militia for service in the War of 1812 under the act of 1850 (courtesy of the National Archives).

The largest run of forty-acre warrants went to Toppan, Carpenter, Casilear and Company of Philadelphia; the eighty-acre warrants were engraved by Danforth, Bald and Company, also of Philadelphia; while the American Banknote Company of New York handled the 160-acre series. Among all the warrant series, the act of 1855 120-acre warrants have the most chauvinistic artwork, a dramatic scene of soldiers rescuing a cowering woman and child from an Indian with a raised tomahawk. The art was set on the warrant face, directly under a portrait of Richard Brodhead.[30]

The Pension Bureau maintained as a second excuse that it suffered from a shortage of clerks. At the time Congress passed the 1850 bill, the Pension Bureau employed about thirty people, with fewer than half at work finishing the 1847 warrant issue. The 1850 act made no provision for implementation or administration, so on

FIG. 7. ACT OF 1855 LAND WARRANT. Engraved 160-acre warrant issued to Priscilla Williams, the widow of Gregory Williams, for his service in the Virginia Militia during the War of 1812. Note that the Pension Bureau had issued over thirty-nine thousand 160-acre warrants under the act of 1855 by August 1856 (courtesy of the National Archives).

his own authority Secretary Stuart hired a head clerk, an assistant head clerk, and thirty-five new clerks to carry out the law. The Robinson committee heard testimony about the daily routine of a clerk in the Pension Bureau and the projected rate of warrants issued per day. A force of thirty (roughly that which administered the 1847 grant) could issue 200 warrants per day, so the committee reasoned that 67 people in the Pension Bureau should be able to issue at least 400 warrants a day, or 10,000 a month. At that rate, the job would be completed in two years, a not unreasonable time. Since the bureau came nowhere near to issuing 400 warrants a day, the committee concluded that the problem lay not with a shortage of clerks but rather with the short hours the clerks worked. Clerks in many Washington offices, including the Pension Bureau, enjoyed a six-hour day as a matter of custom. An average clerk could in six hours fill out twenty-five blank warrants or register and index fifty applications a day. In each case, the committee felt this was too slow a pace.[31]

A third defense offered by the Pension Bureau for its failure to manage properly the 1850 grant rested with the Third Auditor in the Treasury Department. The Robinson committee rejected this on two grounds. First, the committee "found little justification in the apparent condition and efficiency of the Pension Bureau to warrant the allegation of less efficiency in another." Of the 30,000 or so applications received by the end of 1850, only 1,500 had been forwarded to the Third Auditor for scrutiny, about thirty a day and not enough business to keep even two Treasury clerks busy. To make matters worse, the Pension Bureau decided to send every application over to Treasury for checking when it might have accepted discharge papers as sufficient proof. Of the first 30,000 applications, over a quarter came with discharge papers and could have been handled without bothering the Third Auditor.

The fourth and final defense of the Pension Bureau was to blame the slow progress on the Secretary of the Interior. Specifically, Secretary Stuart ordered the bureau to take up and finish each application in the order it arrived. As a result, difficult and complicated applications held up others that might have been completed with less work. Representative Robinson commended the principle of the fairness of the queue but regretted applying such a principle if it slowed movement to a crawl.[32]

Although the Pension Bureau had trouble persuading the Robinson committee of the reasons for its poor work record, the committee did not reach any definitive conclusions about the bureau's behavior. In House debate on the committee's report, Robinson made the partisan but unlikely argument that only a conspiracy within the Executive to defeat the intent of the bounty land act could explain so monumental an administrative failure. Millard Fillmore may have hatched his share of plots, but no evidence has surfaced to show that he or Alexander Stuart ordered the sabotage of the 1850 land warrants. Another committee member thought the delay in bringing out land warrants a comparatively small matter; the real problem, contended Ohio's Representative Miller, was Interior Secretary Stuart's arbitrary appointment of thirty-seven clerks, and the proper solution would be "to prefer an impeachment against the Department for such usurpation of the powers of Congress."[33]

The original intent of the committee's report (to find out what was needed to execute the 1850 act) quickly became lost in congressional denunciations of executive idleness and profligacy. The findings of the committee's investigations were forgotten during a general open season on bureaucrats. The Third Auditor's office, praised by the Robinson committee, came under attack by the Kentucky Whig Humphrey Marshall: "I have been reluctantly compelled to look upon the Third Auditor's office as a sort of Cerbonian bog, in which, when a claim is once ingulfed it is a miracle if it shall ever be extricated." Marshall's solution was to print all the eligible names of potential warrantees as a public document, thus doing away with most of the clerical force. Under this plan, the applicant would do most of the work by checking for his or her name on the comprehensive list. Preparation of a master list involved extra labor and public expense, and Congress preferred to let the private market of agents do the work of facilitating applications. Ultimately Congress gave the Pension Bureau most of the clerks it needed, and, as the warrants began to flow out of Washington by February 1851, the pressure on the bureau eased.[34]

Marshall's idea of publishing a master list bore a similarity to Secretary Stuart's proposal, but neither plan ever made headway. Government publishing was still in its infancy, and Congress and several administrations acknowledged no right of veterans to receive federal help in obtaining their legal reward. Instead, the government showed a preference to reduce, if need be, the value of the land bounty by forcing veterans and their widows to rely on the services of private agents and middlemen. In other words, the government willingly made a process more inefficient rather than risk some fraudulent beneficiaries.

The Pension Bureau did improve its administration of the 1855 act over its 1850 performance. The problems and complications were similar: faulty and incomplete applications, trouble with the Third Auditor, and strict scrutiny of claims. Because of the greater volume and the need to check for previous bounty grants, the 1855 act involved more work. Nonetheless, the bureau avoided the long delay of 1850, and by May of 1855, within two months of President Pierce's signing of the Old Soldiers Act, the Pension Bureau issued the first warrants. Moreover, the office was properly staffed with 153 employees at the start of the new operation, although Commissioner Josiah Minot wanted more help.

The initial surge of applications in 1855 made even the 1850 level seem small. Table 9 shows the volume of applications in the first

TABLE 9

The Land Warrant Business of the Pension Bureau, March–September 1855

Month	Applications Received	No. Briefed	No. Registered	No. Examined	No. Allowed	Letters Received	Letters Sent
March	30,800	. . .	. . .	. . .	. . .	2,530	9,000
April	80,200	29,864	6,000	. . .	. . .	2,733	17,846
May	45,500	38,509	18,733	10,130	4,991	3,721	22,968
June	26,000	42,339	21,188	11,672	6,093	4,611	24,090
July	15,500	32,598	18,371	11,474	6,593	4,787	28,726
August	10,700	28,268	30,668	14,856	8,305	5,188	28,447
Sept.	7,500	24,741	22,655	18,781	11,459	5,250	29,935
Totals	216,200	196,319	117,615	66,913	37,441	28,820	161,012

SOURCE: Report of the commissioner of pensions, 1856.

seven months after passage of the act, together with the volume of warrants processed and issued. The first ninety days witnessed the receipt of over 150,000 applications; by June 1, 1855, the spread between applications received and warrants issued reached 145,000. Not until September did the bureau reach the point where it issued more warrants than it received new applications per day. By various methods, including the use of two shifts, Commissioner Minot managed to raise land warrant output to 11,000 per month, a figure his office maintained steadily throughout 1856. From a high of 185,000 in August 1855, the spread between applications and issued warrants receded to only about 86,000 in September 1856, and below 10,000 one year later.[35]

In his 1856 report, Minot predicted that the bureau would finish the backlog by September 1856. This optimistic forecast was not realized, in part because of a congressional act easing the needed proof of eligibility of widows and minors. Some 50,000 applications had been rejected, but, as Minot unhappily noted, "by that act the past labor on the greater part of the rejected claims was rendered useless, and a re-examination of them under the new act became necessary." The commissioner referred to the language in the act of 1855 requiring "record evidence" from original documents sustaining a claimant. Some applicants who had received act of 1850 warrants on the basis of sworn affidavits, what the bureau called "parole evidence," were turned down for act of 1855 bounties. Revolutionary War veterans and their widows had been drawing cash pensions for two decades on the basis of parole evidence, but they, too, had their claims suspended for act of 1855 warrants. Congress did move to remedy such cases, and in its first action in 1856, during the 34th Congress, it instructed the Pension Bureau to accept parole evidence, incidentally requiring the bureau, as Minot complained, to rework all the suspended applications.[36]

Table 10 shows the acreage in sample warrants issued by the Pension Bureau and gives annual estimates of the total volume of warrants granted. As expected, the heaviest years for warrant issue came after an enabling act of Congress: 1848–49, 1851–52, and 1855–57. The table also shows that most recipients got their warrants within three years after Congress gave its authorization; warrant issue slowed in 1850 as the Ten Regiments Act soldiers were satisfied, again in 1854 as the 1850 act group dwindled, and by 1860 when most of the beneficiaries under the Old Soldiers Act had obtained their bounties. By the outbreak of the Civil War, the Pension Bureau had issued about fifty-six million acres of warrants, or 93 percent of all those ever granted under the acts of 1847, 1850, 1852, and 1855.

Once an applicant had received his land warrant, jurisdiction changed from the Pension Bureau to the General Land Office, also situated in the new Interior Department. The General Land Office faced different problems in the administration of land warrants than had the Pension Bureau. Most of the difficulties appeared at the field office level, not in Washington. The office had comparatively little contact with veterans and avoided the communication problems that plagued the Pension Bureau. For the 1850, 1852, and 1855 acts, Congress sought to make the location of land warrants by veterans easy, and it instructed General Land Office personnel to make locations for veterans by mail. If a veteran could specify the section, township, and range coordinates of a parcel, he merely had to write them at the bottom of the warrant face, and the land office would do the balance of the work without charge and forward his patent. In practice, only a handful of veterans followed this approach, largely because they lacked reliable, current information about western land sites.

Land Office personnel complained most about the fee structure involved in executing the bounty land grants. Initially, land officers in the field received no added compensation for handling warrant locations. In May 1848, in response to stated dissatisfaction by General Land Office personnel, Congress set a new fee schedule for land warrant locations. A person other than the original veteran who located a 160-acre warrant had to pay fifty cents, while the same assignee locating a forty-acre warrant had to pay twenty-five cents.

TABLE 10
Estimated Annual Issue of Sample Land Warrants: Acts of 1847, 1850, 1852, 1855

Year	*Sample Acreage*	*Estimated Projection (X 200)*
1847	7,000	1,400,000
1848	31,800	6,360,000
1849	17,080	3,416,000
1850	2,240	448,000
1851	29,840	5,968,000
1852	28,160	5,632,000
1853	9,520	1,904,000
1854	4,320	864,000
1855	40,200	8,040,000
1856	67,480	13,496,000
1857	25,080	5,016,000
1858	9,440	1,888,000
1859	3,320	664,000
1860	3,920	784,000
1861	4,760	952,000
1862	960	192,000
1863	0	0
1864	960	192,000
1865	720	144,000
1866	320	64,000
1867	1,280	256,000
1868	1,120	224,000
1869	1,440	288,000
1870–79	4,640	928,000
1880–89	1,240	248,000
1890–99	960	192,000
post-1900	160	32,000
Total	297,960	59,592,000

SOURCE: Sample of warrant recipients, acts of 1847, 1850, 1852, and 1855. See App. A.

Later in 1848, and continuing almost yearly thereafter, the commissioner of the General Land Office pressed for higher warrant location fees: "The compensation allowed to the district land officers for their services in the location on these warrants has been found to be wholly inadequate, and many just complaints have been made on this subject." Finally, in 1852, Congress made warrant locators pay to land officers the same 1 percent fee as those who paid $1.25 an acre for cash entries. After Congress made the change, warrant locators paid $2.00 for entering a full quarter-section with a bounty land warrant, $1.50 for a 120-acre warrant, and so forth.[37]

The receiver and register had to maintain a separate set of books for warrant entries and made parallel notations in the cash entry books if an additional fraction of land was entered for cash. The warrants had to be scrutinized for irregularities, and special location forms were required for warrant users. The land office register had to make sure that warrant locators used their warrants only to enter appropriate lands. The sample contains other warrant locations that conflicted with township school lands and thus required additional effort by General Land Office personnel to straighten out the confusion.[38]

The sample reveals a number of conflicting claims cases where a locator used his warrant on land claimed by a preemptor. This should come as no surprise since warrant and preemption policy intersected in confusing ways at several important points in the 1840s and 1850s. The language of the act of 1847 had explicitly prohibited the use of warrants for land that had been claimed as part of a preemption, reflecting a congressional intent to avoid conflict between warrant locators and preemptors. Yet within a year after the act's passage, Commissioner Richard Young instructed land office registers to accept warrants from preemptors wishing to take title to their own claims. In 1848, Young expanded his ruling to allow warrant locations in the name of someone other than the preemptor, thus paving the way for bankers to take title of a parcel and extend credit to the preemptor. Such arrangements, however, extended only to public lands parcels that had been offered for public auction and were then subsequently opened to private entry. The Assignment Act of 1852 included a provision that explicitly authorized the use of warrants as payment for preemption claims, and by administrative decision, General Land Office Commissioner John Wilson allowed preemptors to transfer their claim to warrant holders on land parcels that had not yet been offered at auction. This was a crucial change and opened a huge acreage to warrant operations by preemptors and frontier financiers. In 1855, a different commissioner reversed Wilson and specifically authorized the preemptor alone to use act of 1855 warrants on unoffered tracts. The result of these frequent changes in warrant restrictions was a steady number of cases where two parties laid claim to the same tract.[39]

TABLE 11
Sample Warrant Cancellations—Acts of 1847, 1850, 1852, 1855

Act	*No. Canceled*	*Total (%)*
1847	5	1
1850	47	5
1852	1	1
1855	28	2

SOURCE: Sample of warrant recipients, acts of 1847, 1850, 1852, and 1855.

Each step of the warrant business offered the opportunity for fraud, from the initial application to the receipt (or nonreceipt) of the warrant through assignment. Indeed, each of the warrant acts resulted in cases of fraud and so contributed to the difficulties in administration by the Pension Bureau and General Land Office. Table 11 summarizes the number of warrants issued for each act that were later canceled because of fraud or other irregularity. It is possible to check on the accuracy of this part of the sample by comparing it to the known figures for the 1847 act. In 1850, but before the passage of that year's new bounty land act, the commissioner of pensions issued his *List of Military Bounty Land Warrants Cancelled and Suspended*. This pamphlet listed, by warrant serial number and name of warrantee, the canceled certificates issued under the Ten Regiments Act. It circulated among land office personnel and private brokers and served as a useful reference to halt trading or use of void warrants. The Commissioner's pamphlet, or the "printed Catalogue of fraudulent Warrants," as one dealer called it, listed 1,400 warrants, about 1.5 percent of the total issue, and in line with the sample figure for the 1847 act.[40]

The 1847 act frauds revealed in the sample consisted of simple deceptions. A Mississippi widow, Ellen Reed, with her two children, Thomas and Susan, applied for a land warrant in 1849 in the name of her late husband Richard Reed, a private in Company D of the First U.S. Artillery Regiment. The warrant application was in order, and on June 22, 1849, Mrs. Reed was issued warrant 61,656. In August, she sold the warrant to John Culbertson, a New Yorker involved in Iowa land purchases. Unfortunately for Mrs.

Reed, Richard Reed's mother had applied for a land warrant in her son's name, claiming status as next-of-kin. When she insisted that Richard had never married and had no children, the Pension Bureau sought Ellen Reed and questioned her about the particulars of her marriage. Ellen answered that she had married Richard in Columbus, Mississippi, on a certain date, but Private Reed's mother had little difficulty proving that Richard had gone fishing near his home on the Kennebec River in Maine the day of his "wedding" in Mississippi. Culbertson's warrant was canceled and a new one issued in favor of Reed's mother.[41]

Private Lemuel Kean went off to war in Mexico with the Thirteenth U.S. Infantry and never came back. In 1849, three women claiming to be his surviving sisters, Mary, Jane, and Susan Kean, made an application for a warrant claiming Lemuel's right. They received warrant 62,684 on June 29, 1849, and sold it ten days later to John Dement, a land dealer in the Dixon, Illinois, land district. In 1851, Lemuel's father, William Kean, applied for and received a warrant based on his next-of-kin status. An alert clerk in the Pension Bureau caught the duplication, but too late to prevent the "Kean" sisters from having successfully swindled the federal government.[42]

Only one notary public in the act of 1847 sample, J. W. Earich of Kentucky, was revealed as a swindler. At some point in 1848, John Adams of the same Thirteenth U.S. Infantry as Lemuel Kean appeared before Earich to get help in applying for a warrant. The Pension Bureau issued it August 12, 1848, in care of Earich's office in Louisville. Adams never saw the warrant because he died in Alexandria, Virginia on August 22, yet Earich assigned the warrant, forging Adams's signature, in September, and would have got away with his scheme if Private Adams's mother had not finally made her own warrant application in 1851.[43]

The 1847 sample revealed frauds largely at the beginning of the land warrant chain, at the application stage. A number of 1850 and 1855 act sample warrants were simply stolen from the mail. The front page of *Thompson's Bank Note and Commercial Reporter,* essential reading for those in the warrant business, regularly carried notices of warrants stolen in the mail and even from offices and hotel rooms. In such cases, the General Land Office issued a published caveat against the stolen warrant, in effect a warning to land office registers and receivers to reject the tainted warrant. Some 1850 act applicants faced sufficient delays after the loss of a warrant that they were simply reclassified as beneficiaries of the 1855 act.[44]

The unwitting victim who bought a fraudulent warrant had a difficult time regaining his money. In 1862 R. A. Alger, a Detroit land dealer, bought act of 1855 120-acre warrant 75,199 unaware that a caveat had been filed against it. Alger sought to locate his warrant at the East Saginaw, Michigan, land office, only to have his defective warrant confiscated by the authorities at that land office. For years, Alger tried to recover his money or have another warrant isued in his favor. He persuaded the East Saginaw register to plead his case to General Land Office officials in Washington: ". . . the parties in New York from whom said wt was purchased in New York will not furnish another wt to take the place of wt No 75199 until said wt is returned. Is there no way to enable Mr. Alger to get either his money or another wt from the N.Y. parties? Mr. Alger being an innocent party."[45]

One innovative land warrant agency, Washburn and Woodman of Mineral Point, Wisconsin (with good connections in Boston and New York), offered insurance or a "guaranty" on each land warrant it sold. For an extra five dollars, a warrant purchaser could obtain protection against fraud from the firm. Still Washburn and Woodman had their own troubles with land warrant frauds. In the summer of 1852, Cyrus Woodman wrote his brother George in New York City complaining about being cheated by warrant dealer P. T. Betts. The Wisconsin Woodman urged George not to bother filing suit against Betts but instead to "see him in person and tell him if he does not redeem the fraudulent warrants he sold to you, that you will have him arrested for forgery." Growing angrier at the swindle perpetrated on him, Cyrus then told his brother to "take an officer with you and into his office and tell Betts that he may fork over or go to jail."[46]

Once the warrant had been issued, responsibility for its oversight rested with the General Land Office. That agency worried mainly about frauds and irregularities in the assignment of land warrants. In preparation for the expected deluge of 1855 warrants, the commissioner sent a circular to registers and receivers of land offices in the West about handling warrants. The commissioner summarized the experience with the 1850 act warrants, and his circular urged careful scrutiny of the assignment for the following required information: proper signature or mark of the warrantee; signatures or marks of two witnesses; assignee's name specified; minors stating their date of maturity; certification by a justice of the peace; and the identification of the credentials of the justice of the peace.

The purpose of the General Land Office's circular was to ensure that assignments followed the proper form, consisting of three paragraphs. First, the warrantee acknowledged transfer of the warrant and all rights to another person in return for "value received." On most warrants, there was a blank space left for a name to be filled in, so most veterans or widows who sold their warrants almost certainly never met the end users who located the warrant at a public land office on the frontier. This transfer required two witnesses and a notary public's seal. The second paragraph consisted of a simple statement from the notary public that the warrantee was known to be himself or herself and did execute the transfer or assignment on the date specified. The handwriting of this paragraph throughout the sample almost always matched that of the first paragraph, suggesting that the notary wrote both. The third paragraph was a statement from the judge or clerk of the local circuit court that the notary public was in fact authorized as such in that county.

The object of all the sworn statements, and of carefully examining them at the land office, was to prevent fraud. If one of these checks proved faulty, the General Land Office held up many warrants that may well have been honestly assigned. While some grumbled about the strictness of the clerks, New York land warrant dealer and business press editor John Thompson approved: "I have had warrants rejected for the omission of a single word and in some cases a single letter! That they are severe I am fully aware but I think they wisely foresaw that *some form must be used* to prevent ignorant as well as wise men from using a form of their own."[47]

The most spectacular land warrant fraud case of the 1850s took place in Vermont. A thief with a taste for history acquired muster rolls of the Vermont militia who had fought at the Battle of Plattsburgh in 1814. This category of veteran received special treatment from Congress under the 1855 act because, despite their gallantry, few had served the prescribed fourteen days. More than forty years later, a Mr. Bickford hit on the idea of determining the dead from the Plattsburgh engagement and making applications in their name—an American version of *Dead Souls*. The scheme worked well enough to net the crook 138 bounty land warrants—until the Pension Bureau finally caught on; in the end, Bickford received a four-year sentence and a $500 fine. Although Bickford went to jail, other land warrant cheats got off on legal technicalities. The basic federal fraud statute of 1823 did not specifically make false swearing a federal crime. For a while, land warrant forgers escaped justice by successfully arguing that federal law did not cover the forging of government certificates. In 1859, these problems and others finally led Congress to pass a statute to prohibit the forgery, counterfeiting, or fraudulent use of land warrants, with penalties of up to ten years' imprisonment.[48]

Not all warrant cancellations resulted from fraud. Some warrants were suspended because the Pension Bureau had made an error about the proper acreage due the warrantee. A number of 1850 act applicants appealed their receipt of forty-acre warrants and, on their claims being reexamined, received eighty-acre warrants.[49]

Because of the extensive waiting endured by some veterans, many died before they could have received their warrants from Washington. In anticipation of this problem in administering the 1855 act, the Pension Bureau commissioner issued the following regulation:

> If a party die before the issue of a warrant to which he would be entitled, if living, the right to said warrant dies with him. In such case, the warrant becomes void, and should be cancelled, and the party next entitled in right of the service claimed should make an application; and if there be no such party, the grant lapses under the limitation of the beneficiaries to the bounty.[50]

This particular rule caused numerous cancellations of 1855 act warrants. Widows ignorant of the Pension Bureau's procedure collected their spouses' warrants and only learned of the warrants' uselessness on trying to sell.

Congress did desire to pay off quickly the "just debt" it felt was due to the nation's veterans, but the actual procedures to do so proved complicated and subjected many veterans and widows to delays. Congress also expected that the issuing of land warrants would lead to a more rapid settlement of the public lands and an increase in the nation's wealth. The national legislature did not adequately foresee the burden this would place on field personnel in the General Land Office. This was probably inevitable, since the goal of rapid delivery of warrants conflicted with several features of administrative life in the 1850s. The Pension Bureau faced the task of reviewing hundreds of thousands of applications and, particularly in 1850, fell short of the mark. This was due partly to congressional thoughtlessness in planning for the new law and partly to administrative ineptitude. Improved performance after 1855 suggests that Congress and the Pension Bureau did learn from earlier mistakes. Still, the goal of helping the veteran often conflicted with the goals of preventing fraud or the improper receipt of a warrant and of spending as little money as possible.

4

Westward Who? The Warrantees and Their Bounties

Upon receipt of a warrant from the Pension Bureau, the veteran or heir faced the choice of how best to make use of the bounty. A warrantee had to make two basic choices about employing the warrant, but each option involved other related decisions. A warrantee who decided to sell the warrant had to consider the timing and the place of sale as well as the price offered. If, on the other hand, the warrantee chose to use the warrant to obtain a tract of public land, he or she had to determine the exact parcel out of the tens of millions of acres administered by the General Land Office and then decide how to use the land. The first-named choice was one of converting the warrant into quick income, and the second was of converting it into wealth in the warrantee's portfolio. This chapter examines the breakdown of the income-versus-wealth decision making by the warrantees, with a special focus on those who chose to use the warrant to obtain public land. Chapter 5 looks more closely at the group of veterans, widows, and heirs who sought to realize quick cash from their government bounty.

Beginning in 1848 and annually thereafter, the commissioner of the General Land Office reported to the president, Congress, and the nation the previous year's military bounty land warrant locations. Table 12 shows the annual compilation of warrant locations for 1847–60, based on the commissioner's reports. The table indicates a pattern of locations peaking a year or so after the passage of each congressional bounty land act. Ten Regiments Act warrant locations came bunched in 1848 and 1849, while the heaviest flow of warrants at land offices under the act of 1855 appeared in 1856 and 1857. Only the act of 1850 warrants show a lag: not until 1852 and

TABLE 12
Annual Warrant Locations, General Land Office Returns, and Sample Estimates (Thousands of Acres)

Year	*GLO Returns*	*Sample Estimates*
1847	240	712
1848	2,289	5,228
1849	3,406	4,096
1850	2,168	728
1851	2,454	1,448
1852	3,201	4,532
1853	6,142	4,816
1854	3,403	1,824
1855	1,346	2,968
1856	8,382	7,984
1857	6,284	6,708
1858	5,802	4,088
1859	2,915	2,636
1860	2,783	2,230
Totals	50,815	50,058

SOURCE: Table 2 and sample of land warrant recipients, acts of 1847, 1850, 1852, and 1855.

1853 did this series of warrants appear at western land offices, owing to the eighteen-month ban on warrant assignments. Also, the small number of act of 1852 warrants came on the market at the same time.

The General Land Office headquarters staff in Washington gathered its figures from monthly reports sent in by the district land offices. The Washington clerks double-checked the numbers by having the field agents forward the actual warrants and related papers to Washington for permanent filing. Receipt and possession of the warrant files, and the maintenance of a full parallel set of warrant ledgers and abstracts for each district office, created a new paperwork problem in the General Land Office. By 1858, the commissioner had to beg Congress for new quarters to accommodate the rapidly expanding collection of land records.[1]

The annual warrant locations shown chronologically in table 10 point to a land boom in the mid-1850s that slowed somewhat after

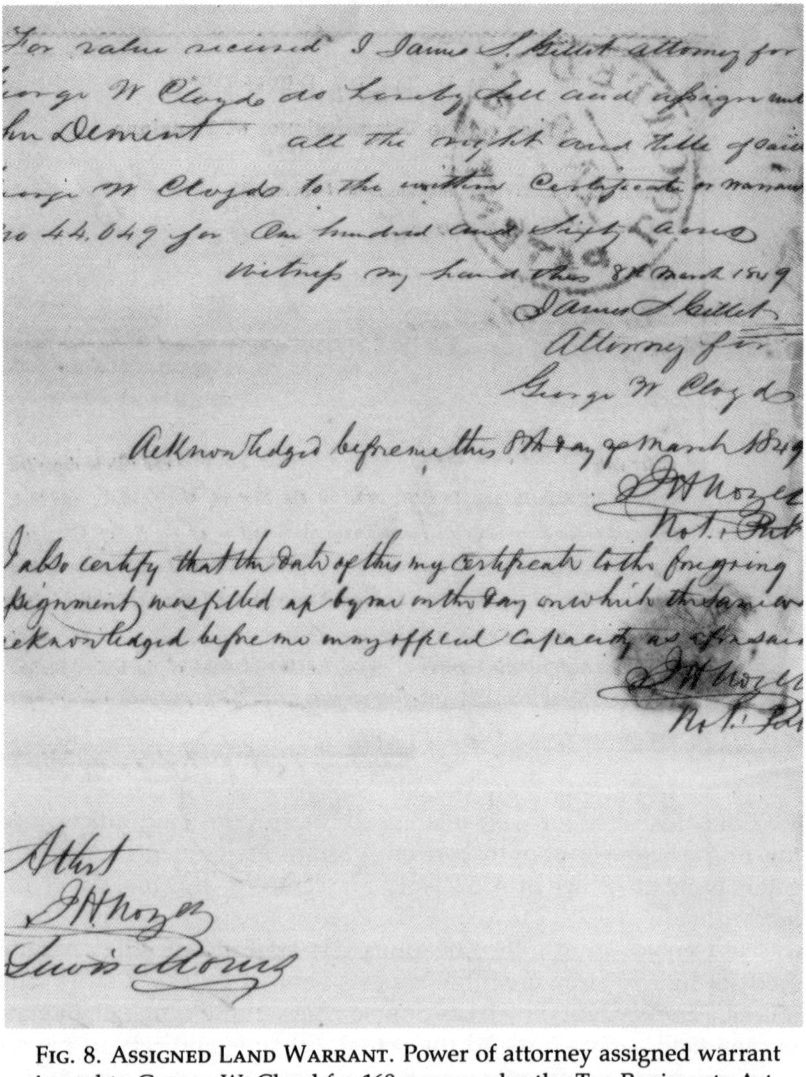

For value received I James S. Gillet attorney for
George W Cloyd do hereby sell and assign unto
John Dement all the right and title of said
George W Cloyd to the within Certificate or warrant
No 44,049 for One hundred and Sixty acres
Witness my hand this 8th March 1849
James S Gillet
Attorney for
George W Cloyd

Acknowledged before me this 8th day of March 1849
J H Mozer
Not. Pub

I also certify that the date of this my certificate to the foregoing assignment was filled up by me on the day on which the same was acknowledged before me in my official capacity as aforesaid
J H Mozer
Not. Pub

Attest
J H Mozer
Lewis Morris

FIG. 8. ASSIGNED LAND WARRANT. Power of attorney assigned warrant issued to George W. Cloyd for 160 acres under the Ten Regiments Act. Note the purchaser is John Dement, who had just lost his position in the Dixon, Illinois, land office in March 1849 and was now using his experience to locate land with warrants in northwestern Illinois (courtesy of the National Archives).

TABLE 13
Land Warrant Locations by State, GLO Returns, and Sample Estimates (In Thousands of Acres)

State	*GLO Returns*	*All Sample Estimates*
Ohio	220	360
Indiana	1,312	1,344
Illinois	7,000	7,048
Missouri	6,000	5,680
Alabama	1,159	984
Mississippi	385	528
Louisiana	1,156	1,240
Michigan	3,933	4,072
Arkansas	1,750	1,008
Florida	466	368
Iowa	14,097	13,968
Wisconsin	6,343	7,236
California	511	644
Minnesota	5,759	6,518
Oregon	68	160
Kansas	4,227	3,744
Nevada	8	0
Nebraska	1,786	2,200
Washington	54	24
Utah	20	32
Dakota	180	168
Colorado	180	280
Montana	*	272
Idaho	*	0
Totals	56,614	57,878

NOTE: GLO 1871 figures are summarized in Paul Gates, "History of Public Land Law Development," p. 275. The GLO figures given here do not include the act of 1812 warrants originally reported. The GLO figures also do not include warrants located after 1871, while the sample figures for the last column include all warrant locations.
*Less than one thousand acres located.

the panic of 1857. Until 1871, the commissioner's annual reports did not show where the warrants found their primary geographical use. In that year, his annual report gave a full breakdown of warrant locations by state (see table 13). The General Land Office report did

TABLE 14
Sample Estimates of Land Warrant Locations by Year and State (In Thousands of Acres)

State	*1847*	*1848*	*1849*	*1850*	*1851*	*1852*	*1853*	*1854*	*1855*	*1856*	*1857*
Ohio	0	160	0	0	40	48	80	32	0	0	0
Indiana	64	480	160	32	56	240	272	8	0	0	8
Illinois	128	1,160	1,256	272	376	1,792	1,664	296	16	40	32
Michigan	0	192	128	32	96	352	320	264	56	480	96
Wisconsin	320	1,048	536	96	80	392	400	160	264	1,540	1,080
Minnesota	0	96	0	0	32	64	32	40	240	1,680	1,336
Iowa	96	1,408	1,032	192	288	724	1,056	600	2,224	3,020	1,012
Missouri	64	224	416	32	272	400	416	176	104	1,088	2,032
Alabama	8	96	48	0	152	240	192	80	40	48	24
Mississippi	0	0	320	0	0	0	80	40	0	0	32
Arkansas	0	192	96	64	32	136	72	32	0	16	128
Louisiana	32	232	104	8	24	16	136	0	24	40	0
Kansas	0	0	0	0	0	0	0	0	0	0	448
Nebraska	0	0	0	0	0	0	0	0	0	32	480
California	0	0	0	0	0	0	0	0	0	0	0
Colorado	0	0	0	0	0	0	0	0	0	0	0
Florida	0	0	0	0	0	128	96	96	0	0	0
Territories	0	0	0	0	0	0	0	0	0	0	0
Totals	712	5,288	4,096	728	1,448	4,532	4,816	1,824	2,968	7,984	6,708

not separate the 1847, 1850, 1852, and 1855 series warrants from the earlier federal issue after the Revolution and those warrants based on the act of 1812. Instead, the GLO reported the location of all warrants issued for military service by the federal government.

The Pension Bureau issued land warrants to veterans from all parts of the country, but particularly to men and women from the states created before the War of 1812; the location of warrants, however, was remarkably concentrated. Table 13 shows nearly a fourth were in Iowa and that more than two-thirds were in the upper Mississippi Valley states. Comparatively few warrants were located south of Missouri.

The random sample of warrants from the four Mexican War–era grants allows one to make a good estimate of how the warrants were distributed geographically over time. The sample data is displayed alongside the data used by the General Land Office to con-

TABLE 14 *(continued)*

1858	*1859*	*1860*	*1861*	*1862*	*1863*	*1864*	*1865*	*1866–1869*	*1870–1879*	*1880–1889*	*1890–1899*	*Post-1900*	*State Totals*
0	0	0	0	0	0	0	0	0	0	0	0	0	360
0	0	0	0	0	24	0	0	0	0	0	0	0	1,334
16	0	0	0	0	0	0	0	0	0	0	0	0	7,048
112	112	24	0	32	224	144	64	568	392	304	64	16	4,072
368	112	24	112	32	64	0	24	400	184	0	0	0	7,236
280	328	942	480	184	64	160	48	192	256	32	32	0	6,518
1,416	172	96	176	88	32	24	32	216	64	0	0	0	13,968
336	104	16	0	0	0	0	0	0	0	0	0	0	5,680
0	56	0	0	0	0	0	0	0	0	0	0	0	984
0	56	0	0	0	0	0	0	0	0	0	0	0	528
112	80	16	32	0	0	0	0	0	0	0	0	0	1,008
112	112	336	32	0	0	0	0	32	0	0	0	0	1,240
1,096	992	536	120	88	0	32	64	176	120	72	0	0	3,744
224	448	208	32	24	32	32	16	176	432	64	0	0	2,200
0	64	32	88	64	64	0	0	64	172	64	32	0	644
0	0	0	0	32	0	0	0	128	56	32	32	0	280
16	0	0	0	0	0	0	0	0	0	0	0	32	368
0	0	0	24	0	0	0	16	0	96	80	56	0	656
4,088	2,636	2,230	1,096	544	504	392	264	1,952	1,772	648	216	48	57,878

SOURCE: Sample of land warrants from the acts of 1847, 1850, 1852, and 1855.

struct the figures reported in tables 12 and 13. The results from the sample alone are displayed in table 14. In the four acts passed between 1847 and 1855, about 25 percent of all warrants were located within the borders of Iowa, while in Illinois, the next-most popular state, only half as many were located. Yet for the years 1847 through 1860, Iowa led the nation in land warrant locations only five times: 1848, 1854 through 1856, and 1858.

In 1847, the first year of locations under the Ten Regiments Act, Wisconsin drew almost half of the warrants used within the nation. The next year saw the first surge of warrant assignments by returning Mexican War veterans and the subsequent tide of locations, with Iowa, Wisconsin, and Illinois all having over one million acres' worth. Indeed, the three land districts in those states abutting one another along the Mississippi River—Dubuque, Mineral Point, and Dixon—alone accounted for over 1.1 million acres in 1848. That year the land district of Fairfield in southeastern Iowa had an additional half-million acres worth of warrant locations. The span from 1849 through 1853 featured Illinois each year as the leading state for land warrant locations, with almost 3.5 million acres located there in 1852 and 1853. After Iowa's dominance between 1854 and 1856, a number of other states had individual years of enormous warrant activity. In 1857, both Missouri and Minnesota easily outstripped Iowa, Missouri alone having more than two million acres located. After Iowa's brief resurgence in 1858, Kansas led all states in 1859; Minnesota did the same in 1860 and through the Civil War years, until Michigan replaced it as the focus of most warrant locations during Reconstruction.

The pattern of warrant locations shows a fairly steady march westward until the Civil War. For example, the easternmost public lands states such as Alabama, Ohio, and Indiana attracted few warrants after 1852. Following the pattern from year to year produces the impression that the movement did speed west, but also to some extent northward or southward along the tier of trans-Mississippi states. Several of the states in question were still federal territories during some of the 1850s, among them Minnesota and Kansas, and all of the public lands states as well as federal territories were divided into land districts by the General Land Office. The opening or closing of land districts could influence the volume of warrants flowing to or away from a state or territory.[2]

Iowa's status as the number one state for warrant locations merits a closer look at its pattern of locations. Table 15 shows the acreage located in warrants at each of Iowa's eleven land offices between 1847 and 1861. The table shows that the state's three leading land offices, in Dubuque, Des Moines, and Council Bluffs, were sited at its eastern boundary, center, and western boundary, respectively (see map 1). The timing of warrant locations shown in table 15 indicates that Dubuque led the field in the years immediately after the Mexican War, with Des Moines garnering most of its locations between 1854 and 1856, and Council Bluffs having its peak year of almost a million acres in the post-panic year 1858. More than in any other state, the Iowa pattern of warrant locations exhibited a steady push west from the Mississippi to the Missouri.

As the acreage in the eastern land districts at Fairfield, Dubuque, and Iowa City passed into private hands, the General Land Office closed those offices and opened new ones further west at Fort Dodge, Sioux City, and Council Bluffs. Something of the same phenomenon occurred north of the Iowa border in Minnesota. Before Minnesota's

TABLE 15

Sample Warrant Locations at Iowa Land Offices, 1847–1860
(In Thousands of Acres)

Office	*1847*	*1848*	*1849*	*1850*	*1851*	*1852*	*1853*	*1854*	*1855*	*1856*	*1857*	*1858*	*1859*	*1860*	*Total*
Chariton	0	0	0	0	32	16	176	56	304	476	0	8	0	0	1,068
Council Bluffs	0	0	0	0	0	0	0	0	416	576	96	992	48	56	2,184
Decorah	0	0	0	0	0	0	0	0	32	824	0	0	0	0	856
Des Moines	0	0	0	0	0	0	152	152	752	448	0	24	36	8	1,572
Dubuque	32	256	416	96	136	268	240	176	448	88	0	0	0	0	2,156
Fairfield	0	640	424	96	80	168	16	32	8	0	0	0	0	0	1,464
Fort Dodge	0	0	0	0	0	0	0	0	128	200	292	240	56	16	932
Iowa City	64	512	192	0	40	272	448	168	0	24	0	0	0	0	1,720
Kanesville	0	0	0	0	0	0	24	16	88	0	0	0	0	0	128
Osage	0	0	0	0	0	0	0	0	0	80	280	96	0	0	456
Sioux City	0	0	0	0	0	0	0	0	48	304	344	56	32	16	800
Totals	96	1,408	1,032	192	288	724	1,056	600	2,224	3,020	1,012	1,416	172	96	13,336

SOURCE: Sample of warrants from acts of 1847, 1850, 1852, and 1855.

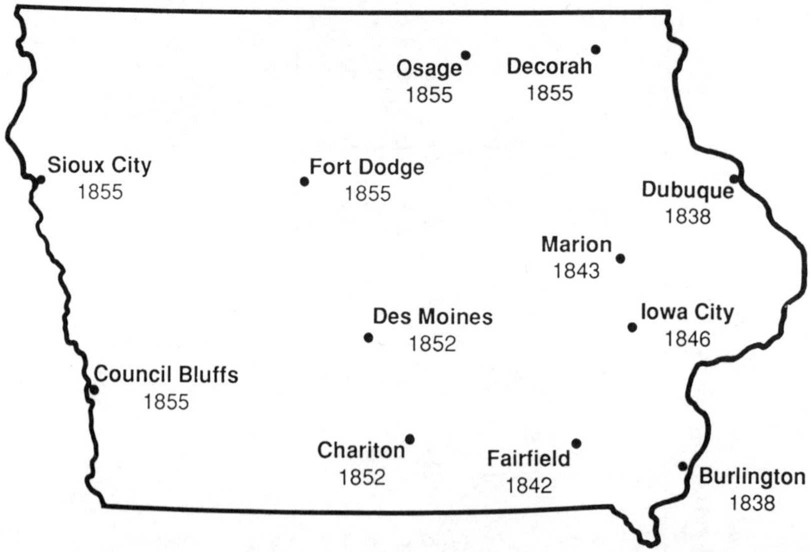

MAP 1. IOWA LAND OFFICES. Years in which new land offices opened in Iowa (courtesy of University of Wisconsin-Eau Claire Cartography Laboratory).

statehood in 1858, the General Land Office established district land offices in the Minnesota Territory at Brownsville, Winona, Red Wing, and Minneapolis, all on the Mississippi River, and at Stillwater on the St. Croix River, east of St. Paul. A tremendous land boom in the southeastern part of the territory in 1856 absorbed most of the public lands in the townships near the Mississippi, so the GLO opened up new offices in late 1856 further west at Chatfield and Faribault. The old offices simply closed, and the new ones commenced business with the same personnel and record books.[3]

The pattern of location does show a decided regional tilt that requires further explanation. Economic historian Stanley Lebergott, borrowing a line from Winston Churchill, calls this pattern of warrant locations part of the "Hinge of Fate" of the American Civil War. Lebergott argues that the North and South stood quite evenly matched until the mid-1840s when two factors, immigration from Europe and land warrant locations in northern free states and terri-

MAP 2. MINNESOTA LAND OFFICES. Years in which new land offices opened in Minnesota (courtesy of University of Wisconsin-Eau Claire Cartography Laboratory).

tories, swung the crucial demographic balance toward the North and freedom. This may be correct, to give the warrants their due; but left unanswered is the question, why did warrants go in such abundance to Iowa and not to Arkansas?[4]

After the Civil War, Congress once again considered rewarding veterans with public land. Indiana Congressman George Julian, a land reformer and self-styled foe of land speculators, opposed new grants on the grounds that antebellum land warrants had been properly used by only one in five hundred of the original warrantees; that is, the other 499 recipients sold their warrants on the open market for cash. Julian's definition of proper use was the veteran's employment of the warrant to begin a new farm for himself and his family. His opposition to further big grants, along with special provisions for Union veterans under the Southern Homestead Act,

TABLE 16
Disposition of Sample Warrants—Acts of 1847, 1850, 1852, 1855

Act	*Number*	*Canceled*	*Assigned*	*Power of Attorney Locations*	*Located by Warrantee*
1847	441	5	410	0	26
1850	945	47	742	86	70
1852	60	1	56	0	3
1855	1,315	28	1,259	5	23
Total	2,761	81	2,467	91	122

SOURCE: Sample of warrant recipients, acts of 1847, 1850, 1852, and 1855.

worked to end talk of more bounty land grants. Since that historical moment in the early part of Reconstruction, Congress has only sparingly used the public domain to aid veterans. In the 1870s, Congress rewarded Winnebago Indians of Nebraska for service on the Great Plains with forty-acre land warrants, and many of the tribe located them on ancestral land in Wisconsin. The great trend in veterans' benefits in the twentieth century, however, has been to offer cash grants along with aid for education and housing as a way of providing veterans with the modern equivalent of a homestead.[5]

George Julian's opposition to another mass bounty land act is of interest here because he offered an informed guess about how warrantees used their bounty under the grants of 1847 through 1855. Indeed, Julian's estimate proved to be only a bit exaggerated. Table 16 presents figures on how beneficiaries of the four bounty land acts used their warrants. The numbers show a near-uniformity of purpose by the veterans and their widows and heirs, much as Julian had argued. Nineteen out of every twenty recipients under the Ten Regiments Act sold their warrants for cash. The rate at which veterans and widows used their warrants to obtain land rose to 7 percent under the 1850 act but fell again to 5 percent under the small 1852 act; under the Old Soldiers Act of 1855, just 2 percent of the recipients located their own warrants. Clearly, most American veterans and their heirs who received a land warrant saw the bounty as providing an opportunity to sell for cash, not as a ticket to a new life in the West. The overwhelming majority of warrant recipients between the Mexican and Civil Wars refused what was in effect a direct invitation from the federal government for them to move to the western public lands states.

Since southern veterans and widows were well represented in the population of warrant recipients, there can be no question of the original warrantees' having been biased against the South. Thus, one answer to the question of why Iowa and not Arkansas is that very few veterans or widows used the warrants themselves. Instead, the market that collected warrants from scores of southern courthouses in turn placed those warrants in Iowa and the upper Mississippi Valley rather than in the antebellum Southwest for a mix of administrative and market reasons. In addition, the slave states attracted comparatively few warrants because Texas, the preeminent southern boom state after 1848, had its own public domain and its own set of public lands laws independent of the United States. This was perhaps the most important material possession Texas retained from the Lone Star Republic, to go with its old national debt. Had Texas been open to U.S. military bounty land warrants, perhaps the figures in tables 13 and 14 might have been less skewed against the slave states.[6]

Two other factors help explain why relatively few land warrants were located in southern public lands states. First, the workings of public lands laws affected the transfer of federal land to private citizens somewhat differently in the South than the North. General Land Office surveyors did their work in the southern states earlier than in the Upper Midwest; more important, the southern public lands were opened earlier to "private entry." That term actually meant sale to the general public at $1.25 an acre; private entry went into effect after townships had been put up for bidding at a public auction and remained unsold. Consequently, southern public lands states had more land open earlier to private entry than northern states, and when the Graduation Act of 1854 dramatically reduced the price of lands long offered at private entry but still unsold, southern buyers preferred to get cheap acres with cash (some selling for as little as 12.5 cents an acre) rather than use expensive warrants costing about a dollar an acre. When the Graduation Act went into effect in August 1854, the United States had 31.6 million acres of fourth- and fifth-class lands that had remained unsold for at least twenty-five years. Of this, slave states contained 29.9 million acres, and free states just 1.7 million. Table 17 shows that warrant locations in the five southern public lands states, Florida, Alabama, Mississippi, Louisiana, and Arkansas, fell from 13 percent of the na-

TABLE 17
Percentage of Sample Warrants Located Annually in Slave States, 1847–1860

Year	*Excluding Missouri*	*Including Missouri*
1847	5.6	14.6
1848	9.9	14.2
1849	14.9	25.8
1850	9.5	13.7
1851	14.4	33.1
1852	11.1	19.7
1853	11.4	19.6
1854	13.0	22.1
1855	2.1	5.5
1856	1.3	14.6
1857	2.7	32.9
1858	5.6	13.4
1859	11.6	15.5
1860	16.6	17.3

SOURCE: Table 14.

tional total in 1854 to just 2 percent the next year, and just 1 percent in 1856, as the full force of the Graduation Act became apparent.[7]

The second reason for the overrepresentation of upper Mississippi Valley states in the location of land warrants is that these states possessed some of the richest farmland for grain growing in North America, and the decade beginning in 1850 was a very good one for grain producers. It was then that mechanical grain reapers first appeared in large number on the prairies. These were also years of heavy food exports to Europe. Cotton producers, too, had prosperous times in the 1850s, but not quite as good as in the mid-1830s. Thus, the market sent warrants to the area of greatest demand in response to an increase in the number of pioneers who sought to begin new farms.[8]

This phenomenon, as it related to the public lands in the 1850s, repeated the booms of the late 1810s and mid-1830s. In the boom after the War of 1812, the greatest land purchases were in the Ohio Valley states, while, in the 1830s, the old southwestern states of Alabama and Mississippi saw the most active land buying. The land rush component of the westward movement between the Revolution and Civil Wars started west from the national center on Chesapeake and Delaware Bays, then moved southwest toward the lower Mississippi in the 1830s, and finally north and west in the 1850s.[9]

Most social groups responded similarly to the government's bounty after each of the four congressional acts. At first glance, it is difficult to find any difference in the personal characteristics between the few who actually located their warrants on the public lands and the many who sold their warrants for cash. Statistical analysis does not show any differences between veterans of particular wars that could have affected the ways they disposed of their bounties. The bounty lands warrant files do not include the ages of recipients, but, on the basis of the particular war served in, it is possible to make a rough classification of the veterans by age-group. For example, veterans of the War of 1812 were mainly in their sixties, Aroostook War veterans in their forties, Mexican War veterans in their twenties, and so forth. The comparable rates of sale among veterans of different wars indicates no difference based on age in the warrantee's decision on how to use his warrant (see table 18). Military rank and literacy, two rough indicators of social class in nineteenth-century America, were not measures of the different ways veterans used their land warrants. Widows who received land warrants on the basis of their husbands' war service, however, did sell their land paper for cash at a somewhat higher rate than surviving veterans and minor heirs.[10]

For the 1847, 1852, and 1855 acts, only geography helped determine which veterans were likely to use their warrants to locate public land. Specifically, residence in a public lands state led a much higher percentage of warrant recipients to locate than would be expected on the basis of chance. Of the 1847 act sample of warrantees who located their land warrants, all but two lived in public lands states. One Kentucky veteran used his warrant to move further west, and a carpenter from Troy, New York, Peter McGlew, abandoned the Empire State and made a new start in Iowa with the help of his 160-acre land warrant. Most of the 1847 series warrants were located at land offices in Missouri, Illinois, Iowa, and Wisconsin. Mexican War veterans from those states were the most likely to use their warrants themselves. In Iowa, two of the four sample warrantees from that state located land with their warrants.[11]

Of the three sample warrants located by their recipients under the small 1852 act, two went to men living in public lands states. One was issued to an Alabamian, William Cook of Talladega County, who located his forty-acre warrant at the nearby Lebanon

TABLE 18
Disposition of Sample Warrants by Age Category
Acts of 1850 and 1855

	War Service before 1820	*War Service, 1820–45*	*War Service after 1845*	*Total*
Act of 1850:				
Assigned warrant	604	125	10	739
Located warrant	44	27	1	72
Power of attorney sale	76	12	0	88
Totals	724	164	11	899
(Missing/canceled = 46)				
Act of 1855:				
Assigned warrant	877	215	134	1,226
Located warrant	29	14	5	48
Power of attorney sale	5	0	0	5
Totals	911	229	139	1,279
(Missing/canceled = 36)				

SOURCE: Calculated from samples of acts of 1850 and 1855 warrants.

land office. Another sample warrant was issued to a Missourian who also used it close to home. The third warrant of the sample used for location went to a Georgian who selected a parcel in Arkansas. The percentage of 1855 sample warrantees using their bounty to locate land was the smallest under all the acts, only 2 percent. Of the twenty-three in the sample who used their warrants to acquire public land, five lived east of the Alleghenies (two each from New York and Pennsylvania and one from Virginia), while the remainder lived in public lands states.[12]

Statistical analysis does suggest that an additional factor influenced the behavior of the 1850 act sample warrantees. The date of each warrant's issue proved important, because those issued before March 1852 suffered from the congressional ban on warrant sales. The 1850 act was the only official effort to discourage the selling of land warrants, and legislative relief did not come until March 1852, when Congress reversed itself in favor of legal assignment. More than a year passed after the Pension Bureau began issuing warrants before recipients could legally sell their bounties. The sample figures reflect this in several ways. The 1850 sample had the highest percentage of warrantees locating land with their bounties, over 7 percent. Many of these locations were on the part of warrantees who received their bounties early in the Pension Bureau's issuing of the warrants.

A look at the seventy 1850 act warrantees who chose to locate their bounties reveals similarities to the warrantees under other acts. Again, the older states provided very few men and women willing to use their warrants to obtain public land. Moreover, the locators lived in public lands states and tended to enter land at a nearby land office. The upper Mississippi Valley states provided a number of men and women locating land with their own warrants; however the 1850 act warrants had an unusual feature in the behavior of veterans from Alabama and Florida. Fourteen veterans and heirs from Alabama located public lands with warrants, fully two-fifths of the sample's Alabama warrantees. Similarly, nine of twenty-three Floridians used their warrants to locate public land at one of the land offices in Florida. This anomaly has no parallel in the other southern public lands states; nor, for that matter, was the pattern forecast by 1847 Alabamians or Floridians or repeated by the 1855 warrantees from Alabama or Florida.[13]

Another group of 1850 warrantees sought value from their bounties in a different way. Rather than use the warrants themselves, they employed the legal device of assigning through a power of attorney. This arrangement featured an agreement whereby the warrantee hired a western land agent to locate the warrant on a parcel of public land, thereby freeing the warrantee to sell the land parcel and realize a cash return. The General Land Office understood the act of 1850 to allow such power of attorney locations as long as the veteran sold neither the warrant nor the land until actual title passed from the United States to the warrantee. In practice, however, western agents paid veterans and widows cash up front for power of attorney warrants. The power of attorney sale yielded a result akin to simple assignment—the veteran got cash for his bounty—but it imposed delays and expenses not faced by the 1847 warrantees.

Power of attorney warrant transactions had been used with act of 1847 warrants, largely to allow the veteran to sell his right to a land warrant before the Pension Bureau issued the actual bounty. This soon brought on complaints and gave the practice a dubious reputation. In the spring of 1849, Washington, D.C., warrant broker Jourdan Maury advised a client in relation to Mexican War warrants, "There has been some frauds discovered in the power of atty warrants, which is the cause of their being less in price than the clean warrants. I would advise you to buy the clean warrants only." After the 1852 act passed legalizing assignments, one western land warrant dealer advised his supplier in the East, "We find that it is no use trying to sell unassigned wts now. People will not have them at any price. If you can get them assigned I should be glad to sell them for you."[14]

The major use of power of attorney warrant locations came in conjunction with the act of 1850 series, as shown in table 16. Analysis of the sample of act of 1850 warrants reveals some details about the recipients who chose to use their bounty in this way. The eighty-eight sample power of attorney warrants, when projected on the basis of the sample size, covered a substantial area, more than 1.3 million acres. Thirty-one of the eighty-eight sample warrants were located at the Dubuque land office, with the Fairfield, Iowa, and the Mineral Point, Wisconsin, land offices following in popularity as destinations. Dubuque was home to Horatio Sanford, among other land agents, and Sanford may have done the greatest nationwide volume of business in power of attorney locations.[15]

The social characteristics of the warrantees who made power of attorney locations were roughly similar to those of the whole sample of act of 1850 warrantees (see table 19). They were a bit older than the entire 1850 sample, as measured by a greater proportion of War of 1812 veterans than veterans of Indian conflicts of the 1830s. The power of attorney warrant locators were also a bit more likely to be the surviving veterans rather than their widows or heirs. When compared with the entire 1850 sample, they were somewhat more likely to come from a New England or middle Atlantic state rather than a south Atlantic state. Also, by a few percentage points, they showed a greater rate of ability to sign their names.

The overwhelming difference, however, of power of attorney locators from those who assigned their warrants after March 1852, was that the former group received their warrants first and disposed of them first. The Pension Bureau's sluggishness in late 1850 and early 1851 had the result that only about 40 percent of all the warrants issued under the act of 1850 reached their recipients before the liberating act of 1852. Of the warrants issued between February

TABLE 19
Profile of the Disposition of Sample Act of 1850 Warrants

	Assigned	*Located*	*Power of Attorney*
Rank:			
Privates	603	79	56
NCOs	64	6	2
Officers	67	13	8
X^2 = 4.93 (missing = 47)			
Literacy:			
Illiterates	200	13	21
Signed name	532	58	66
X^2 = 2.94 (missing = 55)			
War service:			
Before 1820	604	44	76
After 1820	135	28	12
X^2= 21.44* (missing = 46)			

*Significant at .05 level.
SOURCE: Calculated from sample of act of 1850 warrants.

1851 and March 1852, about a quarter were used as power of attorney locations. The sample shows that only three of the eighty-eight power of attorney locations were made after April 1852. Thus, the first 80,000 under the act of 1850 fell into three groups: about 15 percent—mainly westerners—who located their own warrants; another quarter who went the power of attorney route as the only way to gain some income on the warrants before March 1852; and a majority who simply held their warrants until Congress reversed itself with what contemporaries called the "Assignment Bill" in the spring of 1852.

The warrantee willing to sell his or her act of 1850 warrant before March 1852 had to find an attorney willing to work around the ban on sale before issue of the patent. Cyrus Woodman, of the Wisconsin firm of Washburn and Woodman, described at length in March 1851, to George Emery, his Portland, Maine, brother-in-law, the way the procedure worked:

> The new warrants you know are not assignable. You cannot buy them *to hold* to any advantage. . . . The law does not make the Warrants assignable but myself and my partner are buying them and taking the risks. Our plan is as follows: In buying the Warrants we take a Power of Atty. from the warrantee to make the location in his name; a Power of Attorney to convey the land after the location is made; a bond to make a deed of said land when requested—the names of the Attorney and obligee being left blank. . . . In buying in the way proposed we run some risk and it will be well to purchase of parties who you think have some little honor about them. In purchasing, it will be well for you to reserve from $5 to $10 to be paid on the execution of a deed after the issue of the patent, which will not be, probably, until a year after the warrant is located.[16]

Washburn and Woodman also anticipated that some warrantees would actually like to retain possession of the located public lands tract as an investment to be resold at a later date as a capital gain. Cyrus Woodman explained to a New York agent that veterans of this type with warrants in hand, who might "wish to locate them upon western lands," could hire the firm to act as attorney and agent at $5.00 for a forty-acre warrant, $7.50 for an eighty-acre certificate, and $10.00 for a 160-acre grant. Most of the firm's business, however, was directed toward securing power of attorney warrants for resale, that is, of the type described by Woodman to George Emery. Washburn and Woodman were quite specific in telling their eastern agents to "Follow [General Land Office Commissioner Justin] Butterfield's instructions to Registers in taking Powers to locate." Cyrus Woodman wrote his brother George in New York to use care in obtaining power of attorney warrants from other dealers because "if we get Tom, Dick & Harry to buy for us, we shall get the warrants of all sorts of persons stuck on to us & frequently without the signature. . . . "[17]

How did the act of 1850 warrantees who chose the power of attorney method fare in the market? The evidence suggests that they suffered a severe reduction in the prices offered for their warrants in comparison to act of 1847 warrants and to warrants legally assigned after March 1852. In trying to help warrantees escape the power of speculators by barring assignments in 1850, Congress succeeded only in weakening the veterans' market position when the right to sell was finally granted. The business records of John K. Martin, a Richmond warrant agent and broker, show how much warrantees lost by not possessing the legal right to assign in 1851. Martin had almost two hundred clients apply for warrants with his help between October 1850 and March 1852, when Congress made warrant sales legal. These early applicants under the act of 1850 also paid very high application preparation fees: five dollars on a forty-acre warrant, ten dollars on an eighty-acre warrant, and fifteen dollars on a full 160-acre certificate.[18]

These men and women sold their warrants to Martin and another Richmond warrant dealer, William Fulton, for a pittance and received only a fraction of the value that warrants commanded in the market after March 1852. The warrants were purchased using the power of attorney loophole, and Martin saw them as riskier than act of 1847 assigned warants. A few examples will suffice to show the penalty paid by veterans. Edward Clark received 1850 series warrant 1,628 and, after paying the application fee to Fulton, on March 18, 1851, netted just fifteen dollars on a 160-acre warrant, or only nine cents an acre, far below any public price quoted for Ten Regiments Act 160-acre warrants. On June 23, 1851, Fulton bought a pair of eighty-acre warrants, paying to the two veterans, after fees, a mere ten dollars each, or 12.5 cents an acre.[19]

Throughout the fall of 1851, Fulton and Martin bought power of attorney warrants from Virginia veterans and widows and rarely paid more than 35 cents an acre. Their prices started to climb only after representatives and senators convened in December 1851 for the first session of the 32d Congress. The Senate quickly passed a bill to make 1850 act warrants assignable. As for House action, Martin assured a Wisconsin correspondent on January 2, "about the warrants being made assignable under the Act of 28th September 1850 there can be no doubt." Prices by February for power of attorney warrants climbed above 62.5 cents an acre and continued gradually upward after March. Thus, the comparatively low prices that warrantees faced when they finally won the right to sell were actually part of a steady rise. The volume of act of 1850 warrants sold by the end of the summer of 1852, about 70,000, did not depress prices in and of themselves; quite the contrary, western warrant agents welcomed legally sold warrants as much as the veterans did. It does seem likely, however, that higher market prices would have prevailed in the summer of 1852 if assignment of act of 1850 warrants had been legal from the start.[20]

The business papers of Washburn and Woodman also indicate very low prices paid to power of attorney locators. The Mineral Point firm paid twenty-five dollars for a forty-acre warrant throughout 1851, forty dollars for an eighty-acre warrant, and sixty dollars for one issued for 160 acres. Cyrus Woodman conceded to George

Paine, a Poughkeepsie broker and associate of General Leonard Maison, that "these prices may seem to you low," but Woodman stressed the legal risks as well as the anticipated flood of warrants issued under the 1850 act. Just after word reached Wisconsin in the spring of 1852 that Congress had made act of 1850 warrants assignable, Cyrus Woodman wrote his partner, "If Warrants can be bought at the prices we have paid for a year past, you cannot I think get too many of them. . . . I think they must rise."[21]

At the same time that Washburn and Woodman handled as many as 2,000 power of attorney warrant locations in 1851, they sought to fight the ban on assignments in the courts by hiring the most famous legal mind in the country as counsel. The firm never did test in court the legal research that Rufus Choate did in Boston on the constitutional question of the congressional ban on assignments. They did, however, publish the results of Choate's intellectual labor as a pamphlet. In April 1852, Cyrus Woodman sent copies to the commissioner of pensions, the commissioner of the General Land Office, and the secretary of the interior. Moreover, he wrote to several newspaper editors asking them to reprint the eight-page brief, in part because "it will be a valuable advertisement for us."[22]

Abraham Lincoln was one veteran who used the power of attorney method, although in his case the action made little sense since he could legally have sold his warrant. Lincoln arranged for an Iowa land agent to locate his 120-acre warrant issued under the act of 1855 using a power of attorney. Lincoln located his earlier act of 1850 forty-acre warrant, issued for service in the Black Hawk War at the Springfield, Illinois, land office. The warrant was issued in April 1852, but Lincoln did not get around to locating it until July 1854—well after the lifting of the ban on sales. By that time, the General Land Office had closed all its Illinois offices except Springfield, which then served the whole state. Lincoln was quicker to apply for his 1855 warrant, sending in his application for a 120-acre certificate to the Pension Bureau in August 1855. He had the warrant located in Iowa under a power of attorney arrangement. His earlier holding the 1850 act forty-acre warrant for two years before using it suggests that Old Abe had things other than land warrants on his mind. Most people, rather than locating or hiring an out-of-state attorney, chose to wait until the law permitted the sale of warrants. Once the bottleneck on assignments was broken in March 1852, large numbers of 1850 warrants appeared for sale.[23]

Except for 1851 and early 1852, when Congress and the Interior Department forbade warrant asignments, state probate courts decided that selling a warrant for cash represented the best value for an estate. The orphan brothers and sisters of Samuel Woods in Madison County, Florida, received a land warrant after his death in the Mexican War. The Woods children's guardian, Joseph Eaton of Monticello, Florida, received the warrant the first week of January 1853. He asked the Madison County Probate Court for guidance on disposition of the land warrant. The court ordered Eaton to sell "for the best price he can obtain," on the sensible ground that the three Woods children needed cash, not joint ownership of 160 acres of public land.[24]

In only two cases in the sample did the guardian locate the warrant instead of selling it for cash on behalf of a minor child. James Swartwood of Tioga County, New York, received a forty-acre warrant for his father's service in the War of 1812 in June 1852, after it became legal to assign. His uncle and guardian took the warrant and located it at the busy Dixon, Illinois, land office that September. Along similar lines, the minor heirs of Richard Hutchins of Mississippi had their eighty-acre land warrant located at the Columbus, Mississippi, land office by their guardian. In all other sample guardian and probate cases, the warrants sold for cash.[25]

The United Brethren of the War of 1812 and their supporters in Congress made repeated references to the impoverished state of some of the 1812 veterans. General James Nye of New York had posed the political issue as bounty lands or the almshouse for the old veteran. Despite this emphasis, the whole issue of need seems to have gone unquestioned by contemporaries. The Pierce administration, to be sure, presided over four years of general prosperity, and the just debt claimed by General Nye did not reach maturity at a time of mass unemployment and, indeed, could not have done so in the overwhelmingly rural America of 1855. Nonetheless, no one under Franklin Pierce suggested any sort of means test to screen out veterans not in need of a land bounty or its cash equivalent.[26]

Economic historians expect wealth and income to increase with age at least through middle age. With the hindsight of the twentieth century, one might predict that the 1812 veterans would be among the less likely groups in society to need federal aid. Tracing the property holdings of a smaller subsample of five hundred War of 1812 veterans and widows receiving warrants under the acts of 1850 and 1855 reveals that the surviving veterans were relatively well off in the 1850s. The mean value of real estate held by the heads of household in the subsample in 1850 totaled $1,428. The mean value of $1,428 in real property holdings put the veterans in the subsample comfortably above the national mean for free males in 1850 who held real estate worth $1,001. Men who served as officers in militia units during the War of 1812 had an 1850 mean real estate holding of over $1,700, while privates from the same war averaged just under $1,400 in 1850. The occupations listed by the Census of 1850 show that more than half of the veterans were farmers. To a sixty-year-old veteran of the War of 1812 owning, say, a farm worth $1,400, a bounty land warrant worth perhaps $160 was a welcome but not overwhelming gratuity, somewhat like winning third prize in a lottery rather than hitting the jackpot itself. Stated in 1990 dollars, a 160-acre warrant sold for about $1,800.[27]

Widows of War of 1812 veterans stand out as one group that did have a clear need for the government's land bounty. Economic historians have established that nineteenth-century America probably had a wider disparity between men's and women's earnings than does twentieth-century America. Because of legal arrangements, this gap also existed in wealth holdings, and the listings do show a disparity in real estate owned by 1812 veterans and the widows of those veterans. The mean real estate holdings for veterans and widows in the subsample does not reveal this, in large part because the wealthiest person identified was a widow who owned over $41,000 in real estate. When the average is calculated with medians, however, the picture changes: the median for veterans was $500, while that for widows stood at zero.[28]

It is difficult to determine whether the widows without real property had other sources of income, for example, from their offspring. Even if they did, it seems likely that widows in their fifties and sixties were helped considerably by receipt of a land warrant. This especially holds true of the illiterate women. Two-thirds of these women reported no real estate holdings in the returns for the Census of 1850. A sudden windfall of $160 might not have been as satisfying as a lifetime pension of eight dollars a month, Colonel Joel Sutherland's post-1857 idea, but neither should its effect be dismissed.

Why was there so little use of the land warrants to "provide a comfortable home in the twilight years," as Colonel James Porter had put it? The answer is that few gray-haired veterans or widows would move West solely to locate warrants. We know from detailed studies of frontier farming that life was expensive in the West, so much so that few people without sufficient capital or access to credit could easily begin pioneer farming. A careful look at the extent of interstate movement among the veterans of the War of 1812, traced in the 1850 and 1855 samples, shows that most veterans lived out their lives in one state. The Census of 1850 is the first to list all free enumerants by name and also the first to give the place of birth for each free person. Since 1850, it has been possible to gauge geographical mobility by decennial intervals; before that date, researchers are somewhat in the dark. Militia and pension records offer one way of estimating mobility since a comparatively high percentage of young and middle-aged men were enrolled in the various state militias. During the War of 1812, the nation had about 1.1 million white men between eighteen and forty-five, of whom 700,000 were militiamen; of these, about 450,000 were called to active duty against the British or Indians. This may be as good a national sample of American white males as researchers are likely to find before the census of 1850.[29]

Disappointment awaited any congressional granters of bounty land warrants who truly expected the old veterans to move onto new land on the public domain. For those congressmen who saw the warrants as a chance indirectly to give cash to veterans or widows, the fact of the warrant's issue alone was sufficient. This became Senator Richard Brodhead's position in 1856 when he reflected on the effects of the Old Soldiers Act of the previous year:

> It appropriated probably thirty-five millions—certainly thirty millions of acres—of land worth, perhaps thirty millions of dollars to the old States; and therefore, it was a wise measure in my judgement. It gave to the old States their share of the public domain. It distributed them to a very meritorious class of persons.[30]

Here, amid the political bitterness of the spring of 1856, with "Bleeding Kansas" and "Bleeding Sumner" keeping Congress in turmoil, Brodhead the northern Democrat had moved almost to the position Henry Clay had long advocated, namely, "distribution" of the value of the public lands to the non-public lands states.

Brodhead claimed that the bounty land system worked for the "soldier who gets the market value of his warrant, and he gets very nearly the Government price of the land." Behind this statement stood Brodhead's belief that it was a comparatively simple affair for a veteran of the War of 1812 to convert his land warrant into cash. In fact, a fair and efficient market had to be created to pay cash to warrantees and sell the same warrants to buyers on the public lands. In the end, too, the vast majority of veterans who chose to sell their warrants had to prove themselves hard bargainers in the marketplace.

5

Prices, Markets, and Fairness in the Trading of Land Warrants

Astute observers in the 1840s and 1850s were not surprised that warrantees overwhelmingly chose to sell their warrants for cash. Several people noted that a warrant by itself was insufficient to lure men and their families from the seaboard hundreds of miles inland to the West. More heated was the debate over the actual benefit to the veterans of selling their bounties. Contemporaries differed strongly on the likely outcome of warrant sales. In discussing the 1847 Ten Regiments Act, Thomas Hart Benton predicted that the warrants would sell for only a few cents an acre because veterans were no match for speculators. His opponent in Senate debate, Pennsylvania's Simon Cameron, had "no fears about the speculators robbing the soldiers. The volunteers were intelligent men, who were capable of taking care of themselves." Cameron added that for the old act of 1812 land warrants, "the biter had been bit—the speculators had lost by their contact with the soldiers."[1]

Congress repeated the debate in 1850 but now seemed convinced of Wisconsin Senator Isaac Walker's contention that the 1847 warrant assignment practice had worked to the detriment of the veteran. "Examine these returns," challenged Walker, "and see upon how few are the names of soldiers locating their warrants to be found . . . but the soldier who sells his warrant receives but a fourth or at most one half of that value." If Walker was correct, the market price of a warrant to the seller would have ranged from thirty to sixty-two cents an acre, or, for a 160-acre warrant, yielding a total of fifty to one hundred dollars. Though some quarreled with Walker's figures, the sentiment in Congress that year favored a ban on assignments. Congress intended to strike a blow at the despised speculator by pursuing a policy that restricted the benefit of the bounty to the veteran and his heirs.[2]

In 1855, Congress again debated the value to the veteran of an assignable land warrant. Benton, now in the House, and Senator David Stuart of Michigan fought to protect veterans by making the 1855 warrants unassignable. Stuart argued that, if the bill passed, "you cannot sell a certificate for one hundred and sixty acres of land for one hundred and sixty shillings. . . ." Richard Brodhead responded to Stuart on the floor of the Senate: "Sir, I expected a good deal of opposition for the Senators representing the new States. I expected to hear of speculation in land warrants. . . . The value of land warrants is well known and easily understood. They always bring their value or nearly so. . . ." Brodhead, of course, carried the day, but contemporaries wondered whether he indeed had his facts straight.[3]

Veterans never received the full $1.25 an acre for their warrants, but the surviving evidence does not support the contentions of Benton, Walker, and Stuart. Most veterans received a price determined in a competitive market featuring many buyers and sellers, and the recipients genuinely benefited from the federal bounty. In the end, the price a veteran received depended on two factors. First, the decisions and actions taken by officials in Washington directly influenced prices. Specifically, the government set the upper limit on warrant prices by selling public land at $1.25 an acre. No warrant would sell at $1.50 an acre, for example, when a cash purchase of land was cheaper. By determining eligibility standards, Congress also fixed the supply of warrants, although no one knew the exact number in advance. Moreover, actions in Washington could affect the demand for warrants by the way in which public land was offered for sale or entry by warrant.

A second influence on prices was the market sophistication of the veteran, widow, or heir. Veterans willing to sell their warrants for the pittance predicted by Senator Stuart could no doubt find willing buyers; the evidence, however, points instead to careful consideration of the warrants' value by most veterans. The action of brokers in making a market for land warrants also had a related bearing on prices. The strong competition among brokers for warrant business worked generally to the benefit of warrantees. Between the end of the Mexican War and the firing on Fort Sumter, warrant buyers paid veterans and heirs from $50 million to $60 million. Rather than Senator Walker's estimate of a fourth or one-half of the face value of a warrant, 80 percent is closer to the norm.

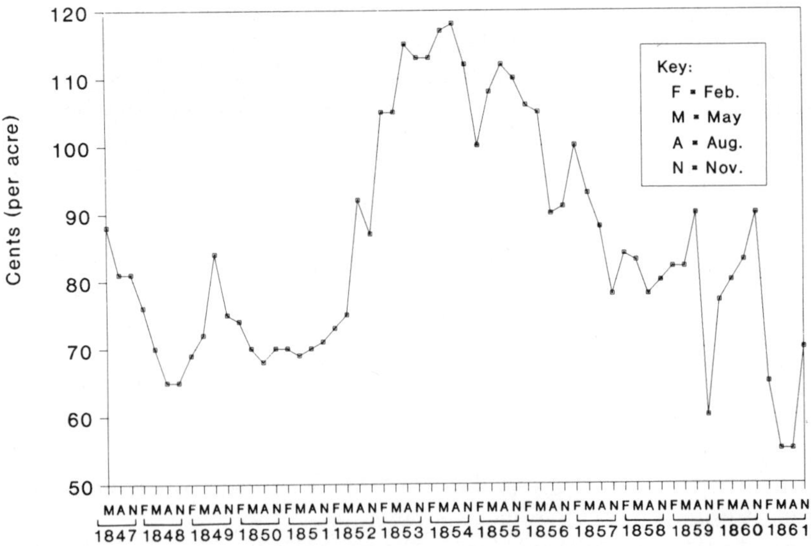

FIG. 9. LAND WARRANT PRICES, 1847–1861.

Thus, as a pension program, military bounty land grants may be said to have worked well in providing veterans and heirs with sizable cash payments.

Figure 9 and Appendix B present land warrant prices from the Mexican War through 1861. The prices charted are an average of quotes from New England, New York, and Virginia dealers. Only once, in 1854, did the asking or buying price reach $1.20 an acre, while on two occasions the price fell below 62.5 cents an acre. Each extreme was something of a limit to land warrant prices. It is unlikely that any warrantee ever received $1.25 an acre; brokers buying warrants maintained a spread between what they paid the warrantee and what they received from someone interested in using the warrant. This spread represented one source of profit for a land warrant broker and placed a cap on buying prices at around $1.20 an acre.[4]

The minimum acceptable price to warrantees set the floor price for land warrants. Contemporaries in the warrant market called this the reservation price; it represented the point below which warrantees would not sell. The figure of 62.5 cents an acre was a more subtle limit than the top price, but, like the ceiling, was subject to influence by congressional action. The reason may be traced back to

1847. A clause of the wartime Ten Regiments Act offered soldiers and their heirs the option of selecting a $100 Treasury note of unspecified maturity at 6 percent interest. This served as a compromise gesture to the Benton forces' apprehension that warrantees would get little for their paper. Sixty-two-and-one-half cents an acre for a 160-acre land warrant (or $100) was exactly the point at which an 1847 land warrant dipped below the value of the Treasury note option. For the 1847 warrantees, the price of 62.5 cents an acre was the point, in the language of the economist, where the warrantee was "indifferent" between a warrant and the Treasury note. If prices for warrants fell below 62.5 cents, this signaled Mexican War veterans to choose the Treasury note option.[5]

Contemporary observers of the land warrant market anticipated that there would be a floor price but, at least initially, they had trouble deciding how far down toward 62.5 cents an acre the reservation price would fall. Cyrus Woodman wrote businessmen throughout the country about this question. He mused to one associate in August 1847 that, "the Soldiers we have no doubt will take the $100 Treasury Scrip, particularly those living in those Sections of the Country where but little Government land remains." Woodman went on to reason that the option "to some extent will fix the value of the land scrip as they will not take the $100 if they suppose their land scrip would convey much more than that." He expected that, at the highest, $150 (or ninety-four cents an acre) would be more than sufficient to buy 160-acre warrants from returning Mexican War veterans; indeed, Woodman made a trip to southern Illinois in September 1847 to buy what he expected would be a few dozen warrants at greatly discounted prices. Instead, he wrote in surprise to a Massachusetts land speculator, many Mexican War veterans "would not sell at that price [$150], intending if they could not get more to make locations for themselves." Some Illinois veterans discharged from the war in the late summer of 1847 demanded $180, or near par value for their warrants.[6]

The bill granting land warrants in 1850, as written in the House, did provide for an alternative of twenty-five, fifty, or one hundred dollars in Treasury scrip in proportion to time served on active duty. The Senate, however, refused to concur in the House provision, and the act that Millard Fillmore signed into law granted only land warrants but no scrip. David Atchison persuaded his fellow senators to oppose a scrip option in 1850 on the grounds that "we treat our lands as of but little value to the Government, and we grant them for almost every and any purpose for which they may be asked . . . but it is certainly no object for the Government to transfer the money in the Treasury into the pockets of individuals." Many certainly did expect warrant prices to sink below 62.5 cents an acre. Some welcomed such a fall as a way "to make public lands cheaper and more easily to be obtained." However, the prices reported in figure 9 throughout the 1850s do show a regular range above the floor level of 62.5 cents an acre, even though the warrantees under the acts of 1850, 1852, and 1855 had no Treasury scrip option.[7]

What explains the fact that warrant prices did not tumble as low as the doomsayers predicted? On the supply side, the Ten Regiments Act may have taught the public that the minimum price for a 160-acre warrant should be $100, and, unless circumstances were extreme, warrantees would not sell below this price. On the demand side, the price buyers paid for land is an indication of their idea of its value. This price, of course, reflected an ongoing debate among contemporaries and, indeed, renewed by writers such as Henry George: did vacant, unimproved land have a value, or was its value due solely to the labor put into improvements? The government's answer in pricing public land at $1.25 an acre was that unimproved land had some value but not much. At a minimum, the $1.25-an-acre price guaranteed security of title in the holding, thanks to the government survey.[8]

The market's answer in buying land warrants between the floor and ceiling prices was that the value of public lands fluctuated in response to other factors, particularly the prospects for future returns. Above all, the expectation of the rapid settlement of an area tended to increase the perceived value of a tract of unimproved land. Cyrus Woodman wrote a New England investor in August 1847 that "we can locate Land Warrants to the amount of $20 or $30,000 on lands that would be worth at least $1.25 per acre, & would pay ten per cent if entered at that rate." He was particularly confident that the land would rise even higher in value when the anticipated Chicago to Galena railroad was completed, "and lands in the vicinity of it or within its influence will greatly advance in value." Other agents made even higher claims for the value of public lands. In 1856, John Clark of Iowa City claimed that warrants located with his help "will be worth I am confident from $2.50 to 5.00 per acre as soon as located, and will rapidly advance upon that price." When enough agents, investors, and settlers agreed, the result was a land rush and a great demand for land warrants, a story told in more detail in chapters 6 and 7 below.[9]

On three antebellum occasions, warrant prices did fall toward the 62.5 cent barrier. The first occurred in July 1850, when dealers became convinced that Congress would pass a vast bill giving land warrants to all veterans and there was no anticipation of a ban on assignments. A more serious price scare came in 1857. During the early months of that year, warrant prices hovered around a dollar an acre. At the approach of summer, warrant prices eased into the ninety-cents-an-acre range, apparently because of a drop in activity by Iowa buyers. A few on Wall Street may have blanched when one editor asked the riddle "Why is *57* like *37*?" His answer: "Because one did and the other will *land* us under the ground." Warrant prices drifted downward over the summer and then tumbled at the news of the failures of the Ohio Life and Trust Company and John Thompson, banker, land warrant dealer, and publisher of *Thompson's Bank Note and Commercial Reporter.* On October 17, *Thompson's* (no longer under John Thompson's control) stopped its weekly summary of the land warrant market because "the market is so unsettled and fluctuating at present, that we cannot quote Warrants without fear of doing more harm than good." The next week *Thompson's* confirmed the bad news: "Land Warrants, during the past fortnight, have been almost unsalable, owing to the demand having entirely fallen off; some lots have changed hands at 60 to 70 cents per acre." Land warrant prices recovered after the panic's end and sold in the ninety-cents-per-acre range throughout 1858.[10]

The only other recorded instance of a prewar buying price's dropping to 62.5 cents an acre came in November 1859 and may have reflected the nervousness of southern investors after John Brown's raid. In addition, and perhaps of greater importance, the Republican-controlled Congress planned to take up a homestead bill that warrant dealers saw as a threat to the value of warrants. After the firing on Fort Sumter, land warrant prices tumbled well below sixty cents an acre (except for forty-acre warrants) and stayed depressed until the Union Army won some battles.[11]

The upper and lower limits on land warrant prices set by Washington denote the restrictions on the market in warrants. The cash sale price of $1.25 an acre, set in 1820, did not necessarily reflect the productive value of land. Until passage of the Graduation Act, a prospective buyer paid the same amount for rich and fertile land as for poor land. Had the figure been $2.00 an acre, as was the case before 1820, warrant prices might have had a ceiling of $1.95 an acre. The floor price resulted from the compromise reached by the

THOMPSON'S

BANK NOTE AND COMMERCIAL REPORTER

BY J. THOMPSON, BANKER, NO. 2 WALL STREET, NEW YORK.

Published at No. 64 Duane St.] NEW YORK, AUGUST 21, 1854. [We have no Traveling Agent.

Foreign Orders.

I must positively decline making drafts on London for amounts less than £5.

J. THOMPSON.

Free Banking.

We have labored long, as our readers well know, to popularize Free Banking. Our influence, our time and our money have been thrown into the scale to insure success. Excepting New England and a portion of the South, Free Banking has triumphed. Occupying this position and foreseeing that the system is in danger of being run into the ground, we have commenced in good earnest to save it from discredit. There are defects in the Free Banking Laws of several States.

In New York, the admission of bonds and mortgages as security for circulating notes, is a defect.

In Indiana, the taking of her own 5 ℔ cent stock at par, is a defect. A thousand dollars Indiana 5 ℔ cent Bonds is not ample security for a thousand dollars of currency.

In Illinois and Wisconsin the currency is well secured, but the Banks and bankers and brokers can ... foreign, insecure and depreciated currency. This is a defect. Owners of foreign Banks and importers of foreign currency should be compelled to redeem at par, in gold or notes of their own States.

These defects are all easily remedied. Let New York drop the bonds and mortgages—let Indiana make her 5 ℔ cent Stocks equal to a 6 ℔ cent by issuing a less per cent on the dollar—and let all the Western States pass an act compelling the dablers in foreign currency to redeem every dollar they ever pay out in gold or secured notes of their own States. This would stop the wheels of the juggernauts and save the people from an insiduous and ultimately a sweeping loss.

A Warning.

PROBABLY no man sees the workings of the Bank note currency so much as we do. Others may see farther and judge better; this is not for us to decide. Our convictions are that a warning should be sounded—that a protest should be made against any further expansion of paper money, until the state of the country, both politically and financially, takes some positive shape. There are now many Banks in various sections of the country whose redemptions rest either on forbearance or on a ruinously expensive system of re-issue. The failure of a few currency mills (no matter how unworthy of the name of Banks they are,) would end the *indulgence* and the *re-issue*, and a Bank panic would seize upon the public mind. There is now danger of this state of things which prudence may avert and imprudence very soon consumate.

Those Banks that have not currency enough, should use such safe currency as they may receive or send to us and buy, which they can do profitably, and those that have too much should convert and contract without delay. We protest against an increase.

The spirit of the people is for gold—ladies pay their servants with gold—the shrewd economist pays all his wages with gold, and he reasons rightly. Nineteen out of every twenty of the laboring classes feel better paid with six dollars per week gold, than with seven paper. We adduce this important fact to give force to our WARNING. We dread a Bank panic and shall do all in our power to avert it, and if it comes we shall do all we can to ameliorate it, but if Banks fail we shall be the first to know it, and as in duty bound the first to announce the fact.

THOMPSON'S
BANK NOTE & COMMERCIAL REPORTER OFFICE,
No. 64 Duane street,
Wednesday Evening, August 16, 1854.

THE notes of the FARMERS' & MERCHANTS' BANK OF MEMPHIS, Tennessee, are not bought in Wall street this afternoon. Whether the Bank will suspend at its counter, we are not able to say.

New York Loan for $1.250.000.

IN answer to the many inquiries about the New York loan which is to be bid for on the 31st inst., I beg to state that, I shall not directly nor indirectly make any bid. I cannot foresee a sure demand for but a small portion of the $1.250.000, except, it be at low figures, say, 110.

There are now on the market about $400.000 New York and United States Stocks, for which the holders are vainly striving to get something like former prices. Currency inveterately presses home for redemption, and I do not feel sure of a let-up until a crisis has swept out of existence many rotton Banks.

There was a great mistake made by the Canal Commissioner in not putting this loan on the market with the former one, while the United States was buying in its Stock at 121.

J. T.

LATEST COUNTERFEITS.

5s, on the **Ashuelot Bank,** N. H.—Vignette female sitting down—a ship on the lower left corner—man with a scythe on the lower right corner.

10s, on the **Mechanics' Bank,** Brooklyn, N. Y., altered from smaller denominations.

5s, on the **Bank of Fort Edward,** N. Y.—Vignette coat of arms and female with Liberty cap—female on the right end.

20s, on the **Grocers' Bank,** Boston, Mass., altered from smaller notes—Vignette female and a vase—a female with a shield on the right end—Indian on a shield on the left end.

5s, on the **Bank of America,** Ind., altered from 1s—Circular die in the centre of the note—arched bridge on the lower right corner.

5s, on the **Oneida Valley Bank,** N. Y.—Vignette female and shield; steamboats on left and locomotive and cars on the right of vignette—female with scales on right end—Indian with bow on left end—well executed.

50s, on the **Southport Bank,** Conn., altered from 1s—Vignette three females and eagle—Washington on the left end—Martha Washington on the right end.

5s, on the **Citizens' Bank,** New York City, altered from 1s—Vignette drove of cattle—female on the left end.

5s, on the **Bank of Montreal,** Canada—Steamer on the upper right corner—cattle on the left end—5 in the centre and on the lower right corner—an eagle between the signatures.

3s, on the **Buffalo City Bank,** N. Y., altered from 1s—Vignette a marine view and a man sitting—canal, &c., on the right end.

20s, on the **Ballston Spa Bank,** N. Y., altered from 1s—Vignette a female and child, with marine view—the figures 20 in red letters across the bill—a house, &c., between the signatures.

THE BANK OF WATERTOWN, Watertown, Wis., was organized and commenced business on the 2d inst., with a capital of $50.000, the circulation of which is secured by North Carolina, Tennessee, Kentucky and Michigan University Stocks. This Bank, we are advised, intends doing a legitimate banking business, and from the high standing and acknowledged worth of its president, A. L. Pritchard, Esq., the public may place entire confidence in the institution. Wm. H. Clark is the cashier.

ANOTHER Bank has been lately organized at Milwaukee, Wis., called the GERMANIA BANK, of G. Papendiek & Co.—G. Papendiek, president, and C. H. H. Papendiek, cashier. This Bank advertises to make collections and remit at current rates without other charges, as will be seen by reference to our advertising columns.

City Subscribers are requested to send notice to No 64 DUANE STREET, of any delay or neglect on the part of our carriers of the REPORTER.

INDEX.

☞ FOR BROKEN, CLOSED and WORTHLESS BANKS, see 30th page.

THE ATLAS BANK, Providence, R. I., is a new institution, and has commenced business under the management of Henry J. Angell, president, and Harvey F. Payton, cashier.

WE are advised that the BANK OF YONKERS, at Yonkers, Westchester County, N. Y., went into operation on the 10th inst., on a capital of $150.000—secured wholly by New York State Stocks. The circulation, $100.000, is redeemed at the MERCHANTS' EXCHANGE BANK, of this city. John Olmsted, president, and Egbert Howland, cashier.

ALL descriptions of Stocks and Bonds bought and sold at the Stock Exchange, at the usual commission. Orders by mail promptly attended to. Any information in regard to the various Speculative or Investment Stocks dealt in, in this market, cheerfully furnished. Address,

A. W. GREENLEAF,
Office of J. THOMPSON,
No. 2 Wall Street.

Land Warrants.

THE passage of the Homestead Bill—the unhealthy state of the country, generally, and the stringency in the money market, combined, compels us to lower the price of Warrants. The following are present quotations for buying only:—

	Buying.	Selling.
160 acre Warrants	$180	$...
80 acre Warrants	90	
40 acre Warrants	45	

All Land Warrants sold at this office are guaranteed in every particular, and without limit, as to time. Orders from the country promptly attended to. Persons sending me Warrants by mail will receive prompt returns at the highest market price.

J. THOMPSON, Banker,
No. 2 Wall st., New York.

THOMPSON'S
Bank Note and Commercial Reporter,
CIRCULATION, 86.000.

Published at No. 64 DUANE STREET, where subscriptions will be received.

Terms of Subscription, in advance:

WEEKLY, $2 per year, with the Coin Chart Manual free of charge.

SEMI-MONTHLY, $1 per year, with Coin Chart Manual free of charge.

MONTHLY, 75 cents per year, with Coin Chart Manual free of charge.

ADVERTISEMENTS, five lines or less, $2 per month.

SOLD BY

D. MURPHY & SONS, 384 Pearl street, New York.
DEXTER & BROTHER, 14 & 16 Ann street, New York.
T. B. PETERSON, 102 Chesnut street, Philadelphia.
FETRIDGE & CO., 72 Washington street, Boston.
LANE & WHEELER, 16 State street, Boston.
W. & H. TAYLOR, Sun Iron Building, Baltimore.
N. TRYON & CO., Little Falls, N. Y.

☞ Bank Officers are requested to inform us of all new organizations; change of officers; new counterfeits, &c.

FIG. 10. *Thompson's Bank Note and Commercial Reporter.* Front page showing land warrant price quotations and brief news about the state of the market (courtesy of the Library of Congress).

Benton and Cameron forces in the congressional debates of 1847. A reading of the 1847 House and Senate debates conveys the impression that legislators spent little time considering a just price for the Treasury note option. Instead of one-half the face value of a land warrant or $100, Congress might as easily have priced the Treasury scrip at $75 or $125.[12]

Within the politically determined limits of 62.5 cents to $1.25 an acre, warrant prices did reflect supply and demand forces. Although Wall Street had the largest concentration of land warrant brokers, that setting should not obscure the difference between the land warrant market and the money or securities market. Unlike the price of a common stock, that of a land warrant did not entirely reflect the value of the commodity or its expected future earnings, either because the government artificially undervalued the land (as in, say, Iowa) or overvalued it (as in parts of Alabama). Though distinct from the money market, the warrant market could not escape disturbances from its larger neighbor. Land warrants were government issued, and even if their price behavior differed from that exhibited by government bonds, they did sometimes act as an index of confidence. The issue of confidence seems to have influenced warrant prices when the future direction of the republic seemed at stake after Fort Sumter or in a much more modest way when Congress acted to undercut the value of land warrants with the Homestead Act.[13]

Congress determined the supply of land warrants by deciding who qualified under the various bounty land acts. After the Ten Regiments Act, each succeeding warrant act involved a political struggle, with market considerations an important element. The 1850 act passed Congress but only with the commercially crippling provision that warrants could not be assigned. The whole point of the 1852 act was to make 1850 series warrants useful to their recipients by making them assignable. By 1855, warrant dealers had largely exhausted their supply of 1850 warrants, and some warrant brokers worked in tandem with the veterans' lobby to get Congress to pass the 1855 act.

The choice left to the warrantee was sale or personal use, and most decided to sell. Thus, the faster the clerks at the Pension Bureau processed applications and filled out blank warrants, the sooner congressionally authorized warrants reached the market. Table 20 estimates the volume of warrants that veterans, widows, and heirs put into the market before the Civil War. The estimates in the table take the amount of acreage in sample warrants assigned each

TABLE 20
Projected Warrant Assignments by Year

Year	*Acres in Warrants Assigned*
1847	712,000
1848	5,080,000
1849	3,488,000
1850	712,000
1851	816,000
1852	5,976,000
1853	3,608,000
1854	1,368,000
1855	5,216,000
1856	10,472,000
1857	5,624,000
1858	2,936,000
1859	1,336,000
1860	1,384,000
1861	1,028,000
1862–69	2,232,000
1870–79	1,568,000
1880–89	432,000
1890–99	256,000
Post-1900	32,000
Total	54,276,000

NOTE: The estimated figure is derived by dividing the sample number of annual assignments by the sample size of .05. Sample of land warrant recipients, acts of 1847, 1850, 1852, and 1855.

year between 1847 and 1861, to arrive at an annual projection of warrant sales by original recipients. The table does not measure warrants resold by subsequent buyers. The peak years for warrant sales, as might be expected, were those following directly the passage of the 1847, 1850, and 1855 bounty land acts. By the outbreak of the Civil War, about 90 percent of all those who would ever receive warrants under any of the four acts had already sold their bounties.

The warrants came in different acreage denominations, ranging from the small forty-acre ones to the full quarter-section warrants worth 160 acres. Under the act of 1847 series, the Pension Bureau issued twelve 160-acre warrants for each forty-acre one. Land agents quickly established a premium price for the smaller denomination for, as one dealer noted, the forty-acre warrants enabled his firm "to select better lands, where we could locate in smaller quantities than where we had to locate a whole quarter sec. in a body." By early 1848, 160-acre warrants had declined in New York City's market to about eighty cents an acre, while forty-acre warrants sold for one dollar an acre.[14]

After the 1850 act warrants came on the market, brokers quoted similar prices in cents per acre without regard to the denomination. After many of the 1850 act forty-acre warrants were sold and located in the West, however, a market differential reemerged. Buyers paid several cents an acre more for forty-acre warrants by late 1856, and the premium increased after the panic of 1857. Indeed, after the fall of Fort Sumter in 1861, when prices for 160-acre and 120-acre warrants plummeted below sixty cents an acre, the price for the few outstanding forty-acre warrants held steady at near a dollar an acre. In contrast, from the passage of the 1855 act, 120-acre warrants sold at a slight discount below the full 160-acre bounties largely because of the inconvenience to western buyers. A person interested in securing 160 acres of public lands felt the drawback of a 120-acre warrant, because he still had to pay cash or find a forty-acre warrant to go along with the 120-acre certificate. Nonetheless, one knowledgeable speculator in the middle of the Iowa land boom notified his supplier in the East that "120's are as good as any and cheaper—so buy 120's and no other kind."[15]

Acquirers of public land preferred warrants to cash because the bounty land paper could usually be obtained below the cash purchase price of $1.25 per acre. The buyer faced only two limitations on using a land warrant. A locator could not employ warrants alone to select special, reserved land that the federal government priced at $2.50 per acre. This was an important category of land in the mid-1850s and after because Congress wished to sell public lands adjacent to land-grant railroads at the higher price. By the end of the Buchanan administration, some twenty-five million acres were potentially valued at the "double-minimum" price. Buyers of this premium land had to pay cash for at least half their acreage and use a warrant for the balance. The other drawback to warrants was that they could be used only on land that had been formally declared open to sale by the president and the secretary of the interior. The tens of millions of acres of land surveyed by the federal government but not yet opened for sale (called "unoffered land") was closed to warrant use. The exception to this rule, and an important one, came when the act of 1852, after administrative interpretation, allowed preemptors to locate parcels up to 160 acres with warrants on the surveyed but unoffered public domain. The 1852 measure expanded an earlier practice by the General Land Office of allowing preemptors to use warrants on their own parcels or to sell their claims to third parties using warrants—as long as the tracts had been part of land districts that the General Land Office had opened to private entry.[16]

Land warrants came onto the market in fits and starts, as table 20 shows, again largely because of events in Washington. Those warrantees fortunate enough to receive their warrants from the Pension Bureau soon after it began issuing a new series, as in 1847 or 1855, usually received the best prices. The first Mexican War veterans demobilized in 1847 did command high prices, but by February 1848, prices had declined to eighty cents an acre, and by January 1849, warrant prices on 160-acre certificates fell to as low as sixty-five cents an acre before recovering in the spring. As the issue of new warrants from the Pension Bureau slowed, warrant prices increased, in the summer of 1849, to 85 cents an acre. The increase was sudden as Cyrus Woodman noted receiving "a telegraphic dispatch from N. York of June 30 saying that Warrants were worth $137 at that date. On the 20th June news was rec'd by telegraph in Galena [Illinois] from N.Y. that they were worth $125 on the 19th. This is going up with a vengeance." Prices then declined a bit for the rest of 1849, and stayed between seventy-five and eighty cents an acre through the summer of 1850, when land warrants were "struck flat in N.Y. having dropped to $100, occasioned by the passage through the House by a large majority giving bounty lands to every body that ever served in any war." Prices soon recovered, however, when dealers learned that Congress made act of 1850 warrants unassignable.[17]

As the supply of 1847 warrants dwindled, the 1850 bill became law, but the new warrants did not reach the market until the spring of 1852 when the no-assignment ban was lifted. By March 3, 1852, the day President Fillmore signed the act, the Pension Bureau had issued over 44,000 forty-acre warrants, some 30,000 eighty-acre warrants, and over 14,000 160-acre warrants. This group of almost 90,000 warrants hit the market with tremendous force in the spring and summer of 1852. Nearly half of all assignments on the sample of 1850 act warrants were made in the last nine months of 1852, and prices reflected the surge in supply by dropping below seventy cents per acre in the early summer, recovering only somewhat in the fall. Once the market had absorbed the warrants and the Pension Bureau had reduced its backlog of new issues, warrant prices rose as the supply of warrants came not so much from brokers' inventories as from new applications by veterans.

After spring 1852, the other great surge in land warrant supply came after May 1855, when the Pension Bureau began issuing the 1855 series of warrants. Curiously, the effect of such a large infusion of warrants into the market did not register dramatically on warrant prices, which remained firm above a dollar an acre until October 1856. The experience of 1852 suggests that massive supply increases would work to press prices to the floor level. Instead, prices ranged up to $1.15 an acre through November 1855 for the new series of warrants. Then prices suddenly dipped ten to fifteen cents an acre, because, as one Washington broker noted, there was now a more than ample "supply of Warrants at all points in the Northwest, where they are required for the purpose of location," and in addition, the Pension Bureau was issuing 60,000 acres' worth of new warrants each day. To some extent also, the break in prices over the 1855–56 winter reflected the ebb of seasonal demand, which picked up again each spring and summer as a new group of settlers contributed to the demand for public land. Still, prices did not sink anywhere near the old floor price, and, as will be discussed in chapter 7 and Appendix D, the absence of a crash in warrant prices resulted from the extraordinary demand for land that characterized much American commercial activity after 1853.[18]

Washington decisions clearly played a major role in shaping price trends. Still, the warrantees had to show themselves competent in the marketplace or, as Simon Cameron had said, "capable of taking care of themselves." If the veterans and heirs possessed no commercial sense, then they would likely be fleeced. Evidence on this point for the half-million warrant recipients is, of course, difficult to assemble, but some information points to an intelligent awareness of the warrant market on the part of veterans. The vast majority of Mexican War veterans eligible under the 1847 act chose a land warrant over the $100 Treasury note. Compared to the almost 89,000 veterans selecting warrants, fewer than three thousand veterans selected the Treasury obligation. With 1847 warrant prices consistently over 62.5 cents an acre, the warrantees had made the proper market choice. Each veteran or heir benefiting under the Ten Regiments Act had to choose and thus calculate that the warrant would exceed

TABLE 21
Holding Time (in days) of Sample Warrants by Assignees, Acts of 1847, 1850, 1852, and 1855

Act	25th Percentile	Median	75th Percentile
1847	14	36	111
1850	50	159	349
1852	23	34	60
1855	22	54	173

$100 in value. Thus, the warrantee was not such an easy mark for the pack of thieving speculators described by Senator Benton. While the 1850, 1852, and 1855 warrantees had no such choice, the behavior of prices during the decade suggests that 62.5 cents an acre still worked as a floor price.

During the 1850 debate, opponents of warrant assignment charged that veterans returning from Mexico had signed power of attorney rights over to unscrupulous dealers within hours of landing at New Orleans. Several Congressmen predicted a repetition of that experience if recipients gained the right to sell warrants. Many in Congress insisted that a pauper veteran suddenly in possession of a land warrant would quickly sell it for a pittance, run through the money, and have nothing left but a bitter memory.[19]

Comparing the date of government issue of the warrants and the date of sale by the warrantee for each sample warrant does allow a rough measure of the recipients' market savvy to be made (see table 21). On average, the sample of Mexican War warrantees who benefited from the Ten Regiments Act let thirty-six days pass from receipt to sale. Warrantees under the 1850 act waited an average of 159 days. The small number of 1852 warrantees unshackled by a ban on sales waited an average of thirty-four days, while those in the sample of 1855 who sold their warrants waited an average of fifty-four days. Each act's sample did reveal a few instances of men selling their warrants less than a week after issue. However, very few warrant recipients rushed out and unloaded their certificates the same day these arrived in the mail. The average warrantee had ample time to investigate prices in the warrant market, compare offers, and make the best deal.[20]

The meeting of veteran and warrant broker in the marketplace constituted the nongovernmental factor influencing warrant prices.

The records of several land warrant agents show that the firm and the veteran could cooperate to secure the bounty from Washington and then negotiate the price of the warrant. The combination provided warrantees with a good price for their bounty land warrants and trading profits to the brokers.

A deal between the Portland, Maine, firm of Freeman Bradford and Zebulon Harmon and War of 1812 veteran Ebenezer Field highlights the various parts of the land warrant business. Born in 1777, Field enlisted at the age of thirty-two in the U.S. Army. He fought Indians at Tippecanoe and the English in Canada, was taken prisoner in 1812, and spent more than a year in a Quebec jail before being paroled in late 1813. His enlistment term expired in early 1814, and the army could not prevail on him to reenlist. His decision to demobilize himself made Field ineligible for the 1812 land bounty that was proffered to men who served the war's duration or five full years after the act's passage. Field's tour of duty covered five years, but only three of them came after 1812.

In late 1851, from his home in Northfield, Massachusetts, Field wrote to Zebulon Harmon asking for help in securing a bounty land warrant under the act of September 28, 1850. Field agreed to appoint "Z. K. Harmon his Atty. who is to obtain a Warrant, locate it, and sell the land & retain one quarter of same for his services and fees."[21] This transaction shows some of the services brokers performed. The firm solicited the business of veterans and heirs by offering assistance in obtaining warrants. The firm also bought and sold warrants. Finally, Bradford and Harmon conducted a small business in locating land in Michigan and Iowa on their own account and for other Maine investors. Because Ebenezer Field in 1851 could not wait until Congress made his warrant assignable, he asked Harmon to execute a power of attorney agreement and do the extra work of locating the land in the West. The partners made money on each aspect of their land warrant operation, although they needed different entrepreneurial skills for the different business tasks.

The business in warrant application services required considerable effort to attract customers. Bradford and Harmon went about this in three ways: through direct mail circulars, through newspaper advertisements, and through local agents. The firm relied partly on the strategy of seeking veterans and heirs by mailing circulars. The partners had a nearby market of Aroostook War veterans, most of whom were still Maine residents in the 1850s. The firm purchased copies of Aroostook War muster rolls from the Maine adjutant general and sent flyers to the several thousand Aroostook veterans. In addition, Bradford and Harmon bought lists of Maine troops from the War of 1812. The firm placed advertisements in a few Maine newspapers to solicit business, and it also dealt with agents throughout the state.[22]

Francis A. Dickins, a Washington, D.C., attorney, followed a different strategy for securing application business. Between July 1848 and August 1850, Dickins placed advertisements for his services in twenty-five newspapers from Boston to Galveston. Dickins also utilized the services of such regional agents as E. W. Tuttle, a Cincinnati warrant broker, Thomas Durden of Montgomery, Alabama, and Samuel Hannah of Troy, New York. These agents forwarded especially difficult warrant applications to Dickins in Washington for prosecution in person. Dickins made use of his experience in the Third Auditor's office of the Treasury during the Jackson administration as well as his friendships with Washington politicians and hostesses.[23]

Washington agents who specialized in securing warrants for applicants included Captain P. M. Henry and the veterans' lobby leader General John McCalla. McCalla handled difficult cases for several New York warrant brokers, and his job was to cajole the Pension Bureau on behalf of clients. On the return of the Democrats to executive power in 1853, McCalla traded on his reputation as an old Jackson man until soured by the Pierce administration's failure to grant him or his son a patronage job; in 1854 he switched his allegiance to the Know-Nothings. Although McCalla admitted, "I am not in favor with the present administration, nor am I favorable to it," he still pressed political solutions to delays in the Pension Bureau. He wrote to a Milwaukee widow, "If you have a friend in any Senator or Representative who will send to the Comm. of Pensions an urgent request, as a favor to him to consider your case and to grant your warrant immediately, I do not doubt that it will be done." Similarly, warrant agents resorted to political help in dealing with the General Land Office. Cyrus Woodman asked his partner's brother, the Illinois congressman Elihu B. Washburne, to intervene with the General Land Office in a case of disputed warrant assignment. The General Land Office commissioner, Woodman wrote, "knowing it came from you he would have no hesitation in passing it—whilst he might possibly reject it were it to go thro the land office with nothing to shew him whence it came" [*sic*].[24]

McCalla and other Washington agents regularly scrutinized the muster rolls at the Treasury to double-check the work of government clerks. The general charged a basic fee of five dollars per warrant application prosecuted, but more if he had to examine the muster rolls. Captain P. M. Henry of Virginia charged ten dollars for the time he spent searching muster rolls in the Tombs, the Treasury building basement. On September 11, 1860, he wrote to a Georgia attorney explaining the nature of his work in securing for his client a 120-acre warrant under the act of 1855 to supplement an earlier act of 1850 forty-acre warrant:

> You will doubtless think it strange that after writing you on the 1st instant, that there was no rolls of Captain Shore's Co. of Georgia Militia, Creek War, that the warrant should now issue for the same service, but as I was not satisfied with the Commissioner's report and knowing that he had received a warrant for 40 acres, I made a personal examination myself at an expense of a great deal of trouble and time, and found the service for which the warrant is now issued. My fee in this case is $10 as I have had a great deal of trouble with the case indeed, and had it not been for my perseverance he would never have gotten the warrant.[25]

Bradford and Harmon charged fees more in proportion to effort than acreage. The partners left special instructions with their clerks under the heading "Warrants to be disposed of as follows." Of 175 applicants claiming warrants on account of 1812 service, forty had special handling instructions, including one notation to send the land warrant of Mrs. Elezar Twitchell to "the Poor Farm in Harrison" (Maine). As for "all others not mentioned place on file, and if they are called for you can deliver them upon payment of $3.50 for 40 (acres) & $4 for all others." The effort to complete an application for a warrant of forty acres was much the same as for a warrant of 160 acres, so the firm charged accordingly.[26]

Francis Dickins set up a progressive fee scale, although his charges varied according to the geographical location of his clients. After the boom created by the 1855 act, Dickins charged Norfolk applicants two dollars for obtaining an eighty-acre warrant, three dollars for a 120-acre warrant, and four dollars for a 160-acre warrant. He demanded the same fees in Ripley County, Indiana, and in Salisbury, Maryland. In Troy, New York, however, Dickins cut his rates to one dollar, a dollar and fifty cents, and three dollars for the three types of warrants.

Dickins engaged only in the warrant application business, neither buying nor selling land warrants. He sought to collect his fees as soon as he had completed his efforts on behalf of clients. Bradford and Harmon operated in a looser fashion. The Portland duo engaged in the applications business primarily to attract customers to a more important business, land warrant purchases. The firm charged fees when warrantees did not later sell their warrants through the firm. On the other hand, they regularly waived all fees (for both application and execution of sale) if the veteran, widow, or heir sold to them. One example of this was their arrangement with Ephraim Cary of Auburn, Maine. Cary had received a forty-acre warrant under the 1850 act and took advantage of the 1855 legislation to obtain an additional 120-acre warrant in October 1855. On October 26, Bradford and Harmon, through their North Auburn agent Peter Noyes, "offered him one dollar an acre & fees." Cary immediately accepted, pocketed $120, and by October 30, the brokers had resold the warrant to Boston attorney Horatio Woodman, who in turn relayed it to his brother Cyrus in Mineral Point, Wisconsin.[27]

Another example is that of Eunice Hammond of East Eddington, Maine, who received an offer January 26, 1856, of "$110 & our fees of $3.25." As in Cary's case, this happened about a week after the Pension Bureau issued her a 120-acre warrant. She agreed to the terms, took the $110, and paid no fee. Among those who availed themselves of the firm's help in applying, most chose to have the Pension Bureau mail the warrant to Bradford and Harmon's Portland office. When Zebulon Harmon mailed a 160-acre warrant to Lydia Shaw, he offered her "$155 & our fees. Our fees will be $4.00 if we do not buy." In March 1856, Harmon forwarded three warrants to veterans in Raymond, Maine, and offered to buy "for one dollar per acre & the fees given in. We want the warrants much."[28]

George Woodbridge ran a Marietta, Ohio, dry goods emporium and sought to build a warrant business by promising to forgo fees in case of a failed application. "Nothing recovered nothing asked" he proclaimed in an 1849 circular. In fact, Woodbridge did exact one fee from all applicants, successful or not—a routine levy for services as notary public on all sworn declarations. When a warrant claim did succeed, then Woodbridge imposed a steep fee: "Joseph McMinus Center Belpre Post Office leaves his declaration paid the charges on the same and is to pay Ten Dollars when the Warrant is delivered to him." On the same day McMinus made his application, Woodbridge attended "Thomas Merrit, his Post Office Lowell Ohio. Merrit leaves his land claim and is to pay for the seal and Ten Dollars for Agency fee."[29]

Woodbridge charged such high fees because he stood at the end of a chain of middlemen, each keeping part of the ten dollar fee.

Examination of the books of the Woodbridge firm reveals that the warrant business was very much a sideline of the firm's main activities of moneylending and fabric retailing. The Marietta operation was quite small and, except for the busy application times, winter 1850–51 and summer 1855, the firm often forwent any warrant business for months. For most of the 1850s, Woodbridge had a standing order to buy warrants for Lyne Starling, an Ohio capitalist and son of the founder of the city of Columbus. Starling in turn sold the warrants he bought from Woodbridge and other small merchants to the big New York warrant brokerage firm Taylor Brothers. When Woodbridge noted in his journal, "Borden Stanlon paid me on Taylor Warrant agency 10 expenses 1.12," five of the ten dollars stayed in Marietta, netting him $3.88, with the balance going to Columbus. During the 1855 crush of applications and sales, the total fee Woodbridge charged dropped to five dollars, a figure more consistent with that charged by other brokers.[30]

The fees charged by warrant brokers no doubt covered administrative costs, but the example of Bradford and Harmon's refunding fees suggests more money was to be found in warrant trading. Western dealers, too, sold a good number of warrants back and forth to one another, but some found the narrow spread not worth the trouble. Cyrus Woodman complained in early 1848 that his firm "should prefer not to sell warrants if we do not get at least five dollars for selling, which is but a small compensation, taking into consideration the trouble, expense & risk which we incur in disposing of them." The warrant brokerage business was structured so that the dealer bought and sold on his own account. Thus, instead of uniting buyer and seller in one transaction, as a true agent or broker might, warrant dealers conducted two independent transactions. Profits resulted from maximizing the spread between the price offered the warrantee and the price obtained by reselling to another buyer.[31]

The account books of Bradford and Harmon give a good picture of the operations of a modest-sized regional broker in the 1850s. The firm bought just over one thousand warrants between 1852 and 1859, but because the firm kept some warrants itself to locate in Iowa, and price data are missing for some others, only 936 warrants separately purchased and sold form the basis for an analysis of the firm's trading and for generalizations about the warrant brokerage business. For those eight years, the 936 warrants covered 104,220 acres of public land, about four and one-half townships' worth in size. To purchase those warrants, Bradford and Harmon paid out

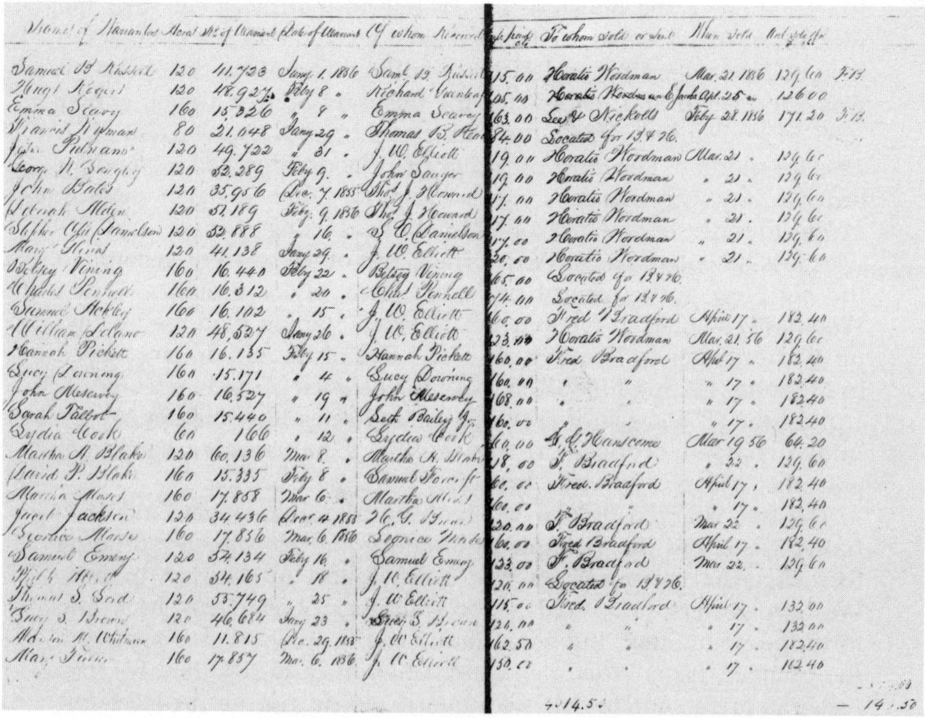

Name of Warrantees	Acres	No. of Warrant	Date of Warrant	Of whom Received	[illegible] paid	To whom sold or sent	When sold	Amt sold for
Samuel B. Russell	120	41.723	Jany 1. 1856	Saml B. Russell	115.00	Horatio Woodman	Mar. 21. 1856	129.60
Hugh Rogers	120	48.927	Feby 8	Richard Greenleaf	115.00	Horatio Woodman & [illegible]	Apl. 25	126.00
Emma Seavey	160	15.326	" 8	Emma Seavey	163.00	Lee & Nickolls	Feby 28. 1856	171.20
[illegible]	80	21.048	Jany 29	Thomas B. Reed	84.00	Located for 13476		
John Putnam	120	49.722	" 31	J. W. Elliott	119.00	Horatio Woodman	Mar. 21	129.60
George W. Dougherty	120	52.289	Feby 9	John Sanger	119.00	Horatio Woodman	" 21	129.60
John Bates	120	35.956	Dec. 7 1855	Thos J. Howard	117.00	Horatio Woodman	" 21	129.60
Deborah Alden	120	51.189	Feby 9. 1856	Thos J. Howard	117.00	Horatio Woodman	" 21	129.60
[illegible] Danielson	120	52.888	" 16	S. C. Danielson	117.00	Horatio Woodman	" 21	129.60
Mary [illegible]	120	41.138	Jany 29	J. W. Elliott	120.00	Horatio Woodman	" 21	129.60
Betsey Vining	160	16.440	Feby 22	Betsey Vining	165.00	Located for 13476		
Charles Penhall	160	16.312	" 20	Chas Penhall	174.00	Located for 13476		
Samuel [illegible]	160	16.102	" 15	J. W. Elliott	160.00	Fred Bradford	April 17	182.40
William Delano	120	48.527	Jany 26	J. W. Elliott	123.00	Horatio Woodman	Mar. 21. 56	129.60
Hannah Pickett	160	16.135	Feby 15	Hannah Pickett	160.00	Fred Bradford	April 17	182.40
Lucy Downing	160	15.171	" 4	Lucy Downing	160.00	" "	" 17	182.40
John Meserve	160	16.527	" 19	John Meserve	168.00	" "	" 17	182.40
Sarah Talbot	160	15.440	" 11	Seth Bailey Jr	160.00	"	" 17	182.40
Lydia Cook	40	166	" 12	Lydia Cook	40.00	G. C. Hanscome	Mar 19 56	64.20
Martha A. Blake	120	60.136	Mar 8	Martha A. Blake	118.00	F. Bradford	" 22	129.60
David P. Blake	160	15.335	Feby 8	Samuel [illegible]	161.00	Fred. Bradford	April 17	182.40
Martha [illegible]	160	17.858	Mar 6	Martha [illegible]	160.00		" 17	182.40
Jacob Jackson	120	34.436	Dec. 4 1855	H. G. [illegible]	120.00	F. Bradford	Mar 22	129.60
[illegible] Morse	160	17.856	Mar. 6. 1856	[illegible] Morse	160.00	Fred Bradford	April 17	182.40
Samuel Emery	120	54.134	Feby 16	Samuel Emery	123.00	F. Bradford	Mar 22	129.60
[illegible]	120	54.165	" 18	J. W. Elliott	120.00	Located for 13476		
Thomas S. [illegible]	120	53.749	" 25	J. W. Elliott	115.00	Fred. Bradford	April 17	132.00
Lucy S. Brown	120	46.684	Jany 23	Lucy S. Brown	126.00	" "	" 17	132.00
[illegible] M. Whitman	160	11.815	Dec. 29. 1855	J. W. Elliott	162.50	" "	" 17	182.40
Mary [illegible]	160	17.857	Mar. 6. 1856	J. W. Elliott	150.00	" "	" 17	182.40

FIG. 11. LAND WARRANT ACCOUNT BOOK, BRADFORD AND HARMON. Records of the Portland firm showing purchases and sales of land warrants (courtesy of the Maine Historical Society).

$94,384, or an overall average price of ninety-one cents an acre. The aggregate selling price of all 936 warrants came to $107,498, or an average of $1.03 an acre. Over the course of the years, this netted the partners a surplus of $13,114 for an average spread of 12.5 cents an acre.[32]

These aggregate figures do not reveal that some years were better than others in the warrant business. As might be expected, the busiest years were 1852, 1855, and 1856, the years of the heaviest national wave of assignments. The 1850 series recipients, it will be recalled, suffered a twofold setback. Scandal and demoralization prevented the Pension Bureau from issuing warrants until well into 1851, and even then, veterans had to wait until the 1852 act gave them the freedom to sell their property. If a claimant chose to ask

Bradford and Harmon to arrange a power of attorney sale, as did the old veteran Ebenezer Fields, then he paid the firm a full quarter of the proceeds of the warrant's sale. The 1855 series warrants began coming onto the market in large numbers the summer of that year and in steady supply throughout 1856. Warrants purchased in 1854 brought the highest prices in part because of heavy demand and the shortage of warrants, and partly because the General Land Office had not brought any new land to market, thus forcing capitalists to stick to older lands and increasing the attractiveness of land warrants. Bradford and Harmon continued to pursue the warrant business in off years but devoted more attention to traditional claims, brokering over old French spoliation cases, pension matters, and general Portland commercial affairs.

The prices offered by Bradford and Harmon followed the same trends as New York prices, although usually a bit lower than posted metropolitan prices. The firm did differ from New York's in the size of the spread between buying and selling prices, and the Portland partnership did manage to extract a bigger spread than New York brokers. This may be seen by comparing Bradford and Harmon's prices to those of the most prominent New York warrant broker, John Thompson, who frequently dealt with Bradford and Harmon, and who published weekly quotes on land warrant prices in his *Thompson's Bank Note and Commercial Reporter.* For example, from January 1857 until his failure in September of that year, Thompson offered 146 separate buy and sell quotes. On six quotes the spread was three cents per acre, eighty-three had a spread of four cents an acre, fifty-five differed by a nickel, while two had a spread of six cents between buy and sell prices. When he returned to the warrant business in 1859, Thompson's spread throughout that year also averaged around four cents an acre. On a 160-acre warrant, this spread of six to eight dollars amounted to a markup of 4 to 5 percent and a slim gross margin of only about 5 percent.[33]

The intensely competitive market in New York City probably offered the best prices for both warrantees and prospective buyers. Bradford and Harmon's spread over the course of the decade averaged thirteen dollars, or twice that of Thompson. This difference may be attributed to both the greater volume and the degree of competition in New York. In Bradford and Harmon's case, it is difficult to determine whether the extra increment came from buying the warrants from the veterans or from selling warrants to big buyers such as the Woodman family. Northern New England veterans (who paid no fees) may have lost up to five dollars for a 160-acre warrant by selling to Bradford and Harmon instead of to a bigger New York firm.

Zebulon Harmon liked to boast that he offered the best prices to warrantees in Maine. In July 1856, he wrote his agent in Boothbay Harbor that several warrantees in the area should "sell to me if I offer as much as anyone else. Will go up if necessary." Such claims of price competitiveness almost always came with a time limit on the offer. As the warrant business began to occupy more of his time during the fall of 1855, Harmon forwarded a 120-acre warrant to John Gray of Stark, Maine, and offered him "$124 and fees if he will return it soon properly assigned." Eager to purchase warrants in January 1856, Harmon nonetheless set a limit on his offer to an agent in Grafton, Maine: "offered him $1—per acre for his 160's & 95 cts for 120's if sent in the course of this week."[34]

Bradford and Harmon emphasized a quick sale because the warrant market could turn fickle and vary by several cents an acre in a short time. At a time of heavy warrant demand in March 1856, Zebulon Harmon made the following notation in his journal: "Joshua Gerrish of Lisbon is offered for one week from Mar 20 56 $1.06 for 120's & $1.09 for 160's properly assigned with certificates complete. Mar 24th wrote him that Warrants have fallen and we cannot pay the prices above named." In reverse fashion, Harmon proved too cautious in December 1855. On December 17 he forwarded the 120-acre warrant of Richard Caswell and, quite unusually for Harmon, "made no offer for it." The same day he sent two 120-acre warrants to two different veterans and quoted each a price of $92 with fees included. This offer produced no takers, and twenty-nine days later, Harmon had to offer the pair $105 and fees, a rise of 15 percent in less than a month.[35]

A rising price trend made bidding for warrants more risky, but it also increased the value of Harmon's inventory of warrants; falling prices for warrants could wipe out profits on inventory without making new warrant purchases any less risky. During a three-week period in the summer of 1856, the firm rode the price roller coaster up and down. On July 29, Charles Campbell received his forwarded warrant with an offer to buy from Bradford and Harmon at eighty-five cents an acre. Two days later, the firm offered another warrantee ninety cents an acre. On August 4, the price offered climbed to an even dollar per acre, and then began to drop. By August 6, the price had dipped to ninety-eight cents an acre bid on new warrants and, by August 11, it had fallen to ninety-five cents. The price dropped another nickel an acre on August 13 and did not stabilize

TABLE 22
Bradford and Harmon's Adjusted Net Revenues from Land Warrant Trading 1852–1859

	1852	*1853*	*1854*	*1855*	*1856*	*1857*	*1858*	*1859*
Warrants bought/sold	223	107	11	205	318	61	9	2
Acreage	10,240	5,840	960	28,900	47,780	8,700	1,440	360
Expenditures ($)	7,370	5,007	925	28,573	44,106	7,131	1,040	232
Revenues ($)	9,453	6,370	1,004	30,966	50,077	8,104	1,259	266
Net income ($)	2,083	1,363	79	2,393	5,970	973	219	34
Rate of return on expenditures	28.2	27.0	8.5	8.4	13.6	13.6	21.0	13.9
Fees forgone* (N × $4)	892	428	44	820	1,272	244	36	8
Adjusted net income ($)	1,191	934	35	1,573	4,698	729	183	26
Adjusted rate of return on expenditures	16.2	18.7	3.7	5.5	10.7	10.2	17.6	11.0

SOURCE: Chapter 5, n. 32.
*It is not possible to determine the exact number of cases in which the firm did not collect a processing fee. The adjusted net income line assumes that no fees were collected as a lower bound.

until eighty-five cents, and only then began to climb back toward the ninety-cents-per-acre range. In less than a month, land warrant prices offered veterans had risen and fallen some 15 to 18 percent.[36]

A market with such periodic volatility, caused by actions from any number of quarters, offered opportunity and danger to the broker. The revenue figures for Bradford and Harmon's land warrant trading tend to support this supposition (see table 22). Bradford and Harmon did not lose money in any year of warrant trading, but neither could they say in advance what would be a good or bad year. Volume or turnover seems irrelevant as a predictor because high-volume years such as 1852 and 1855 could prove to be the high- and low-profit years for the decade. Still, a few generalizations may be advanced to put the Bradford and Harmon numbers into broader perspective. First, the spread between buying and selling prices narrowed for the 1855 series warrants. The act of 1850 warrantees in New England consisted almost entirely of forty-acre recipients who quickly unloaded their warrants after the 1852 act repealed the assignment prohibition. Following national trends, these warrants brought low prices because of a market glut and because of the warrantees' eagerness finally to realize some cash for their bounty. Here were opportunities for shrewd dealers to buy low and still drive hard bargains with western warrant purchasers. In contrast, the spread for 1855 warrants narrowed considerably, in part because of the absence of an administrative block on warrant assignments, and in part because of the greater sophistication of the experienced warrantees.

Success for the warrant broker lay in exerting as much control as possible over purchase prices (by insisting on immediate sales) and by controlling inventory through accumulating standing purchase orders from big capitalists. This is the route Bradford and Harmon followed in successfully trading land warrants. The firm sought to win big customers for sales by claiming the ability to supply warrants in bulk. Most of the firm's sales went to a half-dozen New York and Boston capitalists such as Horatio Woodman and John Thompson and the firm of Green and Sewell. The Portland partners often sent out letters to their large customers asking bids on lots of 5,000 acres of land warrants. While the firm ran some risk of a price collapse in building up its inventory, it gained the advantage of steady buyers easily able to absorb large stocks of warrants at a time.[37]

It is difficult to say what constituted normal profits in the warrant market, but trading seems to have combined those elements economists generally associate with a competitive market, such as the absence of barriers to entry into the field and the free flow of information about the market. A count of newspaper advertisements in the New York press placed by warrant brokers shows an ebb and flow of active dealers, depending on the volume of warrant issue from Washington. For example, in March and April 1855, just after passage of the Old Soldiers Act, more than a dozen firms ran ads in the New York papers.

It took little capital to set out a warrant broker's shingle; a reputation for knowledge of pension and bounty land laws, as well as Washington connections, may have been the most valuable asset to an agent. Brokers certainly made no effort to stifle price information. Most issued price circulars, and *Thompson's Bank Note and Commercial Reporter* effectively disseminated knowledge of prices in the financial world. John Thompson claimed a circulation of 100,000 for his weekly paper, and he openly printed warrant price quotes on his front page. No evidence exists to indicate that a restrictive trade organization of brokers ever came into being. Consequently, the market remained quite competitive through the Civil War, and Bradford and Harmon's profits may be viewed as normal even if comfortably over the rate of return on readily available alternative investments. The matter of profits in warrant brokering leads directly to one of the central issues of the economics of the land warrant market, namely, whether veterans and heirs received a fair price for their bounty land warrants. If firms earned normal profits and exploited neither buyer nor seller, then the warrantees may be said to have received a fair price. This contention contradicts the conventional wisdom of the 1850s that speculators and sharpers would fleece the hapless veterans, widows, and orphans.

Advocates for the veterans, like Richard Brodhead, argued in Congress that warrantees would receive fair prices, and the evidence bears this out. Opponents of land warrant grants, however, had a more involved criticism of "speculators" gaining hold of millions of acres of warrants. Their charge was that western states would suffer from land warrant speculators using cheap warrants to take control of the public lands. Senator Brodhead's answer to this complaint was perhaps less assuring, namely, "What is the difference between a speculator who enters land at $1.25 an acre under our laws and the speculator who gives $1.15 or $1.20 an acre for a land warrant?" The answer to that question, rephrased as who bought warrants—and why—is one of the other questions about the economics of the land warrant trade and forms the subject of the next chapter.[38]

6

Land Sharks and Loan Sharks, Squatters and Sawyers: The Users of Land Warrants in the Upper Mississippi Valley

Military bounty land warrants passed through several hands before they reached the people who would actually employ them to become owners of public lands. From the veteran's or widow's assignment, the warrant went to an eastern broker. If the brokerage was small in operational scope, like Bradford and Harmon, then the warrant would in turn be sold to a bigger metropolitan dealer. The big brokers shipped warrants west to buyers or agents in frontier land office towns. Warrants in the hands of frontier entrepreneurs might be sold for cash to prospective farmers or to lumbermen interested in the timber on the public lands, or even be located by the agent with a view to reselling the land itself for a profit in the near future. Some frontier agents, known in the vernacular as land sharks, sold warrants on one year's credit to farmers, often at very high interest rates. This arrangement was known as a time-entry loan. The lender kept title to the land, giving the borrower a bond that title would pass on the payment of the loan.

It is difficult to include all warrant locators in a single profile, if only because of the diversity of more than half-a-million separate warrant purchase transactions. Study of the land warrant location papers in the records of the General Land Office, however, suggests that frontier land agents found three types of local users for warrants, and although there was some overlap, the three groups followed one another in rough chronological order. First and most prominent were the time-entry credit locations to settlers. The warrant location files, along with surviving records of private business firms, point to the importance of this practice for the acts of 1847 and 1850 warrants, and to a lesser extent for the act of 1855 warrants. A second use for warrants was found in the need of frontier preemptors of public land, that is, men and women engaged in farm making on public lands without first possessing title. Preemptors ultimately did have to pay for their claims, using either cash or warrants—and sometimes on very short notice from the General Land Office. This group accounted for a sizable portion of warrant locations in 1856, mounting each year in importance until the outbreak of the Civil War. The third and smallest group of warrant users were the lumbermen of the Upper Midwest who used military land bounties to acquire tracts of public land for the value of the timber, not for settlement. This group came to some prominence in the warrant trade after the Civil War.

How important were the big purchasers of land warrants in the national market? Contemporaries, particularly those in the National Reform movement for free land, seemed to think that most land warrants were used to benefit big speculators. After passage of the Old Soldiers Act in 1855, James Gordon Bennett of the *New York Herald* asked the "Commissioner of Pensions [to] oblige us by an estimate of the probable amount of these bounties that will be absorbed by Washington spoilsmen and speculators . . . and what provisions are to be applied against speculators buying up millions of acres for a song, and locating them in a solid body to the prejudice of actual settlers?"[1]

Proponents of free homesteads argued that the system of land warrants tended to promote land monopoly. This was an effective political charge, given the concern in Jacksonian America with the dangers to the republic from the concentrated control of land by a minority. Americans thought that a minority control of land was incompatible with liberty, as demonstrated by aristocratic Europe and despotic China. Recent economic historians have pointed out that "land monopoly" by speculators was an impossibility since the federal government offered a huge amount of territory and farmers could always choose to buy directly from the General Land Office. While true, this economic fact did not necessarily prevent capitalists from achieving a dominant position in the supply of assigned warrants. This would constitute a more modest version of land monopoly if a small number of men controlled sixty million acres of the paper instruments for land entry that were cheaper than cash.[2]

In effect, editor Bennett identified two types of alleged monopolists at work in the acquisition and resale of the public lands. The first type made extra profits through control of cheap bounty land warrants; profits came from buying cheap more than from selling dear. The second type Bennett charged with obtaining a block of land in the path of settlement and charging extra-high prices for land that settlers had to have in order to be nearer to established markets.

Given the volume of acreage for sale, the second type of attempted monopoly could not have been successful too often or for too long. Can the same judgment be made for the first type? An answer may be obtained by investigating the names of the buyers of land warrants in the sample. The sample for each legislative act from 1847 through 1855 includes one of every two hundred warrants, and if the name of a buyer appears more than once in the sample for each act, the conclusion may be drawn that the person was actively engaged in the land warrant business. For example, a man who bought two 160-acre warrants that appear in the sample more likely bought two times two hundred 160-acre warrants, or 64,000 acres worth of warrants. A man who bought two sample forty-acre warrants may actually have bought a minimum of 16,000 acres' worth of warrants.

Thus, one rather crude check on the extent of monopoly in the warrant business is to count the number of repeat buyers. The sample land warrants issued under the Ten Regiments Act show a pattern: about 5 percent went to purchasers who bought more than one. This increased somewhat over the next few years, as may be seen by looking at the big act of 1855 issue of warrants. Purchasers who bought two or more warrants under the Old Soldiers Act accounted for 2.93 million acres of warrants out of a total of thirty-four million issued, a rate of just under 9 percent. The number of multiple buyers who bought more than one sample warrant jumped considerably after the 1847 act but did not vary by much between the two big acts of 1850 and 1855: seven for the Ten Regiments Act, forty-seven for the 1850 act, and forty-five for the Old Soldiers Act of 1855.

It does appear that the number of big buyers was large enough that they competed against one another. This does not sustain a charge of monopoly but does show that, with time and experience, big buyers became more involved in the use of land warrants for locating public land; and, at the local level of the western land office, the big buyers did stand out for their relatively large purchases. The estimate of 9 percent should be considered the minimum extent to which big buyers controlled the purchase of warrants. It includes eastern and western investors or agents who located land on their own account for later resale, and land located as part of a time-entry loan. The locations in the sample of land warrants do not show the extent to which agents and investors resold warrants at western offices for cash to settlers or straight mortgage loans where the borrower located the warrant in his or her own name.[3]

The records of Wisconsinite Cyrus Woodman give a vivid demonstration of how a frontier land agent used land warrants. Woodman utilized his family connections in Boston and New York to obtain warrants for building an empire in Wisconsin land. From 1845 through part of the mid-1850s, Woodman maintained a partnership in Mineral Point with Cadwallader Washburn, a member of the remarkable Washburn political family, that at one time had Cadwallader serving in the House of Representatives along with his brothers Elihu of Illinois (later, Ulysses S. Grant's patron) and Israel of Maine. All of the Washburn brothers invested in land warrants for use in western land speculations. Cyrus Woodman went west to Illinois in 1840 as an agent of Massachusetts investors seeking to recoup their money from land purchases in 1835 and 1836. After struggling for years to make money for the capitalists of the Boston and Western Land Company, Woodman eventually decided to become his own land agent in partnership with Washburn. They faced a basic business challenge common to many western land agents: how best to make money from public land priced at $1.25 an acre at a time of rising in-migration to their area. One way was to help new settlers who had cash to select the best tracts of land, in this way making money from the agent's expert knowledge of the countryside. The preferred way, however, and the one that Washburn and Woodman chose, was to advance credit to cash-poor settlers as an aid in acquiring land.[4]

The partners faced two difficulties in lending money to new settlers in the Wisconsin Territory. First, the firm had a limited capital and so had to find willing investors from the East to advance funds. The New England duo found this hard, in part because their associates from Boston and northern New England had in many cases lost money on earlier western land investments. In addition, Boston from the mid-1840s onward offered capitalists ample opportunities to invest in alternative enterprises such as railroad securities. A second problem that Washburn and Woodman faced was that the Wisconsin territorial legislature had enacted a usury statute limiting the rate of interest to 12 percent. This was insufficient to attract eastern money, given the distance and risk involved. Time-entry loans offered a way around the usury law, and the partners had been active in making such loans at 25 percent interest well before Congress authorized the issue of land warrants under the act of 1847.[5]

The attraction of bounty land grants for Washburn and Woodman was that the warrants eased the problem of raising capital and provided a way of circumventing the usury laws. In 1847, Woodman immediately perceived that warrants could be purchased at a discount below the General Land Office price of $1.25 an acre, thus making an investment of money good for acquiring additional land. Also, buying warrants made time-entry loans appear to conform with the territorial usury laws. A settler who borrowed from Washburn and Woodman to buy a quarter-section agreed to pay $225 in one year. Although the warrant may have cost only $130, the partners could say that the higher figure was simply a 12 percent loan on the par value of public lands ($200) and a one dollar conveyance fee, when in reality the rate of interest was closer to 70 percent. The partners persuaded several New England investors to put up money for the purchase of warrants and their resale on credit. As the Mexican War warrants came onto the market, Washburn and Woodman concentrated more on credit sales and less on cash sales, as "we are convinced that the best disposition that can be made of Warrants here is to sell them on credit to persons who have valuable claims to enter."[6]

Washburn and Woodman offered several investment plans to New England capitalists for warrant operations. To Aziel Chandler of Boston and others, Cyrus Woodman explained the following arrangement:

> If you will furnish us with warrants, calling them worth $125 each, without charge of interest, we will transact all the business of examining the land, locating the warrants & collecting the money of the purchaser for one-half over and above $125 & hold ourselves responsible for one half of any losses. . . . On reflection & further consideration, instead of agreeing to bear our half of any loss that may arise, we will do what we suppose you would prefer, to wit: we would guaranty that within four years from the time the warrants come into our hands you should receive the price of the warrants, say $125, and at least six per cent interest from that time.[7]

Washburn and Woodman persuaded Jacob B. Merrick of Thorndike, Massachusetts, to invest $6,000 in warrant time-entry loans in 1848, and ultimately Merrick added another $5,000, sufficient to buy eighty-eight warrants. The partners and Merrick at first considered entering land for Merrick and holding it for a rise in value, a strategy that Woodman assured Merrick would produce "a profit of from eighty-to-ninety per cent . . . but you might have to hold the lands for some time & have taxes to pay," so instead Merrick took the firm's advice and chose to invest in one-year time-entry loans for "a certain profit with a speedy return." Henry Hubbard, Jr., of New Hampshire, son of a Supreme Court justice, also invested $6,000 with the Mineral Point land agency in time-entry loans, purchasing warrants in Boston and New York at $130 for a 160-acre certificate and asking $225 at the end of a year.[8]

The lure of high rates of return drove Washburn and Woodman to seek warrant location possibilities outside the Mineral Point land district. In July 1849, Woodman asked an Oshkosh, Wisconsin, agent, "Should a man visit Oshkosh with from $5000 to $10000 how could he get rid of it so as to pay him a smashing big interest with perfect certainty?" Woodman went on to inquire about the truth of rumors that "a man has been doing something in this line with your settlers on the Canal lands at from 50 to 75 per ct. int. Is this so?" Clearly, the usury law was insufficient in limiting interest rates to 12 percent, and in January 1849, the new Wisconsin state legislature abolished the law, prompting Woodman to write Hubbard in New Hampshire, "take all you can get—that's the law now." Woodman did express the hope that the usury law's end would "have a tendency to bring in capital here," but the firm continued lending on time-entry warrant locations at $225 for one year, throughout 1849 and into 1850. Credit remained difficult to obtain, and Woodman complained at the end of December 1849 that, despite the new era of unregulated lending, "it is too bad that we are daily obliged to turn away persons who will borrow money at 25% on undoubted security." He urged Washburn, then traveling in New York, to "find anybody soft enough to lend us money at from seven to ten per cent," and if successful, "sign the firm's name for all you can get from two to five year's time." Starting in late 1848, Washburn and Woodman began making time-entry loans with funds reinvested by Jacob Merrick, Henry Hubbard and others. The terms remained $225 for a year's credit on a 160-acre warrant, but the firm also allowed two years' credit if the borrower paid $125 after one year, with another $125 due in the second year. When act of 1850 warrants became assignable in spring 1852, the firm was forced by competition to drop its credit price to $200 for one-year time-entry loans.[9]

The time-entry loan was something of an act of faith by both lender and borrower, and its success depended only in part on the care with which the loan was made and the exertions of the borrower. The lender was of course attracted by the high rate of return, and the borrower hoped that land values would rise as fast or faster than the rate of interest, so as to make repayment easy. The process depended to a large extent on a steady increase of in-migrants and population. A population outflow could ruin the entire calculation. Washburn and Woodman experienced both phenomena in something of a wave, starting with a boom in population and land values in 1848, followed by a crash during the next three years caused by out-migration of southwestern Wisconsin lead miners headed for the goldfields of California, and in 1852, another boom. These experiences left the partners very cautious about making time-entry loans for, as Woodman recognized as early as 1847, "What we want to be sure of is to get the $225 when the note becomes due."[10]

The warrant location business peaked in the spring, when roads and weather cleared, but the spring of 1849 produced a setback for the firm as "the California fever is raging here & many are selling their property at half-price." New time-entry sales came to a halt, and the firm had great difficulty collecting its debts from settlers, many of whom abandoned their farmsteads for California. For those unable to pay in full or at all in 1849, the firm extended their loans at an additional 25 percent, provided some payment was made. For example, the partners offered to carry Warren Brewster's time-entry loan in Adams County, Wisconsin, for another year at that rate if he paid fifty dollars on his debt. At the end of the harvest season, Woodman wrote Merrick in Massachusetts that the "Land Warrant business being so dull that we think it best to close our investments on joint account."[11]

Collections slowed even more in 1850, with Woodman despairing at one point about a debtor that "he made so much noise about the interest on his bond that I gave up, thinking that we should perhaps lose more than we should make by collecting it." The firm coaxed one minister into paying something on his time-entry loan by appealing to Scripture, but to another settler, Woodman threatened, "Do you intend to pay up or must we sell to the first man that wants" the land.[12]

As the public lands in Iowa County around Mineral Point filled up, Washburn and Woodman looked further afield in the land district for tracts upon which to make time-entry locations. In 1851, the firm again began making extensive locations with power of attorney warrants, relying on George Woodman in New York to secure the warrants and on a network of local agents throughout southwestern Wisconsin to find good land and good credit risks. Cyrus Woodman urged his brother George, in April of that year, "For God's sake, send us some [warrants] if they are to be had . . . and I want you to attend to nothing else but supplying us for a few weeks to come. Within the next 90 days we can use 100 forties 25 eighties & as many quarters. . . . We beg you to move heaven and earth." The partners instructed their Wisconsin agents to make sure not "to make entries that would be likely to be left on our hands." For guidance, Cyrus Woodman let his field agents know that he and Washburn preferred to make time-entry loans with warrants to settlers already on an unlocated tract with "improvements worth $25 or more on the place." The experience of 1849 and 1850 taught the firm the lesson that the safest loans were to those settlers already engaged in farm making and thus less likely to up and leave for California. Washburn and Woodman, like other Wisconsin agents, had experienced trouble with timber depredations on lands they owned or oversaw, and Woodman instructed his La Crosse agent, Ole Knudsen, "Timber lands we do not care to enter at all unless there is considerable improvement, and unless there is a moral certainty that they will be paid for and the timber not cut off." In the end, the two Maine-born partners looked for time-entry borrowers who they supposed were honorable men, which in general meant other New Englanders and, wherever possible, Yankees who came with references from the East.[13]

Just as Woodman and Washburn figured prominently in the land business at Mineral Point, so too did one or more agents at nearly every active land office in the public lands states and territories. The firm's business records show clearly the extent to which warrants were used as instruments of frontier credit, and were used similarly in other land districts. For example, Cyrus Aldrich and the Dement brothers, John and Charles, dominated the Dixon, Illinois, land district just south of the Wisconsin border. Colonel John Dement served as register for the Dixon land office under every Democratic president from Jackson to Pierce; when out of office because of Whig victories in 1840 and 1848, Colonel Dement and his brother turned their full attention to land purchases in northern Illinois. The Dements located over 150,000 acres at Dixon between the Mexican War's end and 1853.[14]

Further west, in Davenport, Iowa, the firm of Cook and Sargent was the leading land agency. Ebenezer Cook and his partner, the one-time U.S. surveyor-general for Iowa, George Sargent, bought and sold warrants and corresponded with eastern bankers and brokers interested in Iowa land. Two weeks after the passage of the bounty land grant of 1850, the Davenport partners advertised their willingness to use the power of attorney loophole to help warrantees sell their bounties:

> The late act of Congress granting Bounty Land Warrants making it necessary that the lands should be located in the name of the party to whom the Warrants may issue, before they can be made available, we take this means of offering our services as Agents for the selection of Lands and location of Military Bounty Land Warrants in the flourishing State of Iowa.[15]

Fairfield in east-central Iowa also had a busy land warrant brokerage business, led by Henn, Williams and Company. Bernhardt Henn had served two terms as a Whig congressman from Iowa and also held the post of receiver of the Fairfield land office under the Taylor-Fillmore administrations. While Henn served in Washington, his partner Jesse Williams tended to the land business. The principal competition in Fairfield came from a young Massachusetts emigrant named Ward Lamson. Years later, Lamson recalled the warrant-selling business, "When I charged the current high rates, I felt like a hog, and I guess that many who paid them thought I was one." In Iowa City, the leading land speculators were LeGrand Byington and John Culbertson. In the older area around Dubuque, Horatio Sanford and William Joshua Barney maintained the leading land agencies.[16]

In Michigan, three men dominated the land warrant trade from Detroit: Eber Ward, David Preston, and Charles Merrill. Preston dealt in land warrants before the Civil War and for many years after as well; in the 1870s, when the Saginaw River Valley was opened to large-scale lumbering, he acquired tens of thousands of acres of warrants for resale to the timber companies who needed to acquire extensive land.[17]

One of the most prominent speculators from the Northeast was Francis Daniels, who split his time between New York City and Vermont. Robert Ives of Providence invested extensively in Illinois lands before moving his interest west to Iowa. His fellow Providence merchant John Carter Brown was also an active speculator in Illinois land warrants.[18]

In his years of research into the history of the public lands, historian Paul Gates found that southerners were among the most prominent investors in midwestern land before the Civil War. Study of land warrant locations at midwestern offices shows many southern men, especially from the upper South, who made extensive investments in warrants and frontier lands. Among southerners, Charles Pairo of the District of Columbia located 40,000 acres in Iowa before suffering a setback in the panic of 1857. Elias White and his sons entered over 175,000 acres in Iowa land from their base of operations in Baltimore. Joseph Loose from Hagerstown, Maryland, also saw and seized the opportunity for profit in Iowa land.[19]

Surviving business records of the Halifax, Virginia, firm of James Easley and William Willingham give a detailed picture of the absentee southern investor in midwestern land. Easley and Willingham invested more than $400 thousand in land warrants between 1853 and 1856 and used the bounties almost exclusively to make time-entry loans to settlers in Iowa. The firm records show the role of warrant brokers in New York and Washington in supplying absentee investors like Easley and Willingham as well as the critical role of local agents in Iowa land office towns who supervised the Virginians' loans. Starting in the spring of 1853, the south side Virginia firm made time-entry locations in eastern and central Iowa, and each year for the next four advanced their operations further west, so that by 1856 they had concentrated their entries in the Sioux City and Council Bluffs land districts bordering the Missouri River. After the panic of 1857, the partners moved further afield into the Nebraska Territory, dealing in some cases with former Iowa land agents who had also removed to the new territory.[20]

The business correspondence and financial records of Easley and Willingham show that the firm adjusted its time-entry loan rates both to the cost of warrants and to other competitors in the market. When the Virginia investors began their warrant entries in the Iowa City land district in May 1853, they charged $60 for a one-year loan on a forty-acre warrant, $120 for a loan on an eighty, and $240 for a time-entry quarter-section loan. The absence of any premium on the forty-acre warrants attests to their abundance after the acts of 1850 and 1852 brought them into the market by the tens of thousands. The credit rate of charging $1.50 an acre on a year's time may be compared with the firm's cost of buying warrants in New York and Washington that same month, May 1853, for 87.5 cents an acre, or $35 for forty-acre warrants, $70 for eighty-acre warrants, and $140 for 160s. Before adjustment for commissions, profit divisions, exchange, and other costs, the gross profit on the basic time-entry loan of May 1853 was 71 percent. By October 1853, Easley and Willingham had increased their time-entry charges seven cents an acre to $63 for a forty-acre warrant, $126 for an eighty, and $250 for a 160-acre warrant-based loan. By the fall of 1854, the firm raised its time-entry charges again, this time to $68, $136, and $272, for forty-, eighty-, and 160-acre warrants, respectively. This rise, however, did not compensate for a bigger rise in warrant prices to $1.13 an acre, reducing the gross profit to about 50 percent. Easley and Willingham settled on $1.75 an acre ($280 for a 160-acre warrant) as their basic time-entry charge by late 1854 and stayed at that rate throughout the next several years.[21]

When Wisconsin and Iowa entered the Union as new states in 1848, the former promptly chose to repeal its territorial usury law, while the latter chose to maintain a legal ceiling of 10 percent interest. Easley and Willingham had no intention of limiting themselves to that low rate; they found time-entry loans attractive throughout the 1850s for, among other reasons, the contracts they signed with settlers circumvented the usury law. Moreover, in case of problems with a borrower, the partners kept control of the land, and in a time of rising land values, they were confident of quick resales on new time-entry loans. A traditional mortgage, by contrast, was subject to the usury law, and when conflict arose over the loan, the title might be placed in jeopardy from the lender's point of view.[22]

The time-entry lending business proved immediately profitable for James Easley and William Willingham in 1853. Out of thirty-six loans advanced in May of that year, all but two were repaid on schedule. Indeed, many of the time-entry borrowers repaid their loans before a year's lapse so as to lower their debt burden. The Davenport land agency of Cook, Downey and Sargent wrote Easley in August 1853 that "We cannot restrict the settlers from paying up their notes in advance . . . the privilege of paying in advance at a proportionate rate of discounts is inseparable from these transactions." Agents like Cook, Downey and Sargent, or Dubuque's William J. Barney worked for Easley and Willingham much as Cyrus Woodman and Cadwallader Washburn did in Wisconsin for their eastern clients. The local land agent made the time-entry in the absentee investor's name, found a willing settler in need of credit, and agreed to pay the investor the cost of the warrant, 10 percent interest, and one-half the profits of the settlement cost beyond the warrant's cost and the interest. The result was a net rate of return for the Virginians of at least 30 percent.[23]

The years up to 1857 were quite successful for time-entry lenders, agents, and borrowers. The panic of 1857 put a brake on the business as the volume of settlers going west slowed and land prices tumbled. Land agents in Iowa had difficulty collecting time-entry debts, much as Washburn and Woodman had had during the California fever in southwestern Wisconsin. Easley and Willingham continued time-entry lending in 1858 and 1859, but not nearly on the scale of the mid-1850s. By the end of the decade, an increasing percentage of land warrants in the market were being directed away from time-entry lenders and to settlers taking advantage of the preemption laws to acquire public land.[24]

Time-entry lending between the Mexican War and the panic of 1857 in Iowa, Illinois, Wisconsin, and elsewhere depended on several simultaneous developments. The first and most important was the influx to a land district of settlers in need of credit. In addition, local land agents had to coordinate the flow of warrants for location from absentee investors interested in a high rate of return on what appeared to be safe loans. A third factor that fueled time-entry lending was the common belief of both debtor and creditor that the land was underpriced at the General Land Office rate of $1.25 an acre; this offered security to the creditor in case of a failure to repay the loan and, at the same time, made the high rate of interest charged seem not so onerous to the borrower because of an anticipated large capital gain from the expected sharp rise in land values. The final ingredient was the General Land Office's practice of bringing new ranges of public land onto the auction market and thereafter open to private entry with warrants.

The sample of warrant files shows a number of prominent political figures involved in the business of buying warrants. Among the 1847 sample, John Sherman, the young Mansfield, Ohio, congressman, bought a 160-acre warrant just as he embarked on a fifty-year career in national political life. Charles Brodhead, a nephew of the senator who led the fight for the 1855 grant, bought and sold warrants in Easton, Pennsylvania, before he moved on to the iron business in nearby Bethlehem. While senator from New York, John Dix actively invested in Iowa land with the aid of land warrants. The champion land speculator and land warrant buyer of the Senate, however, was Louisiana's John Slidell, who nonetheless strongly supported the homestead bills before the Senate. Together with his New York banker friend August Belmont, Slidell located 25,000 acres of public land in the 1850s. In the House, Tennessee's William B. Stokes has the name appearing most frequently in the sample of land warrant buyers.[25]

A common arrangement in the land warrant location business was to have one member of a family go west and act as the frontier land agent for other family members in the East. Hamilton Fant, the biggest land warrant dealer in Washington, D.C., had his son open a land agency in Lecompton, Kansas, in the 1850s. The Woodman family of Maine is another example, though Cyrus Woodman in frontier Wisconsin actually gave directions to his younger brothers George and Horatio in New York and Boston. Perhaps the most interesting family in the warrant business was that of Jay Cooke and his brother Pitt. Historians know Jay Cooke as the "financier of the Union" in the Civil War and as the famous banker ruined by the panic of 1873. Before he became so well known nationally, Cooke actively invested in Iowa and Minnesota land, relying on his younger brother Pitt to make the actual locations with warrants supplied from the banking house of E. W. Clark, Dodge and Company in Philadelphia where Jay was a partner.[26]

Pitt selected Dubuque as his base of operations, making occasional trips home to Sandusky, Ohio, where he struggled to pay off a debt of over $40,000. He had many adventures in Iowa from 1855 to 1857, and his letters to Jay give a lively picture of warrant locating, the land office business, and frontier life. Pitt spent April and May 1855 examining over 40,000 acres in the Dubuque land district and decided to locate 34,000 acres with warrants. The brothers agreed to wait on their purchase of warrants in Philadelphia until autumn of 1855 since they mistakenly expected that the vast new issue of act of 1855 warrants would depress warrant prices to seventy cents an acre. Pitt did locate three thousand acres with cash, but almost all the other acres he had spotted were taken by rival speculators who had not waited for warrants to fall in price. When the Dubuque office closed in the late summer, Pitt transferred his base to the new office at Decorah and reported back to Jay:

> Speculators are as thick as Blackberries in term and 100s at Decorah. We have an awful time to get a place to sleep & anything to eat. . . . Sold 2-40s = 80 acres for 3$ per acre & had so many nibbles for more. I wish we had not waited for those confounded warrants, the small difference is nothing.[27]

Over the winter of 1855–56, Pitt identified over 45,000 acres in the Decorah land district which he divided into three equal lots he called first, second, and third choice. He wrote to Jay before Thanksgiving, "We hope to secure the whole of the first choice & if not fill up with 2nd choice what we fail to secure of 1st choice. There is great competition—the fastest nag wins."[28]

The spring of 1856 saw Pitt Cooke achieve his greatest success in Iowa land speculation. He located seven thousand acres with warrants in the Decorah district that he later sold for $4.00 an acre, while the warrants had cost Jay only from $1.01 to $1.05 an acre. Moreover, Pitt managed a clever stroke in convincing the voters of Chickasaw County, Iowa, to move the county seat from Bradford in the far southwest corner of the county to centrally located New Hampton. The latter site was on land donated by Pitt and surrounded by thousands of acres the Cookes owned. The political maneuver cost about $250 in campaign expenses to bring off, but it quickly raised the value of the brothers' land holdings.[29]

Pitt traveled widely across Iowa, Minnesota, and Missouri during the summer of 1856. He used eight thousand acres of warrants to locate lands in the district at Winona in the Minnesota Territory. He also inspected lands in the Iowa districts of Fort Dodge, Iowa City, and Osage. At Osage (an office opened to continue the work of the recently closed Decorah office), Pitt managed to locate over three thousand acres in warrants, but his account of events to Jay tells something of the nature of the frontier land business:

> There are 400 or 500 thousand acres of Warrants in hands of Greedy land agents, settlers, Speculators & Everyone else. . . . I got every one of my entries just as I wanted them while 100's did not get an acre, but keep this quiet. It was all done by paying something for it.[30]

Jay and Pitt Cooke continued their land speculations into 1857 but curtailed the size of their investments because Pitt found that securing first-choice lands proved harder than it had in 1855 or 1856. Still, the brothers were caught holding thousands of acres of land they could not sell in Missouri, Iowa, and Minnesota when the panic of 1857 hit in the fall. The basis of speculation as practiced by the Cooke brothers was to find good land, enter it with warrants (with the help of bribes, if need be), and then resell it for a few dollars an acre in a short time. Pitt described the business to Jay as follows:

> We find a great many things to be done preliminary to making any actual locations and that it is an arduous undertaking any way. Many old farmers come to Iowa I find & after running around to the different counties & back to the Land Office end off in many, in fact in more than half the cases by buying at second hand from previous purchasers or pre-emptioners, at 2, 2½ & 3 $ & in many cases at $5.00, many of them that I have talked with say it is hard work to hunt up land & get it located to suit them.[31]

For the most part, Pitt and Jay Cooke bought lands for resale and occasionally put out money at interest to other land agents, usually at 15 or 20 percent. The brothers did not engage in time-entry lending, but Pitt knew of such arrangements and described their workings in an early letter from Dubuque to Jay:

> The way a large amount of money is made here is by entering lands for settlers. A settler comes & wants you to enter 160 acres which he has not the money to pay for, you do it take title in your own name, give him the refusal for say 1 year for $80. That is 40%, the settler as soon as he can raise the 280, will pay it—some times in 30 days, 90 days & so on & in ⅔ the cases within six months. This makes it equivalent to 60 or 70 percent.[32]

One who did engage in making time-entry loans was the Minnesota agent and banker Jason Easton. Operating out of the land office town of Chatfield, Easton made arrangements with such big New York land warrant brokers as Taylor Brothers and Le Huray and Company to lend money on warrants. As with Easley and Willingham in Iowa, the practice was to sell a warrant at the par or "government" price of the full $200 for 160 acres, and to charge 40 percent interest so that the borrower had to pay $280 at the end of twelve months. Easton made time-entry loans himself and also served as middleman for eastern investors who sought such high returns in moneylending. In the latter case, he charged 10 percent, or twenty-eight dollars, as a fee for arranging loans between eastern investors and settlers on the Minnesota frontier.

The Easton business records show a number of warrants returned to his New York suppliers because of confusion or legal difficulties. As much as anything else, mistakes and irregularities reflect the crush of business in the Minnesota Territory in 1856 and 1857. From time to time, Easton felt moved to complain about unwanted purchases on his account or about worthless warrants. In May 1857, Easton wrote somewhat peevishly to the Wall Street firm of Le Huray and Company, "We return you herewith six 160 acre Warrants rec'd in yours of April 30. We did not order these Warrants and cannot use them. We are unable to see the 'advantage of low rates' to which you refer as your prices range higher than quotations of other Houses in your City of the same date." Later in the fall of 1857, when tempers were short among all land dealers, Easton returned a warrant to Le Huray "which has been refused at the Land Office in this place 'on account of the assignment being made in such a bungling manner.' "[33]

Jason Easton's operations peaked between the end of June 1856, when the Chatfield land office opened after the removal of the old office from Brownsville on the Mississippi River, and June 1857. The General Land Office opened over one million acres to private entry in the Chatfield land district, although in spring 1857, some land was withdrawn to fulfill the terms of a federal railroad grant to Minnesota. Still, Easton had a busy year; analysis of his business records shows he bought 295 warrants for use in a twelve-month span. Those warrants, almost all of them 120- or 160-acre warrants purchased from New York brokers, totaled just under forty thousand acres.

Forty-four of the 295 warrants were sold on time-entry loans, almost all of them 160-acre warrants at a price of $200 with the standard interest charge of 40 percent. Easton insisted in August 1856 that a 60 percent return on time-entry loans was routine and, more to the point, safe:

> I am aware that these figures will surprise our Eastern friends. They wonder how a man can run in debt for a farm and contract to pay such interest. But this is so and the borrowers are frequently making more money than the lenders.[34]

The 60 percent interest figure, and similar rates at other land districts, represented scarce credit and were a market expression of the riskiness of such investments. Those who borrowed from a Jason Easton to cover the cost of the warrant and a year's money were, Easton's optimism notwithstanding, potential candidates for failure. Indeed, study of Easton's land business records shows that a large number of the time-entry borrowers defaulted in 1857 when their loans came due. The panic of 1857 explains some of the failures, but, even in the absence of commercial turbulence, the fact remains that time-entry lending could be a risky business.

Time-entry locations constituted only 15 percent of Easton's total warrant dealings; most of his sales went to the large number of settlers known as preemptors, or pejoratively as squatters, who created a demand for the cash purchase of warrants. The relatively small percentage of warrants that Easton used in time-entry loans is one indication that the time-entry business was not as extensive after the act of 1855 had passed, allowing preemptors to use warrants on unoffered land not open to nonresident buyers or warrant locators. This pattern serves as another reminder that Washington decisions shaped the use of warrants on the frontier. Time-entry warrant locations may well have dominated the employment of act of 1847 and act of 1850 warrants. The 1855 series, however, was characterized by

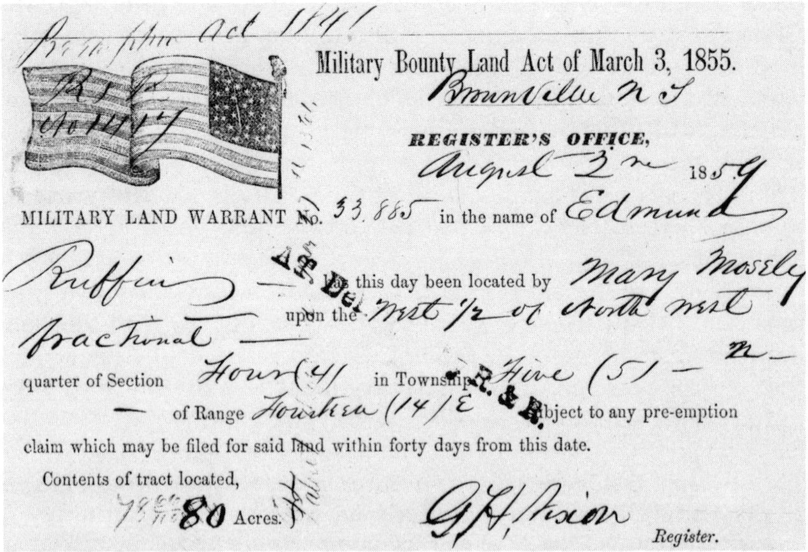

Military Bounty Land Act of March 3, 1855.
Brownville N. T.

REGISTER'S OFFICE,
August 2nd 1859

MILITARY LAND WARRANT No. 33,885 in the name of Edmund Ruffin — has this day been located by Mary Mosely upon the West 1/2 of North West fractional — quarter of Section Four (4) in Township Five (5) — N — of Range Fourteen (14) E subject to any pre-emption claim which may be filed for said land within forty days from this date.

Contents of tract located, 80 Acres.

G. H. Nixon
Register.

FIG. 12. LAND OFFICE REGISTER'S RECEIPT FOR LAND LOCATION USING A LAND WARRANT. Issued to Mary Mosely, a Nebraska preemptor who paid for her claim by using the eighty-acre warrant sold by Edmund Ruffin (courtesy of the National Archives).

extensive use of warrants to secure preemptions. Table 23 shows that 287 sample warrants, which represent about 57,000 individuals, were used to secure the right, under the act of 1855, to obtain title to their preempted land parcels. This involved about nine million acres, and the group constituted only the preemptors who successfully acquired public land—an unknown fraction of the total number of preemptors. The sample of warrant files in the National Archives does not measure those who claimed a parcel but left before receiving title.

After 1855, preempting with the help of a warrant flourished especially in two parts of the West: eastern Kansas and Nebraska, and in the counties in eastern Minnesota and western Wisconsin along the Mississippi River. The Kansas preemptors are best known for their part in precipitating the Civil War because of the frontier violence in the years after 1854. The Minnesota and Wisconsin preemptors are less well studied, and investigation of the role of land warrants in the history of preempting and settlement on the upper

TABLE 23
Profile of the Use of Sample Act of 1855 Warrants

Private entry locations	988
Preemption claims	287
Homestead commutations	5
Missing/cancelled	35
Total	1,315

SOURCE: Sample of 1855 warrants. See App. A.

Mississippi reveals much about the character of pioneering in this region. Table 24 breaks down the use of act of 1855 warrants by preemptors on the public lands, showing both the state and the year the warrant was located. Nearly two in five of the group called Minnesota their home; about another quarter settled in Kansas. Better than 80 percent of these warrant-based preemption locations came before the outbreak of the Civil War, with about two million acres' worth in 1857 alone. More than half of the preemptors using warrants in 1856 and 1857 lived in the Minnesota Territory, and they were particularly active in the Chatfield land district, as Jason Easton's business records show.[35]

By 1858 and 1859, the center of preemption payments with warrants had shifted to the Kansas Territory, especially to the Lecompton land district. More than half of all the warrants used for preemptions in the second and third years of the Buchanan administration were in Kansas, a connection that was not coincidental. The administration, led by Interior Secretary Jacob Thompson, determined to punish free-soil Kansas settlers for rejecting the Lecompton Constitution. Thompson decided to force the preemptors in Kansas to pay for their preemptions by having the president declare their lands open to auction and private entry. Those preemptors who had been on their parcels for more than fifteen months had to obtain cash or a warrant to pay for their claims or risk losing the lands. Paul Gates found it one of the more outrageous abuses of executive power and one of the factors that turned Kansas into a solidly Republican state for the next century. In 1860, Minnesota preemptors, especially those in the Henderson land district, received the same treatment from Buchanan and Thompson. The ad-

TABLE 24
Geographical Distribution of Sample Act of 1855 Warrants Used for Preemption Claims, 1856–1899

State/terr.	*1856*	*1857*	*1858*	*1859*	*1860*	*1861–65*	*1866–69*	*1870–79*	*1880–89*	*1890–99*	*Total*
Michigan	1			1						2	4
Wisconsin	5	7	1			1	2				16
Minnesota	19	34	7	8	28	11	2	1	1		111
Iowa	5	9	6			1		1			22
Missouri			2								2
Arkansas				1							1
Louisiana	1			1			1				3
Dakota								1			1
Nebraska		14	5	5	3		3				30
Kansas		8	32	18	5		3	2			68
Colorado						1	4	2			7
California			4	1		4		7			16
Oregon						3		1			4
Montana							1				1
Total	31	72	57	35	36	21	16	15	1	2	286

SOURCE: Preemption claims in act of 1855 warrants.

ministration in Washington retaliated against Minnesota preemptors for voting Republican in local elections by throwing open large tracts to auction and private entry (see table 25).[36]

The basic source for identifying squatters is a document called the Register of Declaratory Statements, part of the records compiled by the register at each district land office. A preemptor who wished to stake his claim and secure legal protection for his preemption had to appear personally at the district land office and make his declaration of preemption. He was required to do this within three months of settling on the parcel, though many in fact waited much longer. After he filed his declaratory statement, he then had a grace period of one year to make improvements on his parcel and either obtain a warrant or accumulate sufficient cash to buy the land from the United States.[37]

After the year's grace period ended, the preemptor had to come forth with proof of his improvements to the tract and the necessary payment, or forfeit his exclusive right to the land. In the latter case, the General Land Office reopened the parcel to other preemptors, or, if

TABLE 25
Leading Land Districts for Sample Act of 1855 Warrants Used for Preemption Claims, 1856–1899

Year	*Office*	*N*	*Annual National Total (%)*
1856	Winona, MN	11	35
1857	Omaha, NE	12	17
1858	Lecompton, KS	19	33
1859	Lecompton, KS	8	22
1860	Henderson, MN	10	28
1861–65	Winnebago City, MN	5	24
1866–69	Denver, CO	4	29
1870–79	San Francisco, CA	6	38
1880–89	Worthington, MN	1	50
1890–99	Marquette, MI	2	100

SOURCES: Preemption claims in act of 1855 warrants and table 24.

the tract was for sale as part of an already offered township, the General Land Office opened it to private entry by outright buyers. The terms of the 1841 Preemption Act (the basic law of "squatting") stated that only heads of families, single men over twenty-one, or widows were eligible to preempt a parcel of public lands. Moreover, those who owned more than 320 acres of land anywhere in the United States were declared ineligible to benefit from the privilege of preempting. This stipulation reflected the congressional desire to limit speculation in land to those in need of a farm.[38]

Investigation of the Registers of Declaratory Statements at eight Mississippi Valley land offices in Minnesota and Wisconsin shows that about sixty thousand men and women filed preemption claims between 1852 and 1862, covering about 8.5 million acres of public land. On the Minnesota side, nearly every tract in some townships was claimed by a preemptor (see table 26). The table also shows the extent to which preemptors remained on their claimed parcels and gained a patent (title) to the land, as well as how many of these preemptors-turned-landowners acquired their land on the basis of a land warrant. The benefit to the preemptor in using a warrant was clear: he or she could obtain a substantial discount, perhaps 10–20 percent off the government's cash price of $1.25 an acre, by

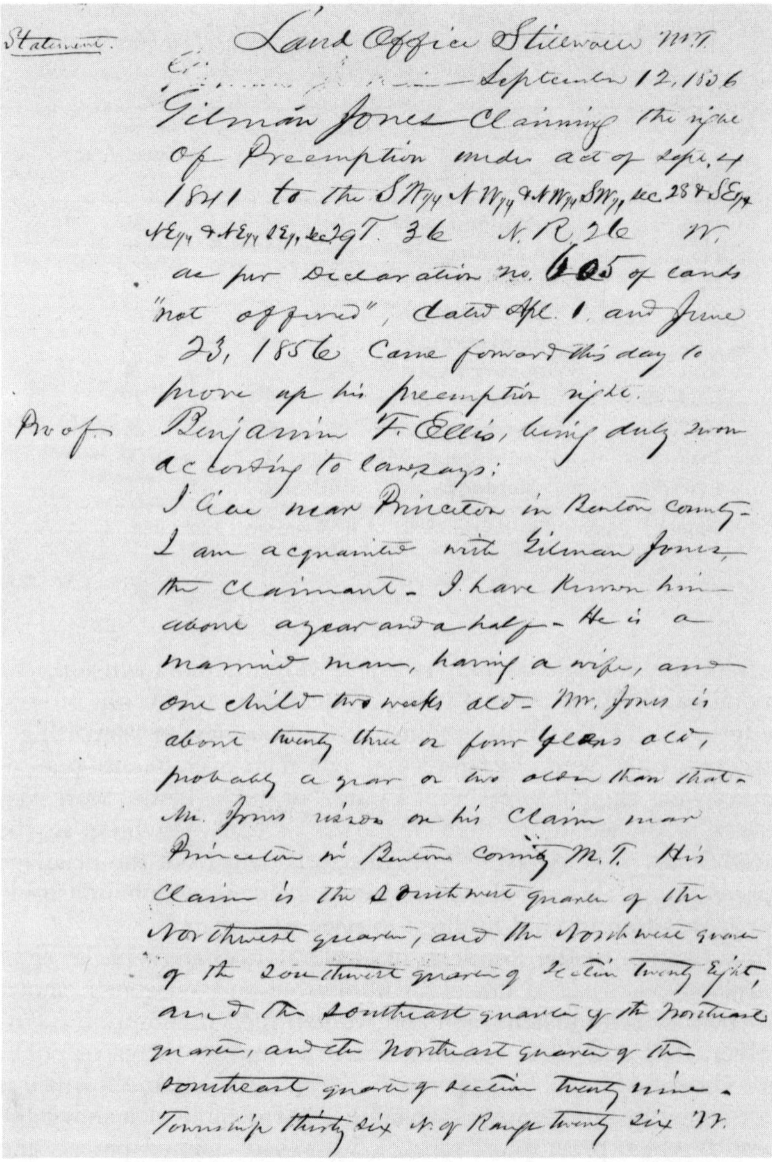

Statement. Land Office Stillwater M.T.

September 12, 1856

Gilman Jones Claiming the right Of Preemption under act of Sept. 4 1841 to the SW 1/4 NW 1/4 & NW 1/4 SW 1/4, sec 28 & SE 1/4 NE 1/4 & NE 1/4 SE 1/4, sec 29 T. 36 N. R. 26 W. as per Declaration No. 605 of lands "not offered", dated Apl. 1. and June 23, 1856 Came forward this day to prove up his preemption right.

Proof. Benjamin F. Ellis, being duly sworn according to law, says:

I live near Princeton in Benton County. I am acquainted with Gilman Jones, the Claimant. I have known him about a year and a half. He is a married man, having a wife, and one child two weeks old. Mr. Jones is about twenty three or four years old, probably a year or two older than that. Mr. Jones resides on his Claim near Princeton in Benton County M.T. His Claim is the Southwest quarter of the Northwest quarter, and the Northwest quarter of the Southwest quarter of Section Twenty Eight, and the Southeast quarter of the Northeast quarter, and the Northeast quarter of the Southeast quarter of section twenty nine. Township thirty six N. of Range twenty six W.

Fig. 13. Preemption Proof Claim. Eyewitness statement of Benjamin Ellis supporting the 1856 preemption claim of his neighbor Gilman Jones to 160 acres of public land in the Stillwater, Minnesota, land district (courtesy of the National Archives).

TABLE 26
Preemptions by Selected Land District in Wisconsin and Minnesota, 1852–62

District	Number of Preemptions	Percent of Sample Gaining Title	Percent of Title Gainers Using Warrants
LaCrosse	7,918	27	38
Eau Claire	1,070	27	33
Hudson	3,125	42	40
Minneapolis	7,274	65	70
Brownsville/Chatfield	11,864	64	90
Red Wing	10,095	64	83
Stillwater	1,639	41	29
Winona/Faribault	16,647	75	79
Total	59,632		

SOURCES: Registers of Declaration, Records of the Bureau of Land Management, Record Group 49, National Archives; U.S. Land Entry Books, State Historical Society of Wisconsin and Minnesota Historical Society.

using a soldier's bounty land warrant. Those who chose to pay cash frequently preempted smaller parcels, sometimes at the minimum entry of forty acres, and these people may have had difficulty obtaining forty-acre warrants. Also, the discount on the small-denomination warrants was not as great as that available on the larger ones. Still, some preemptors did pay cash for a full quarter-section; in retrospect, one must wonder about their business sense.[39]

The records created to keep track of the preemptors tell much about the social history of the pioneer settlements of the upper Mississippi Valley region. For example, the sex ratio of male to female preemptors reflects the fact that the law favored men and prohibited any but widowed women from preempting. About 97 percent of this sample of Minnesota and Wisconsin squatters in the 1850s were men. Two of the women squatters in the sample had adult sons preempting an adjoining parcel of land in the same township, suggesting a family strategy of acquiring considerable contiguous land at a low price. Among the men, the records of the General Land Office show a rather even split between married and unmarried men making declaratory statements of preemption.[40]

The sample of preemptors shows a relatively narrow age distribution. The median age of a preemptor in antebellum Wisconsin and Minnesota was twenty-nine. Very few heads of families or single men over the age of forty-five appear in the records, although fifty-nine-year-old Maine-born Jonas Brown made a preemption in frontier Wisconsin in 1856. At the other end of the spectrum that same year, young Giles Rathburn was only twenty when he and his eighteen-year-old wife and infant child made a preemption claim on 120 acres in Monroe County, Wisconsin.[41]

Historians of Wisconsin and Minnesota have long thought of their two states as immigrant outposts of central and northern Europe. Interestingly, immigrants appear quite infrequently in the records of preempting. Under 20 percent of the preemptors in the two-state sample were foreign-born, quite a bit below the percentage of foreign-born in each state in 1860. Of the immigrant squatters, the largest number came from England—not Norway or Germany, as one might expect. Perhaps the ability to speak English as a native language gave the American-born and immigrants from the United Kingdom an advantage in obtaining the best lands through preemption. The Scandinavians and Germans who eventually filled the upper Mississippi Valley did not constitute the first wave of white settlers into the area. Their turn would come later.[42]

Usually the first activity a squatter engaged in was the construction of a dwelling. The proof statements filed by preemptors in the General Land Office land warrant location records show how tiny these houses or shanties were: the average square footage of a squatter's shanty was 215, smaller than many Americans' living rooms today. The typical squatter's cabin had one door and one window and was inexpensively constructed of hewn logs rather than cut boards. Planks or boards would be used only for the floor. After constructing the cabin, the preemptor could turn his attention to his land and exploit its potential.

Inventories showing personal belongings of preemptors indicate that they enjoyed the use of few material comforts. The example of Edward Peno gives some idea of the squatter's standard of living. Peno immigrated from England in the summer of 1854 and made his way to Anoka County, Minnesota, the next spring, where he quickly preempted 160 acres of land. The unmarried Peno built a rather spacious cabin twenty by sixteen feet, with two windows and a board roof, all in the span of six days. After squatting for eighteen months on his parcel, Peno finally acquired the land with a land warrant at the downriver Minneapolis land office. In the year and a half between the time he settled his parcel until the day he finally tendered a warrant for it, Peno cleared and brought under cultivation ten acres of land and built a stable for his livestock. At the time he used the warrant, late in the fall of 1856, Peno's personal belongings consisted of a table, four chairs, a bed and bedding, stove, and some dishes and cooking utensils. In Peno's case, and that of many other squatters, all available labor went into expanding the improved acreage. Only when a farm was solidly established could the ex-squatter turn his attention to remaking or expanding the living quarters.[43]

This phenomenon is most quickly apparent in a few instances where fire destroyed the original squatter's cabin. For example, John Wage, with his wife and four children, preempted a quarter-section in Monroe County, Wisconsin, in April 1856, and built what an eyewitness described as a "log shanty," twelve by fourteen feet with one door and one window. That summer, the family cleared four acres of land and sowed it with wheat. They also planted another acre with potatoes and turnips. In September, the shanty burned, and the Wages had to rebuild. Rather than reconstruct a simple log hut to last through the winter, the Wages devoted sufficient time, energy, and money to build themselves a frame house, two stories high, eighteen by twenty feet, with one door and six sash windows, all covered by a shingled roof![44]

How successful were the preemptors in obtaining title to the public land they preempted? Follow-up research in the official land entry books (records that show how every forty-acre tract of public land in the United States passed to private hands) shown in table 26 indicates that a bit more than three-fifths of the upper Mississippi squatters received title to the land they sought, usually within a year of the time they first went to the local land office to make their declaratory statements. This is an impressively high figure and suggests at first glance the ease with which men could obtain land. It compares very favorably, for example, with the rate at which homesteaders under the 1862 law were able to acquire successfully title to their land. Indeed, it is hard to think of other times and places in American history where 60 percent of incoming migrants could be landowners in a little more than a year.[45]

The registers of declaratory statements, proof statements, original land entry books, and other General Land Office records do not, regrettably, give uniform information about the number of children, their ages, or the wives of the squatters. As a result, we do not know all the details about the family situation of preemptors for each land district at the time of settlement or declaration. Such information must be pursued in the manuscript census for 1860. The eighth decennial census, taken in the summer of 1860, came four to five years after most of the preemptors had settled on the public lands. By that time, only about 30 percent of the preemptors remained on their parcels of land. This comes as something of a surprise since the initial news from 1855 and 1856 was the ease of acquiring title to new land. One might expect the preemptors who did not gain title to move on, but nearly half of those who did get title also migrated out. The characteristics of the preemptors who persisted deserve some scrutiny before we ask why there was such high out-migration among "successful" in-migrants and how this may have influenced decisions about matters like family size.[46]

First, it is worth noting that the rate of success in gaining title among the persisting preemptors was nearly identical with that of those who had migrated out by 1860, 61 percent as opposed to 60 percent. Certain variables distinguish the preemptors who remained on the parcel they came to own from those who gained title but did not stay long. The most important predictor was the year of settlement. Those who arrived in Wisconsin or Minnesota in 1855 had better chances for success in gaining and keeping title than did those who came in 1856, and both years' group of "squatters" fared far better on this point than did the 1857 arrivals. The persisting former preemptors of 1860 were much more likely to be married than the original migrants of the mid-1850s. Indeed, 80 percent were married in 1860. Some, no doubt, had been single men who found mates after settlement, but there also is evidence that those who came as married men with families were more likely to persist. The outcome of gaining title is positively correlated to family size at the time of settlement and preempting. Moreover, there is a sizable difference in the median 1860 ages of married men and single men who had once been Minnesota and Wisconsin preemptors: the figure for married men was thirty-five, while for single men it was twenty-eight. This suggests that, among squatters on this frontier, there were at least two streams of migrants, men around the age of thirty with families, and younger unattached men, just past the legal minimum age for preempting. The family men, for a variety of reasons, were more likely to stick out the pioneer life than the single men.[47]

There existed a striking difference in ethnic origin between the persisters and those who had squatted and gained title but left. Forty-three percent of the persisting men in 1860 were foreign-born; Germany, Ireland, and Norway were the leading countries of origin. England and Scotland made up only 15 percent of the immigrant population. This finding is repeated in the ethnic background of the wives of the persisting preemptors: 38 percent of these women were foreign-born, with Norway as the leading home country.

One reason so many apparently successful preemptors failed to last as long as five years on their farms was the hardship caused by the panic of 1857. Those most likely to succeed and persist were the early in-migrants, especially those who brought some capital, usually men in their thirties with families. The 1860 Census information on persisters also gives some background information on those who succeeded in getting title to their plots and those who failed to do so. There is a striking difference in wealth between the two groups: those who gained title had a mean total estate of $2,073, while those who did not gain title had a mean total estate of $992. This disparity may reflect a greater degree of material success while working on the frontier; in a sense, proving by circular reasoning that the wealthier group did manage to hold their lands through the panic of 1857. Another possibility is that, having moved to the frontier with more capital, they were able to finance their own land acquisition without the need to borrow from a frontier "shark." The disparity in ages between the two groups lends some credence to the latter explanation. The mean age of title-gaining preemptors in the 1860 census was 39.4, while that of non–title holders was 36.0.[48]

To sum up, those who were most likely to preempt, gain title to, and stay on their lands through 1860 were those who came to Wisconsin and Minnesota early in the land rush, and came older and wealthier. Preemptors used land warrants quite extensively in obtaining title to frontier land, though landownership did not guarantee economic success. Some preemptors no doubt sought a quick resale of their tracts to take advantage of a rise in the value of their lands.

After the end of the Civil War, the pace of land warrant locations picked up once again. By the late 1860s, settlers began taking possession of the Great Plains in Kansas and Nebraska; in the next decade, warrants were used in the Rocky Mountain states and territories. Yet, as table 15 showed, there was also a northern frontier after the Civil War for the employment of land warrants. Indeed, the most active state for postbellum warrant locations was Michigan, and the busiest land office for warrants was also in that state, at East Saginaw. The explanation for this alternative frontier was the extensive lumbering in the western Great Lakes states in the postbellum period up to the depression of the 1890s.

Scattered throughout the land warrant location files in the National Archives are the names of lumbermen and lumber companies active in the pine forests of Michigan, Wisconsin, and Minnesota, including the biggest in scale of operations, the German immigrant Frederick Weyerhaueser. A few lumbermen, like Minneapolis's Dorilus Morison, had used warrants before the war to locate pineland; but for the most part, the great timber rush came later. Sawmill operators had not been in the habit of acquiring extensive landholdings before the Civil War, relying instead on a mix of lumber purchases and outright depredations on the public lands. As the size and scale of sawing grew, millowners began to become concerned about maintaining a steady supply of timber to supply their investment. The only certain way to do so was to acquire land. Warrants as well as cash purchases were used for this purpose, as was scrip similar to warrants, issued to states under the Agricultural College Act of 1862. Some lumbermen resorted to fraud or chicanery to acquire public lands by filing false preemption and homestead claims simply so they could cut the timber.[49]

The postbellum history of the use of land warrants places them more firmly in the story of the "Big Barbecue," that is, the corporate exploitation of natural resources with the aid of the federal government. Still, most of the warrants were issued and located before the firing on Fort Sumter. What remains to be shown is the extent to which warrants aided or hindered the volume of western settlement and land acquisition.

7

Land Warrant Grants in Historical Perspective

In 1924, Benjamin Hibbard wrote of the bounty land grants of the 1850s, "As an example of how not to dispose of public land it was excellent." Hibbard's judgment reflected in part his political orientation as a Turner student sympathetic to the homestead idea and, like George Stephenson, scornful of obstacles placed in the way of the free land policy. In addition, Hibbard's training as an agricultural economist convinced him that bounty land grants were a profligate use of the public domain and positively harmful to the interests of settlers. Should this judgment be reaffirmed today? One response to Hibbard is to measure the bounty land grants against Congress's stated aims in public lands policy. The national legislature before the Civil War could agree on only two principles for disposition of the public lands. The first was that the federal government should strive to turn the public domain into private property, while the second held that land policy should aid the settlement of new farmers. Judged by both these standards, bounty land grants succeeded. Sixty million acres given away to veterans did soon pass into private hands. As to the second point, issuing land warrants reduced the government's selling price of $1.25 per acre, especially in the upper Mississippi Valley where the Graduation Act had little effect.[1]

Historians have the job of explaining how change happens over time and sometimes claim too much influence for a particular decision, policy, or idea. I wish to resist the urge to claim more importance than is deserved for the history of military bounty land warrants of the Mexican War era, yet I do think this history is worth telling. The federal bounty land grants do represent an aspect of change and a turning point in late antebellum America's politics, society, and economy. More to the point, study of the warrants from their creation to their final use offers a different way to look at some of the problems in nineteenth-century America.

The political changes brought about or highlighted range from the immediate to the long run. The rapid westward movement into the Mississippi and Missouri valleys after 1850 led to the troubles in Kansas, both for the Native Americans relocated there by the Jackson administration and for the white settlers, who helped start a civil war. Four million acres' worth of land warrants found their way to Kansas land offices, many during the period of strife between free-soilers and proslavery men. To the extent that land conflicts exacerbated an already existing tension between the two groups and that warrants made land acquisition simpler and cheaper than cash, it may be said that warrants were a small part of the coming of disunion.

At the same time that the crisis of the old republic became clear, the warrants and the new land policy represented an end to the old debates between Hamiltonians and Jeffersonians and between Whigs and Democrats about how the public lands should be used. The bounty land grants played a part in moving the United States from relying on the public lands as a revenue source for the government itself to viewing the public lands as a source for broader economic and even social development.

Another political consequence of the land grants to ex-soldiers is more subtle, but part of something more far-reaching. The key point here is that a group of older men formed a pressure group to demand pecuniary benefits from the federal government. Though couched in the language of old-fashioned republicanism, the veterans' lobby in fact represented the forerunner of the more modern organizational society in which individuals form groups to acquire privileges and awards from government. Moreover, the United Brethren of the War of 1812 raised the matter of grants and pensions to old soldiers as a political issue. Thus, the one-time pension grant of 1832 to Revolutionary War veterans became reinforced. Wars from then on would ultimately carry the obligation to provide in some way for the veterans. In this sense, there is a direct connection between the relation of the United Brethren and the Pension Bureau, and today's veterans' groups and the Department of Veterans' Affairs.

The land warrant grants represented something of a test of the willingness and ability of Americans to pick up and move west. The test was, of course, unfair, and the results should not surprise us today. Most elderly 1812 veterans or their heirs had little interest in a move to the frontier despite the federal invitation. Less obvious but also evident is the resistance of young Mexican War veterans to using their bounties as Senator Benton wished. Employing the bounty records as a source for study confirms the aggregate decision reached by a half-million people. The value of the warrants was its convertibility into cash. Veterans did not use their warrants to emigrate to public lands because typical moves were not long-distance ones from settled areas to the frontier, but tended to be short distance.

Were preemptors helped by the availability of land warrants, or, put another way, was the interest of the veteran of the War of 1812 at odds with that of the settler who wished to obtain new land? Contemporary politicians like Thomas Hart Benton and subsequent historians like George Stephenson have assumed that the warrants were used by speculators to the detriment of actual settlers—in other words, that warrants necessarily were weapons against the settlers. The warrants themselves, of course, were neutral instruments available for use by anyone with the money to purchase them. As a result of competitive pressures to minimize the spread between purchase and sale prices, the prices posted on warrants for sale, both in New York and by frontier agents, almost always remained at a discount from the government's cash price of $1.25 an acre.

Common sense suggests that any discount below this level could only help settlers in the eventual purchase of their land. It is hard to see any cost to the pioneer settler from the issue of a half-million warrants and also quite easy to see the benefit to him of cheaper land. Preemptors on land surveyed by the General Land Office, but not brought to auction or opened to private entry, did not face any competition from nonresident buyers. The preemptors could be hurt by a vengeful Buchanan who forced them to pay for their claims on short notice and at a time of tight credit and low commodity and land prices. Yet this same vulnerability would have held true in the absence of military bounty land grants. The warrants, in this case, were simply the preferred method of payment at the land office. Settlers on public lands open to private entry did face competition from absentee investors like the Cookes for the best land, but then Senator Brodhead's question of 1856 is pertinent: What is the difference between a land speculator paying $1.10 an acre for warrants or $1.25 an acre in cash? At most, the discount in price would allow the absentee investor to engross 12 percent more public land with warrants than without.

The advantages and drawbacks should be examined from more than just the perspective of the settler. It may be helpful to do the same for the other actors involved in the bounty land grants. The federal government actually bore the direct costs of the land warrant program in revenue forgone from land sales, in land unavailable for other giveaways, and in the cost of administering the bounty land grants. Of these three costs, the first was the greatest. Many, perhaps most, of the fifty million acres' worth of warrants located before the Homestead Act had passed would doubtless have been sold for cash had there been no bounty land grants. The maximum loss to the Treasury before the Civil War would be on the order of $62 million, assuming that all the warrant acres sold at the private entry price of $1.25 an acre charged by the General Land Office.

The second cost, the sixty million acres in warrants given away to the old soldiers, represented about 4 percent of the public domain from Ohio to the Pacific. The federal government was not at all constrained in further land giveaways by the warrants; quite the contrary, as argued above in chapter 2. The cost of administering the programs from Washington amounted to surprisingly little. For example, in 1855 Congress authorized spending about $190,000 for processing the Old Soldiers Act. The Pension Bureau received an extra $100,000 for new clerks and office supplies, while the General Land Office was granted an additional $90,000 for its expenses.[2]

Some settlers in the West did feel that they paid a price for the land warrant grants, specifically in the distortions in western land holdings. The existence of land warrants encouraged speculation in western lands and gave rise to the time-entry system of lending. Here, however, one must be careful not to project an ideal West free from land speculation in the absence of military bounty land warrants. Short of a homestead policy coupled with entail, nothing could have curbed Americans from buying and selling western land in the hope of making large gains. Also, usury prevailed on the western frontier during the land boom of the 1830s, and no doubt Iowa and Minnesota settlers would have paid 40–60 percent interest, whether or not warrant-based time-entry loans existed. Cyrus Woodman's use of time-entry loans before act of 1847 warrants became available is worth recalling on this score. The point to be emphasized is that political action in Washington could slow or fuel the natural urge of Americans to speculate in land. Bounty land grants, a clear case of interest-group politics, threw sixty million acres' worth of warrants on the market, and so may have encouraged some additional speculation, but they also effectively lowered land prices.

Paul Gates's early writings on the history of the public lands focused extensively on speculation and how this led to what he considered the un-American phenomenon of tenancy. More recent writers have pointed out that tenancy served to prepare young farmers for eventual landownership and farm proprietorship. Economists challenge the Gates view on the evils of land speculation. Writers like Edward Rastatter and Stanley Lebergott deny that "land monopoly" (the bugaboo of Thomas Hart Benton and George Julian) actually existed. Economists point out that no true monopoly could exist when the federal government made available tens of millions of acres at low cost. If the "old farmers" in Iowa Pitt Cooke described preferred to pay $3.00 an acre for good, privately owned land rather than find land unspoken for at $1.25 an acre, then such a situation would not be so much monopoly as convenience.[3]

The irony of "land monopoly" in historical perspective is that it could flourish only if the federal government withheld new land from the market. When the General Land Office put much of Iowa up for auction in the early 1850s, then nothing like land monopoly could emerge. But when the Pierce administration brought to auction very little land anywhere on the public domain in 1856, then speculators who had obtained land stood in a stronger position. The Buchanan administration, in this sense, did not aid speculation when it dumped thirty-six million new acres onto the market in 1858, 1859, and 1860. Buchanan's intent, of course, was to punish Kansas and Minnesota squatters for voting Republican, but the volume of new land also reduced the bargaining position of those with privately held frontier land to sell.[4]

In judging the bounty land programs, one must be exact and precise about which intended policy succeeded and which failed. Clearly, the grants did not induce even a sizable fraction of veterans to take up new homes on the public domain. Thus, as a public lands policy promoting veteran settlement in the West, the Mexican War–era bounty land grants failed. When evaluated from other perspectives, however, the land warrant policies worked quite well. The 1847 grant succeeded in both its immediate and its larger aims, namely, raising ten regiments of volunteers for the successful prosecution of the war against Mexico. The testimony of ordinary private soldiers in the Mexican War indicates that many joined volunteer units precisely to take advantage of the government's bounty.[5]

The 1850, 1852, and 1855 grants should be thought of as a one-time pension payment and evaluated accordingly. On the basis of price information, one must conclude that land warrants were an effective way for a land-rich, cash-stingy government to reward its veterans. If an average buying price of one dollar an acre is projected nationally over the course of the 1850s, then the aggregate money received just by the War of 1812 veterans amounted to about

$34 million, based on 211,800 warrantees receiving 160-acre warrants granted them under the acts of 1850 and 1855.[6]

The total federal budget in 1850 was only $39 million and, even under the Pierce administration, the 1855 budget only reached $59 million. Appropriating $34 million in one year was beyond federal powers. For example, the ten million warrants assigned in the year 1856 fetched better than dollar-an-acre prices in the market. Had that been a direct cash grant from the federal government, the amount would still have come close to 20 percent of the budget for the final year of the Pierce administration.

A program of issuing federal debt certificates of fixed maturity to veterans of the War of 1812 and the various Indian wars would have required a large expenditure. Simply to take care of the more than 210,000 surviving 1812 veterans and widows who benefited from the bounty land acts with a one-time cash grant of $200 (the face value of a full land warrant) would cost $42 million in principal and another $42 million in interest, assuming the government borrowed the money for twenty years at 5 percent interest. With the exception of the 1850 act and its ban on assignments for eighteen months, the land warrants worked efficiently to put cash speedily into the veterans' pockets. At a dollar an acre, a veteran would net $160, a tidy sum in the 1850s. One estimate of antebellum wages and salaries put the average annual earning of all American employees at about $363 in 1860. Thus, receipt and sale of a quarter-section land warrant provided nearly half of an average year's earnings. The actual net to the veteran might be higher or lower, according to the timing of assignments and market prices, and so the value of the warrants would obviously differ among individual warrantees.[7]

Another way of looking at the size and effect of the bounty land grants is to compare the extent of the bounty land grants to the nation's existing acreage in farmland. The 1850 Census measured the size of the nation's farmland at 294 million acres, most of which was in woodland. Only 113 million acres at mid-century were cleared for crop planting. The warrant grants loosed another sixty million acres of public land before the Civil War, of which fifty million were taken up by purchasers. Even if most of this new acreage was yet in woodland by 1860, it still represented about 17 percent of the nation's farmland. When the census takers came to do their job again in 1860, they counted 407 million acres of total farmland, both cropland and woodland. Up to half of the expansion of the decade may be traced to the use of land warrants.[8]

The view advanced here is that the Progressive school concentration on the speculative use of land warrants is of limited value to understanding the bounty land grants. Above all, the last three bounty land acts, of 1850, 1852, and 1855, must be understood as a pension program as well as a public lands policy. Congress closely guarded public money but happily bestowed land on the veterans as a measure of thanks. Not until 1871 did Congress vote cash pensions to the 1812 veterans, and not until 1878 did men who had served short terms in the war qualify. By that time, most War of 1812 veterans were dead.

How much additional settlement was directly produced by the effect of warrants lowering the cost of public lands? This question is not so simple as would first appear since it raises several related issues about the agricultural economy of the North in the years before the Civil War. General Land Office figures confirm the finding from the sample that about fifty million acres in land warrants were entered at western land offices between 1848 and 1860. Yet the 1850s constituted a decade of high demand for public land, so the problem is to estimate how much of the additional acreage alienated from federal to private hands came about solely as a result of the military bounty land warrant grants.

A number of historians and economists have studied the late antebellum demand for public land, and they have made different assumptions about the effect of land warrants. Arthur H. Cole's 1926 article, "Cyclical and Sectional Variations in the Sale of Public Lands, 1815–1860," argued for the existence of a regular eighteen-to-twenty-year cycle in the antebellum demand for public land. Cole saw peaks in demand in 1818, 1836, and 1856, years that, he noted, preceded financial panics and general downturns in the economy. This view put westward expansion, land speculation, and financial instability at the center of economic growth in the early republic. Nearly forty years after Cole's article appeared, Paul Gates offered a rebuttal to the thesis that increased land sales in the 1850s represented a distinctly cyclical phenomenon. His "Charts of Public Land Sales and Entries" insisted that the presence of the land warrant grants distorted sales figures so that they could not be a reliable guide to the public's demand for land. Moreover, Gates pointed to the role of the federal government's control of the supply of new public lands as a factor in overall sales. The large quantity of public lands brought to market by the Fillmore and Buchanan administrations, Gates reasoned, might better explain high sales than a theory invoking long swings of economic activity.[9]

An econometric study by Stephen Schoene of the antebellum land market takes issue with Gates's contention that the federal government's supply of new land offerings influenced demand. Schoene's work does not, however, return our state of knowledge to Cole's speculation-based cyclical theory because Schoene's careful estimates show the relative unimportance of land speculation. He concludes that land sales in the 1850s reflected "real economic forces rather than purely financial speculative motivations." Schoene's main interest lay in testing whether the demand for land reflected the expected present returns from agricultural commodity prices or the expected future returns from speculative purchases. His research established that rising agricultural prices after 1850 spurred an increased alienation of public land to private owners. His work recognized military bounty land warrants as a factor in the market, but his intent was not to test the importance of warrants in the overall demand for land.[10]

The problem of measuring the importance of warrants in the market remains to be solved. The historical implications of the answer may extend beyond economic history to one of the central facts of U.S. history: that the North won the Civil War, ended slavery, and preserved the Union. Stanley Lebergott's argument for the "Hinge of Fate," it will be recalled, implicitly assumed that much of the acreage located with warrants would have remained untouched in the absence of bounty land grants. In other words, the fifty million acres located with warrants before the firing on Fort Sumter in mainly free states and territories would have stayed unsettled. Such an amount of additional settlement would have produced a large number of Union Army soldiers and aided the northern cause. If, on the other hand, settlers had paid $1.25 an acre anyway for the same fifty million acres, then one might dismiss the warrants, though not the migration to the Old Northwest and trans-Mississippi, as part of the hinge of fate.

The importance of the warrants in attracting settlers westward must lie in the fact that discounted warrants made public lands available for less than $1.25 an acre. To some extent, this depends on how frontier land locators actually used the warrants. Those who borrowed on time-entry loans reaped no savings at all from warrant prices below $1.25 since lenders charged the full face value of $200. In economic terms, the questions to be answered are, first, how much money did purchasers save by using warrants, and second, did that savings draw forth more settlers? In other words, was the demand for public lands price elastic?[11]

Table 27 presents annual estimates of the savings to settlers from using land warrants. The price differential was substantial early and late in the 1850s but narrowed in the middle years, 1854

TABLE 27
Estimated Annual Savings to Users of Land Warrants

Year	*Average Price per Acre ($)*	*Estimated Savings ($)*
1847	1.20	138,050
1848	.92	1,378,410
1849	.85	1,894,000
1850	.93	1,143,680
1851	.94	1,333,310
1852	.92	1,568,820
1853	1.08	1,228,420
1854	1.22	313,170
1855	1.22	278,500
1856	1.16	1,225,306
1857	1.00	1,441,368
1858	.88	1,710,301
1859	.93	1,431,378
1860	.88	1,252,057
Total		16,336,770

NOTE: Average price calculated from a weighted average of the ratio of warrants sold at market prices (from table 3) and the number of acres sold by warrants and at the minimum price of $1.25 an acre, from Gates, "Charts and Entries," p. 28. Estimated savings remainder of $1.25 an acre minus average price per acre X total acres (from table 1).

through 1856. In a year like 1849, when the supply of relatively cheap warrants was abundant, the average cost of public land fell to about ninety cents an acre. Yet in 1855, when warrants were also plentiful, their relatively high price combined with heavy sales at $1.25 raised the average cost of newly offered public lands to $1.22 an acre, or near the ceiling price.

The trend of rising and then falling average public lands prices followed rather closely the price of wheat during the same years. This tends to confirm Schoene's finding that real factors (in other words, agricultural prices) led the demand for public land. In addition, and contrary to Gates, Schoene found that the volume of new land brought to market by the General Land Office was not an important factor in the demand for public lands. The years of greatest land transfer were precisely the years of the highest warrant prices. The explanation is that warrant prices moved in sympathy with wheat prices and not independently. Overall, the figures in table 27 show an estimate that the average land price for new public land throughout the decade was sufficiently below $1.25 that purchasers saved an estimated $16 million. This leads to the next question: Did the savings go toward additional public lands purchases or to other investment or consumption? Regression analysis suggests that the lowered price for public lands led to the purchase of only about an additional four million acres, mainly in the upper Mississippi Valley. It seems, therefore, that not much of the $16 million in savings caused by cheaper average land prices through the introduction of soldiers' warrants went toward further land acquisitions. The demand for land was relatively price inelastic.[12]

What do the findings here suggest for Lebergott's hinge of fate thesis? High grain prices and cheap warrants together helped the North's expansion after the Mexican War. However, it should be recalled that most people after 1800 moved in a more or less straight westward direction along lines of latitude. The people who moved into the upper Mississippi Valley before the Civil War came largely from parts of the United States loyal during the Civil War. Only the foreign-born component of the population lured to the upper Mississippi by cheap land and high grain prices was a net addition to this part of the North's population and economic resources. Thus, as Lebergott notes, it was the response of peasants to the Hungry Forties that swung the hinge toward the Union.[13]

Finally, study of the purchase and sale of warrants shows that, at least in the nineteenth century, markets worked. In the absence of federal assistance, veterans and heirs managed, with private help, to obtain their bounties, although it is unclear how many of the 200,000 denied warrants were wrongly denied. Those who did receive the bounty proved on the whole that they could successfully negotiate a sale in an impersonal market. The agents who bought and sold warrants earned their profits in a competitive market through careful buying and effective sales to frontier agents. In a very short time, the national network centered in New York established a distribution system that sent warrants to the areas willing to pay the most for them. In so doing, the brokers combined two sometimes contradictory traits, fairness and efficiency.

Appendix A
Sampling Methods and Sources

Research done on the sample of land warrants underlies much of the discussion in the text, so an explanation of the records used and the sampling approach may interest the reader. The warrants were in the files of the General Land Office for eighty years until accessioned by the National Archives as part of Record Group 49. They are primarily used by local officials seeking to trace land titles in public lands states. Some genealogists have tried using the warrants to trace ancestors, although, for this purpose, the warrant applications that are part of the records of the Department of Veterans' Affairs are more useful. The historian's immediate impression of the warrant files is their vastness. The most useful way to study them is by sampling. I drew as large a sample as possible, and, given the labor in transcribing information from warrants to note cards, then to coding sheets, and then to computerized data files, I set the sample size at .5 percent, or 2,761 warrants.

I drew four samples, one from each legislative act, using a random-numbers table. Since each act had several subsets of warrants based on differing acreage, I combined the serial numbers consecutively and treated the warrant samples only by act. For example, the Pension Bureau issued 88,274 warrants under the Ten Regiments Act of 1847, 80,689 for 160 acres and 7,585 for forty acres. I took the 160-acre lot as numbered, and for purposes of the sample, gave the forty-acre group serial numbers 80,690 through 88,274.

The samples are unweighted (except to reflect acreage, as discussed), and they are replacement random samples. With one procedural exception, each warrant had the same chance to be drawn as any other. The exception is in the treatment of missing warrants. I wanted to determine the extent of missing warrants from the National Archives, since my research in manuscript collections of land speculators turned up occasional assigned but unlocated land warrants. For the four legislative acts, about 4–6 percent of the warrants selected in my random-numbers drawing were missing from the National Archives. They may have been lost, burned, misplaced by the

General Land Office, or sitting never used in attics today. An unassigned warrant today, alas, has even less value than an 1850 act warrant before assignability; Congress set 1964 as the deadline for the final location of all outstanding land warrants. In the case of missing warrants for the 1847 act, I selected additional random numbers to fill the sample of 441. Once I had established that the files were nearly complete, I used a less stringent procedure for the other three samples and simply alternated and took the next numbered warrant up or down in serial sequence.

The accuracy of the sample in representing the universe of warrant recipients may be gauged in a few ways. The 1847 sample fits closely the profile of the Mexican War soldier's type of unit (volunteer or regular) and wartime death rates. The other samples closely follow certain aggregate tabulations of locations compiled by the General Land Office as shown in tables 12, 13, and 14.

The warrant files are arranged in Record Group 49 by legislative act, by acreage allotment, and finally by serial number, and, in volume, total well over one thousand cubic feet of records. The warrant files contain some or all of the following information: name of the veteran, relationship if an heir, service rank, military unit (usually down to the company level), war served in, issue date of the warrant, assignment(s), land office location forms, patents, preemption claims and proof statements, homestead commutation claims and proof statements, court papers, and General Land Office correspondence. I coded all the data susceptible to numerical counting. Copies of a tape containing the sample and codebook are available from the Inter-University Consortium for Political and Social Research, Ann Arbor, Michigan.

Appendix B
Measuring Land Warrant Prices

This appendix discusses how I arrived at the data to construct figure 9 and table 28. As discussed in chapter 5, contemporaries differed considerably in their estimate of how warrantees fared in selling their warrants for cash in the market. Until the early 1960s, most historians who dealt with the matter simply repeated the comments of particular politicians or editors. For example, Benjamin Hibbard quoted Horace Greeley's *New York Tribune* to the effect that warrant prices were low at one point, and extrapolated from this comment that warrant prices were always low. My research in newspapers has convinced me that editors, with one exception, knew little and cared little about warrant prices. The *Tribune* rarely carried news of the warrant market, though it regularly printed the advertisements of brokers seeking business. Neither did business periodicals such as *Hunt's Merchants Magazine* cover the prices offered in the warrant market. The only publication routinely to cover prices and news from the warrant market was John Thompson's *Bank Note and Commercial Reporter. Thompson's* was the forerunner to the present-day *American Banker* but, sadly, few issues of the paper have survived until the present. The Library of Congress owns the most complete set of *Thompson's Bank Note and Commercial Reporter,* but even its holdings cover only two complete years, 1857 and 1859, and a fragment from 1854. Other institutions reporting their holdings of *Thompson's* have only scattered issues throughout the 1850s; Baker Library at the Harvard Business School, for example, possesses less than a full year's run.

Since a continuous published price series no longer exists, the historian must consult manuscript records to reconstruct the change in prices. Natalie Disbrow, a graduate student at Cornell University in the 1950s, began a dissertation on land warrants under the supervision of Paul Gates. She never completed her work but did go so far as to construct a price index for buy and sell quotations from the manuscript records in the papers of William W. Corcoran at the Library of Congress. She generously shared this price series in draft form with other historians, and, for the first time, researchers could see the movement of prices throughout the 1850s. My

TABLE 28
*Median Monthly Warrant Prices Quoted to Warrantees, 1847–1861**
(In Cents per Acre)

Year	*Jan.*	*Feb.*	*Mar.*	*Apr.*	*May.*	*Jun.*	*Jul.*	*Aug.*	*Sep.*	*Oct.*	*Nov.*	*Dec.*
1847	0	0	0	0	94	0	0	81	88	81	81	78
1848	78	76	0	0	70	0	70	65	65	65	65	65
1849	65	65	69	67	72	78	86	84	78	75	75	73
1850	73	74	65	65	70	70	70	68	0	68	70	76
1851	0	70	0	72	72	72	0	69	0	0	71	77
1852	77	73	79	84	75	81	83	92	93	90	87	88
1853	93	105	105	104	105	107	112	115	114	113	113	113
1854	107	113	114	115	117	118	118	118	114	110	112	113
1855	113	100	101	105	108	111	111	112	111	109	110	100
1856	102	106	110	106	105	95	93	90	93	92	91	91
1857	88	100	97	97	93	89	91	88	86	65	78	78
1858	84	84	86	78	83	83	80	78	75	75	80	76
1859	83	82	84	80	82	82	86	90	82	78	60	70
1860	0	77	80	80	80	80	87	83	81	91	90	90
1861	75	65	55	55	55	55	53	55	66	65	70	70

SOURCE: Appendix B.
*Includes prices for legally assigned warrants only; quotes are average for all acreage denominations.

figure 9, and the more detailed table 28, show trends similar to Disbrow's research. Prices remained near the floor level from the Mexican War through the summer of 1852, and then rose and remained high until the panic of 1857 temporarily brought them down. In the years that followed the panic and up to the Civil War, prices remained in the eighty- to ninety-cents-an-acre range.

The object in creating a price series is twofold: (1) to get an idea of the prices warrantees received, and (2) to measure the discounted price of public land below the minimum price of $1.25 an acre. In the eastern market, the first is measured by "buy" quotes, and the second by "sell." The Corcoran quotes are the best surviving single source since they cover the entire period in question for buy and sell, but they do not always cover every month over the years. Corcoran had many other business and political interests beyond land warrant trading, and when I began this project, it seemed an open question to me whether his firm was entirely representative. I decided to seek out other manuscript sources against which to check the Disbrow price series. The result is that the prices reported here are from seven sources: (1) Alfred Churchill of upstate New York, 1848–50; (2)

John Martin of Richmond, Virginia, 1848–56; (3) Bradford & Harmon of Portland, 1852–59; (4) *Thompson's Bank Note and Commercial Reporter* of New York City, 1854, 1857, and 1859; (5) Le Huray & Co. of New York City, 1858–61, as preserved in the Jason Easton Papers; (6) Cyrus Woodman and his brothers George and Horatio in Mineral Point, New York, and Boston, respectively, from 1847 to 1855; and (7) James S. Easley and William Willingham of Halifax, Virginia, who dealt with numerous New York and Washington brokers from 1853 to 1859. The sources reflect my main interest in chapters 5 and 6, to determine the prices paid to warrantees, and so I only report a price series of buy quotes. As I maintain in chapter 6, the spread between buy and sell was narrower in New York City and wider in the provinces, but the reader interested in using this series to gauge the cost of public land in western states may simply add a nickel or so an acre to the buy series reported here, and have a reasonably accurate sell series.

Appendix C
Congressional Voting on Public Land Issues in the 33d Congress

Statistical testing can help determine whether attitudes fell on a continuum from solidly antibounty and prohomestead, on the one side, all the way to solidly antihomestead and probounty land on the other. Thus, the first task is to determine whether there were consistent attitudes among the legislators as a whole. If so, the next task is to explain the pattern of voting by testing the competing hypotheses of region, section, and party.

The bounty land issue reached the floor of each chamber only in the second session of the 33d Congress, and I took all five Senate and all three House votes on the bill as the first basis of study. I then selected an equal number of homestead bill votes from the previous session to match against the bounty land votes. When scaled, each chamber of Congress showed a pattern of dividing along a continuum of probounty land to prohomestead; in each case, the coefficient of reproducibility was .90, or at the minimum acceptable level to proceed with further statistical analysis.

The votes in the Senate include, in the order of the most probounty land to the most prohomestead: (1) Gwin motion to postpone the bounty land bill, December 1854, at page 150 of the *Senate Journal* for the 2d Session of the 33d Congress; (2) Brown amendment to bar aliens from benefits under the Homestead bill at page 1746 of the *Congressional Globe*, 33d Congress, 1st session; (3) Stuart motion to tighten eligibility rules on bounty lands at pages 94–95 of the *Senate Journal* (2d sess.); (4) final vote on the bounty land bill at 556 of the *Globe* (2d sess.); (5) Benjamin amendment to allow minors to qualify for homesteads at page 1748 of the *Globe* (1st sess.); (6) Dixon amendment to forbid aliens' heirs from homestead benefits unless they became citizens at page 1746 of the *Globe* (1st sess.); (7) Dodge amendment to limit locations to 320 contiguous acres using land warrants at pages 559–60 of the *Globe* (2d sess.); (8) Brodhead's motion to postpone the homestead bill at page 1662 of the *Globe* (1st sess.); (9) Brodhead's amendment to charge 50 cents an acre for homesteads at page 1792 of the *Globe* (1st sess.); and (10) Brodhead's amendment to ease rule of eligibility for relatives on bounty lands at page 78 of the *Journal* (2d sess.).

On the House side, again in descending order of bounty land sentiment, the votes include (1) final vote on the bounty land bill at page 1004 of the *Globe* (2d sess.); (2) Benton amendment prohibiting assignment of warrants at page 1003 of the *Globe* (2d sess.); (3) motion to commit the bill back to the Committee on Public Lands at page 1002 of the *Globe* (2d sess.); (4) amendment restricting the homestead bill to whites only at page 455 of the *Globe* (1st sess.); (5) final vote on the homestead bill at page 549 of the *Globe* (1st sess.); and (6) motion to table the homestead bill at page 455 of the *Globe* (1st sess.).

To analyze the votes in each chamber, I used the technique of discriminant analysis. I gave each legislator a numerical score between 0 and 1.0 with 0 representing a completely prohomestead and antibounty land attitude, and 1.0 as the reverse. I used this score as the dependent variable, and then applied the discriminant analysis to produce unstandardized coefficients that would indicate the statistical significance of the influence of section, region, and party.

For the purposes of the analysis in tables 29 and 30, section and region are defined in the following way: section—North (Maine, New Hampshire, Vermont, Massachusetts, Rhode Island, Connecticut, New York, New Jersey, Pennsylvania, Delaware, Ohio, Indiana, Illinois, Michigan, Wisconsin, Iowa, and California), South (Maryland, Virginia, North Carolina, South Carolina, Georgia, Florida, Alabama, Mississippi, Tennessee, Kentucky, Louisiana, Arkansas, Texas and Missouri); region—public lands states (Ohio, Indiana, Illinois, Michigan, Wisconsin, Florida, Alabama, Mississippi, Louisiana, Arkansas, Missouri, Iowa, and California), non–public lands states (Maine, New Hampshire, Vermont, Massachusetts, Rhode Island, Connecticut, New York, New Jersey, Pennsylvania, Delaware, Maryland, Virginia, North Carolina, South Carolina, Georgia, Tennessee, Kentucky, and Texas).

TABLE 29

Multivariate Analysis of Senate Voting on Public Land Issues, 33d Congress (Dependent Variable = Vote 1 to Vote 10; O = pro-homestead, 1 = pro bounty)

	Unstandardized Coefficients			
	Party	*Section*	*Region*	*Function* χ^2
Vote 1	1.01	−.43	1.85	
	(3.62)	(.57)	(6.88)*	8.62*
Vote 2	−1.70	2.13	.98	
	(18.83)*	(18.46)*	(.21)	24.62*
Vote 3	−.55	1.26	2.37	
	(.88)	(5.01)*	(12.37)*	13.84*
Vote 4	1.65	.70	.61	
	(3.72)	(.93)	(1.31)	6.27
Vote 5	−.60	2.05	.57	
	(2.78)	(7.03)*	(.30)	6.77
Vote 6	−.32	3.56	.21	
	(4.60)*	(21.71)*	(1.36)	13.57*
Vote 7	1.56	.13	1.92	
	(15.68)*	(.32)	(16.25)*	23.12*
Vote 8	−.16	−1.65	2.34	
	(.61)	(1.75)	(5.91)*	7.23
Vote 9	−1.05	.18	2.11	
	(1.50)	(1.28)	(6.55)*	8.88*
Vote 10	−.51	.34	2.13	
	(.09)	(.35)	(5.36)*	5.44

f-values in parentheses.
*Significant at the .05 level. Coefficient of reproducibility = .92
Note: See Appendix C for description of the scaling of Senate votes, and their sources. The three independent variables were coded as follows: Party = Democrats (0) Whigs (1); Section = 17 free states and Delaware (0) 14 slave states (1); Region = 14 public land states (0) 18 non-public land states (1). The votes that make up the dependent variable are Vote 1 = Gwin motion to postpone the bounty land bill; Vote 2 = Brown amendment to bar aliens from homesteading; Vote 3 = Stuart motion on eligibility for bounty lands; Vote 4 = final vote on bounty land bill; Vote 5 = Benjamin amendment to allow minors to qualify for homestead; Vote 6 = Dixon amendment restricting foreigners from homesteading; Vote 7 = Dodge amendment limiting warrant locations; Vote 8 = Brodhead motion to postpone homestead bill; Vote 9 = Brodhead amendment to charge 50 cents an acre for homesteads; Vote 10 = Brodhead amendment on eligibility for bounty lands.

TABLE 30
Multivariate Analysis of House Voting on Public Land Issues, 33d Congress (Dependent Variable = Vote 1 through Vote 6; 0 = pro-homestead, 1 = pro-bounty)

	Unstandardized Coefficients			
	Party	*Section*	*Region*	*Function* χ^2
Vote 1	.74	−.38	1.98	
	(1.40)	(.10)	(7.06)*	8.43
Vote 2	1.31	−.41	2.14	
	(12.58)*	(.94)	(27.13)*	40.08*
Vote 3	1.30	−.48	1.91	
	(12.44)*	(1.31)	(20.71)*	32.97*
Vote 4	−.68	2.54	−.75	
	(10.04)*	(76.88)*	(.14)	61.02*
Vote 5	−.91	1.57	.95	
	(4.02)*	(11.40)*	(3.59)*	16.17*
Vote 6	−.85	1.24	1.27	
	(4.84)*	(8.68)*	(7.13)*	16.93*

f-values in parentheses.
*Significant at the .05 level. Coefficient of reproducibility = .90
Note: See Appendix C for description of the scaling of House votes, and their sources. The three independent variables were coded as follows: Party = Democrats (0) Whigs (1); Section = 17 free states and Delaware (0) 14 slave states (1); Region = 14 public land states (0) 18 non-public land states (1). The votes that make up the dependent variable are Vote 1 = final vote on the bounty land bill; Vote 2 = Benton amendment prohibiting assignment of warrants; Vote 3 = Motion to recommit the bounty land bill to the Public Lands Committee; Vote 4 = amendment restricting the homestead bill to whites; Vote 5 = final vote on homestead; Vote 6 = motion to table the homestead bill.

Appendix D
The Demand for Public Land, 1847–1860

Economic theory suggests that the quantity of public lands demanded by Americans before the Civil War should have increased as warrants reduced the price and shifted the supply curve to the right. This prompts the question: How much additional public land was acquired because of warrants available at below the General Land Office price of $1.25 an acre for land open to entry after the auction? The answer may be estimated by a regression equation setting the volume of total acreage located (with warrants and cash sales at the minimum price of $1.25 an acre) as the dependent variable. Table 31 displays the results of the regression. The independent variables tested include the average price of land (from table 27), wheat prices lagged one year, the volume of warrant sales in the private market, the volume of land newly offered by the General Land Office, and a dummy variable for the Graduation Act.

The chief finding summarized from table 31 is that the wheat variable proved statistically significant, while the other predictor variables did not. The coefficient measuring the effect of wheat prices points to an outcome where, for each rise of one cent in the wholesale price of wheat, nearly 79,000 additional acres of public lands were located by private individuals the next year, either using warrants or paying cash at $1.25 an acre.

The Graduation Act's effect did not change the demand for new land in the North, in large part because graduating public land prices was a largely southern phenomenon, while most land sales at the full price and warrant locations came in free states and territories. As noted in chapter 4, relatively few land warrants were located in the South, and after graduation in 1854, few acres sold at the $1.25 minimum for new land.

No variable that represents the supply of land proved to be statistically significant. The number of acres that the General Land Office opened to auction and private sale each year at $1.25 an acre did not usefully predict the volume of cash and warrant locations. Despite much contemporary comment about speculators eager for new tracts to be opened by federal

TABLE 31
The Determinants of the Demand for Public Land, 1847–1860

Independent Variable	*B*	*T-Ratio*
Constant	−4,797.65	−.74
Wheat prices	78.93	2.14*
Average land price	−11.18	−.19
Volume of warrants sold	0.25	.77
New land offered by GLO	0.10	.50
Graduation Act	−2,804.87	−1.39

NOTE: Wheat prices in cents per bushel (lagged one year) from *Historical Statistics of the United States,* p. 209; average price of land in cents per acre from table 27; warrants sold in thousands of acres from table 20; new land offered in thousands of acres by the General Land Office from Gates, "Charts and Entries," p. 28; the Graduation Act dummy variable measures the effect of the 1854 Graduation Act on land sales at $1.25 and warrant locations (0 = before 1854, 1 = after). R^2 = .69; F = 3.52*; and DW = 1.56. Dependent variable = total acres located with cash sales at $1.25 and with warrants, in thousands of acres.
*Significant at the .05 level.

authorities, the calculations shown here suggest that the supply of new land did not drive land acquisitions, at least not in the short run. Similarly, the number of warrants assigned by veterans in the private market each year did not immediately lead to additional land acquisitions. In sum, increases in the supply of land, either from the General Land Office or from privately marketed land warrants, did not increase demand. This confirms Stephen Schoene's finding that demand reflected real factors, such as agricultural prices, not excessive supply or speculative purchasing.

If the regression coefficient for the average price of public land of −11.18 is multiplied by the remainder of $1.25 an acre minus the average land price of combined warrant and cash locations, the resulting estimate is that about 3.7 million excess acres were located because of cheaper land prices between 1848 and 1860. To give this figure some context, it should be noted from table 1 that, for the same years, the total acreage located with warrants and at the minimum cash price was over eighty-five million acres. Thus, a crude estimate is that, in a hypothetical world where new public land was available only at $1.25 an acre, then about eighty-one million acres would have been acquired by private buyers.

TABLE 32
The Effect of Wheat and Land Prices on the Quantity of Public Land Acquired, 1847–1860

Variable	*Adjusted Predictor*
Range of wheat prices:	
108–30	−2,201
131–65	−1,536
166–200	691
201–45	8,651
Range of average land prices:	
85–91	−163
92–98	779
99–105	1,124
106–12	3,335
113–19	−1,129
120–25	−6,387

NOTE: Grand mean = 6,091; R^2 = .72. Multiple classification analysis: dependent variable = total acres located with cash at $1.25 an acre or with warrants, in thousands.
SOURCE: Table 31.

The test of the average price of public lands variable requires a bit more comment. The coefficient of this variable was not statistically significant, but, as one would expect, it did show a negative sign. Why was the standard error of the regression coefficient so high? Table 32 extends the regression analysis with a multiple classification analysis that shows the expected effect of average land prices after controlling for lagged wheat prices, the sole significant variable in the regression equation.

Table 32 makes it clear that average land prices moved in a way consistent with expectations only at the upper end of the price spectrum. For example, average land prices at 122 cents an acre produced smaller acquisitions of public lands (controlling for wheat prices) than did lower prices. However, as the price rose from 85 to 112 cents an acre, the amount of land acquired also increased, contrary to expectations. This bulge in the middle and lower price ranges accounts for the high standard error in the regression coefficient and thus makes it risky to say flatly that a decrease of one cent in the average price of public land led to an extra eleven thousand acres alienated from federal to private control. Still, this will suffice as a very rough estimate of the effect of cheap warrants. Perhaps the lowered price of public land led to an additional acquisition by Americans of four million acres of public land, located mainly in the upper Mississippi Valley. It does not seem, however, that much of the $16 million in savings caused by cheaper average land prices through the introduction of soldiers' warrants went toward further land acquisitions. Thus the demand for land was relatively price inelastic.

Notes

INTRODUCTION

1. The starting point for nineteenth-century public lands history remains Thomas Donaldson's *The Public Domain: Its History with Statistics,* and its more interpretive update by Paul W. Gates, *History of Public Land Law Development.* Other classics of the field include Benjamin Hibbard, *History of the Public Land Policies,* esp. chaps. 8, 9; Roy Robbins, *Our Landed Heritage,* esp. chaps. 1–5; and the collected essays in parts I and II of Vernon Carstensen, *The Public Lands.* A modern analysis of the thinking behind government policy toward the public lands is Mary Young, "Congress Looks West: Liberal Ideology and Public Land Policy in the Nineteenth Century," in David Ellis, ed., *The Frontier in American Development.* A good recent treatment of the intricate political wrangling between 1819 and 1841 is Daniel Feller, *The Public Lands in Jacksonian Politics.* See also William N. Chambers, *Old Bullion Benton,* pp. 190–93; Robert Swierenga, *Pioneers and Profits: Land Speculation on the Iowa Frontier;* and Reginald Horsman, "Changing Images of the Public Domain," in *This Land of Ours.* Another useful introduction to the literature is Lawrence B. Lee, "American Public Land History," pp. 284–99. See also Marion Clawson and Burnell Held, *The Federal Lands: Their Use and Management,* chap. 1; John Opie, *The Law of the Land,* chaps. 1–4; Dyan Zaslowsky, *These American Lands,* and Bernard Shanks, *This Land Is Your Land.*

2. Many books seek to describe the political and economic philosophy of the Democrats and Whigs, starting with Marvin Meyers, *The Jacksonian Persuasion;* Daniel Walker Howe, *The Political Culture of the American Whigs;* Bray Hammond, *Banks and Politics from the Revolution to the Civil War;* Robert Remini, *Andrew Jackson and the Course of American Democracy.*

3. See Frederick Jackson Turner, *The Frontier in American History* and *The United States, 1830–1850.* See also George Stephenson, *Political History of the Public Lands;* Raynor G. Wellington, *The Political and Sectional Influence of the Public Lands;* Helene S. Zahler, *Eastern Workingmen and National Land Policy.* Stephen Hahn and Jonathan Prude's introduction to the essays in *The Countryside in the Age of Capitalist Development* gives a clear account of how the "new rural history" differs from Turner's earlier work. Stated briefly: Turner saw a timeless story of three centuries of continuous renewal on the frontier, with the 1890s marking the end of American history as he

knew it. The authors in the Hahn and Prude volume seek to understand the nature of change in rural America brought on by the spread of markets and prices, particularly how old traditions fell before or resisted exchange relations. The work presented here takes an issue of great interest to the Turnerians—public land policy before the Homestead Act—and reinterprets it from a more modern standpoint.

4. Donaldson, *The Public Lands,* pp. 234–37; Gates, *History of Public Land Law Development,* chap. 11; Swierenga, *Pioneers and Profits,* chap. 6.

5. Alice Hanson Jones, *Wealth of a Nation to Be,* establishes the high standard of living at the close of the colonial period. The importance of the growth of population and land cultivation for the colonial economy is made clear by several recent writers, including Edwin Perkins, *The Economy of Colonial America,* chap. 3; the same theme is sounded for the early republic in Stanley Lebergott, *The Americans: An Economic Record,* chaps. 8, 9. See also William N. Parker, "From Northwest to Midwest," in David Klingaman and Richard Vedder, eds., *Essays on Nineteenth Century Economic History.* A recent view emphasizes the importance of foreign trade alongside domestic sources of growth. See John McCusker and Russell Menard, *The Economy of British America, 1607–1789,* esp. chaps. 3, 4.

6. Stanley Lebergott makes this argument with more specific reference to the South in "The Demand for Land: The United States, 1820–1860," pp. 181–212.

7. See "Statement of the Quantity of Land Likely to Be Claimed under the Bounty Land Bill Recently Passed by the Senate and Now Pending before the House," *House Executive Document* no. 79, 33d Cong., 2d sess., Serial Set 788. For other guesswork on the potential number of veterans entitled to warrants, see "Annual Report of the Commissioner of Pensions, 1850," *Senate Executive Document* no. 1, 31st Cong., 2d sess., Serial Set 587, p. 179.

8. The records are briefly described in Harry Yoshpe and Philip Brower, comps., *Preliminary Inventory of the Land-Entry Papers of the General Land Office.* See also Richard Maxwell, "The Public Land Records of the Federal Government," in *National Archives Reference Information Paper no. 57* (Washington, D.C.: National Archives, 1963); Robert W. Harrison, "Public Land Records of the Federal Government," in Carstenson, *The Public Lands,* pp. 487–98. Appendix A describes the method I used to draw the sample.

9. See Turner's *The United States, 1830–1850* for a reflection of his more mature views; Ray A. Billington's *Frederick Jackson Turner: Teacher, Historian, Scholar* gives a helpful explanation of Turner's two ideas concerning the frontier and sectionalism; see also Reginald Horsman, *The Frontier in the Formative Era.* Gates's *History of Public Land Law Development* summarizes much of his life's work up to 1968; Allan Bogue's *From Prairie to Cornbelt* may well be marked as the beginning of a newer history of the public lands; indeed, as part of the new rural history discussed in n. 3 above.

CHAPTER 1

1. Lewis C. Gray, *History of Agriculture in the Southern United States to 1860,* pp. 386–92; Jerry O'Callaghan, "The War Veteran and the Public Lands," pp. 163–68; Rudolph Freund, "Military Bounty Lands and the Origins of the Public Domain," pp. 8–18. See also Gates, *History of Public Land Law Development,* chap. 3; Donaldson, *The Public Domain,* pp. 232–33; Everett Dick, *The Lure of the Land,* chap. 1. For a comparative view, see Isser Woloch, *The French Veteran from the Revolution to the Restoration,* chap. 8.

2. Gates, *History of Public Land Law Development*, pp. 251–57; Benjamin Hibbard, *History of the Public Land Policies*, pp. 116–18; William Hutchinson, "The Bounty Lands of the American Revolution."

3. Act of Feb. 16, 1812, 2 *Statutes*, pp. 671; Gates, *History of Public Land Law Development*, pp. 262–63.

4. J. C. A. Stagg, "Enlisted Men in the United States Army, 1812–1815," pp. 615–45, gives an estimate of the number of men in the regular forces and some detail about their background. On the bounty land grants under the act of 1812, see Theodore Carlson's *The Illinois Military Tract*, pp. 7–9, 24–28; Malcolm Rohrbough, *The Land Office Business*, pp. 68–78, discusses how the General Land Office managed the bounty land program from Washington.

5. Hibbard, *History of the Public Land Policies*, pp. 119–20; O'Callaghan, "The War Veteran and the Public Lands"; Edgar B. Wesley, *Guarding the Frontier: A Study of Frontier Defense from 1815 to 1825*, chap. 9.

6. The recruiting story of the Mexican War is passed over in most histories of the conflict in favor of the more exciting events in Congress and on the battlefield; see, e.g., Singletary, *The Mexican War*. A recent treatment of the Mexican War argues for the importance of volunteers in the war but seems to reflect the sentiment of the summer of 1846 rather than the winter of 1847. See Robert Johannsen, *To the Halls of Montezuma*, pp. 63–66. The law's terms are spelled out in the act of Feb. 11, 1847, in Peters, *Statutes at Large*, 9:125.

7. The debates may be followed in the *Congressional Globe*, 29th Cong., 2d sess., pp. 172–73, 195, 215–16, 285–86, 294. Benton had nothing to say about the debate on the Ten Regiments Bill in his two-volume memoirs *Thirty-Years View*. Instead, he dwelt at length on the politics of the Wilmot Proviso, introduced in the House just a week after President Polk signed the bounty-granting bill.

8. Cyrus Woodman to Horatio Woodman, March 14, 1849, in the Cyrus Woodman Papers, Outgoing Correspondence Letterbooks, vol. 171, State Historical Society of Wisconsin. I have made extensive use of the manuscript volumes 169 through 191 that are in chronological sequence from 1847 through 1855, when the firm of Washburn and Woodman dissolved. Subsequent citations will list only the dates of the correspondence. For a description of the collection, see Larry Gara, *Westernized Yankee: The Story of Cyrus Woodman*, pp. 239–43.

9. The Senate debated the operation of warrant provisions under the Ten Regiments Act as the army demobilized, with Democratic and Whig views apparent. See *Congressional Globe*, 30th Cong., 2d sess., pp. 263–65; see also Feller, *The Public Lands in Jacksonian Politics*, pp. 194–98.

10. 80,689 veterans or heirs received 160-acre warrants and 7,585 90-day volunteers in the Mexican War received forty-acre warrants. See "Annual Report of the Commissioner of the General Land Office, 1906," in *House Executive Document* no. 5, 59th Cong., 2d sess., Serial Set no. 5117; on agriculture before the Civil War, see Paul Gates, *The Farmer's Age*, and Clarence Danhof, *Change in Northern Agriculture, 1820–1870*; and Jeremy Atack and Fred Bateman, *To Their Own Soil*.

11. The events in Congress from 1848 to 1850 are carefully recounted in David Potter, *The Impending Crisis*, chaps. 3–5; in Holman Hamilton, *Prologue to Conflict*; and in James McPherson, *Battle Cry of Freedom*, chaps. 2, 3.

12. *Congressional Globe*, 30th Cong., 1st sess., p. 1691.

13. Committee of Officers of the War of 1812, *Bounty Lands to the Surviving Officers of the Late War of Second Independence*; Committee of New York Association of Officers of the War of 1812, *To Officers of the Late War*. For the Pittsburgh officers' plea, see *Senate*

Miscellaneous Document 182, 25th Cong., 2d sess., Serial Set 316. Freund argues that the exclusion of officers under the bounty land acts of the War of 1812 reflected a lingering fear of an officer corps organized like the unrepublican Society of the Cincinnati; see Freund, "Military Bounty Lands and the Origin of the Public Domain."

14. This figure represents the considered estimate of the leading historian both of the War of 1812 and of the state militias. See John Mahon, *History of the Militia and the National Guard,* p. 77. See also "Officers and Soldiers of Militia, Late War, etc." *House Documents* 20 (24th Cong., 2d sess.), Serial 302 gives a total of 471,622 soldiers, noncommissioned officers, and commissioned officers, but the report acknowledges some double counting; Marvin A. Kreidberg and Merton G. Henry place the exact number of militiamen who served in the war at 458,463 (p. 50 of their work).

15. "Soldiers of the Late War," Petition referred to the Senate Committee on Military Affairs, 31st Cong., Accession Senate 31A-H11, Record Group 46, National Archives (hereafter petitions cited only by accession number).

16. "Soldiers of 1812 of Van Buren, Arkansas," Accession Sen. 31A-H11. For state legislatures' resolutions on bounty lands after the Ten Regiments Act, see *Senate Miscellaneous Document* 101, 30th Cong., 1st sess., Serial Set 511; *Senate Miscellaneous Document* 93, 31st Cong., 1st sess., Serial Set 563; *Senate Miscellaneous Document* 16, 31st Cong., 2d sess., Serial Set 592; and *Senate Report* 297, 30th Cong., 2d sess., Serial Set 535. For a listing of the petitions of 1849 and 1850, see *House Report* 246, 31st Cong., 1st sess., Serial Set 584.

17. "Meeting of the Officers and Soldiers of the Last War with England," Accession Sen. 31A-H11, and "Officers of the War of 1812," Accession Sen. 31A-H11.

18. For a discussion of the samples used in this study, see App. A; see also GLO Report, 1906; act of Sept. 28, 1850, 9 *Statutes*, 520–21.

19. *Congressional Globe,* 30th Cong., 2d sess., p. 265; Gates, *History of Public Land Law Development,* pp. 273–75.

20. *Congressional Globe,* 31st Cong., 1st sess., p. 2000; see also the account of the incident given by an involved eyewitness, Illinois Congressman John Wentworth, in *Congressional Globe Appendix,* 31st Cong., 2d sess., pp. 35–36. At the last hour of the first session of that Congress, Wentworth rose in the house to demand dramatically that the speaker order the floor be cleared of the many land warrant brokers so that business could be conducted. See *Congressional Globe,* 31st Cong., 1st sess., p. 2074; Swierenga, *Pioneers and Profits,* pp. 132–35, offers a thorough analysis of the congressional maneuvering surrounding the end of the session in September 1850.

21. Act of March 21, 1852, 10, *Statutes at Large,* pp. 3–4; Gates, *History of Public Land Law Development,* pp. 274–275; *New York Tribune,* Feb. 5, 1852.

22. "GLO Report, 1906"; Act of March 3, 1855, 10 *Statutes at Large,* pp. 701–2; Gates, *History of Public Land Law Development,* p. 276.

23. Lebergott, *The Americans,* p. 227.

CHAPTER 2

1. Early twentieth-century writing on the history of the public lands tended to stress 1862 as the great divide in policy between cash sales and free land; e.g., James DuBois and Gertrude Mathews, *Galusha Grow: Father of the Homestead Act.* Paul Gates, "The Homestead Act in an Incongruous Land System," pp. 652–81, marked one break in this interpretation by arguing for a series of conflicting land policies after 1862. In *Our Landed Heritage,* Roy Robbins pushed the argument back to the 1840s

and 1850s by sketching a northern industrial-agrarian "alliance" that prompted ample grants of land to corporations and settlers, see esp. chaps. 10, 11.

2. Hibbard, *History of the Public Land Policies*, chap. 9; Gates, *History of Public Land Law Development*, chap. 10; Robbins, *Our Landed Heritage*, chap. 5; Dick, *The Lure of the Land*, chap. 5. The general 1841 preemption law is found at 5 *Statutes*, pp. 453–58.

3. *Historical Statistics*, p. 1106; Barry Poulson, *Economic History of the United States*, chap. 16.

4. See "Report on the Subject of a Change in the Management and Disposal of the Public Lands," *Senate Report* 167, 31st Cong., 1st sess., reprinted in *New American State Papers: Public Lands*, 3:475. For the changing view, see also Millard Fillmore's 1850 message to Congress in James Richardson, ed., *Messages and Papers of the Presidents* 5:83–84; Thurlow Weed, *Memoirs of Thurlow Weed* 2:441–42.

5. *Congressional Globe*, 33d Cong., 1st sess., p. 560; Holman Hamilton, *Prologue to Conflict*, pp. 119–21; 9 *Statutes at Large*, 466–67; Gates, *History of Public Land Law Development*, pp. 357–59.

6. A durable discussion of the evolution of the proprietorship idea to the give-away philosophy is in Lewis Haney, *Congressional History of Railroads*, vol. 1, esp. chap. 19. For a discussion of the earlier land policy, see Jerry Van Atta, "Securing the West: Public Lands and Political Economy in America, 1784 to 1841"; Feller, *Public Lands in Jacksonian Politics*, chap. 8. See also the debate in *Congressional Globe*, 33d Cong., 1st sess., pp. 456, 519.

7. Richardson, *Messages and Papers of the Presidents*, 6:2780–89; 7:3142. See also Dorothy Clarke Wilson, *Stranger and Traveler: The Story of Dorothea Dix, American Reformer*, pp. 169–81, 205–12.

8. *Congressional Globe*, 30th Cong., 1st sess., p. 547.

9. Ibid., p. 733.

10. Holt, *The Political Crisis of the 1850s*, esp. chap. 5. William Gienapp attributes the collapse of the Second Party System to the sudden urgency of issues related to foreign immigration such as temperance legislation and residency requirements; see his *Origins of the Republican Party*, chap. 2. Gienapp, too, sees no role for the land issue in the collapse of parties in 1853 and 1854 or in the new party system that emerged in 1856.

11. Johanssen, *To the Halls of Montezuma*, chap. 5; Russell F. Weigley, *History of the United States Army*, chap. 7; Mahon, *History of the Militia and National Guard*, pp. 67–77; Edward Coffman, *The Old Army*, p. 40; Lawrence Cress, *Citizens in Arms: The Army and the Militia in American Society to the War of 1812*.

12. Charles Jared Ingersoll, *History of the War of 1812;* Charles J. Peterson, *Military Heroes of the War of 1812*, is similar in outlook to Ingersoll. The standard modern account is John Mahon, *The War of 1812*.

13. Studying citizen petitions to Congress or to state legislatures is one way to gauge nineteenth-century public opinion. Examples of the scholarly use of petitions include Jean Wilburn, *Biddle's Bank;* Norman Risjord, *Chesapeake Politics, 1781–1800*, pp. 208–15.

14. See the petitions sent to the House Committee on Public Lands and Military Affairs, 33d Cong., Accessions HR33A-G20, HR33-G20.5, HR33A-G20.10, and HR33A-H1.7, Record Group 233, National Archives.

15. A historian of postbellum patriotic societies observed of the local 1812 veterans' corps that "These movements seem to have arisen simultaneously but independently, as if in obedience to the law of multiple invention." Wallace Davies, *Patriotism on Parade*, p. 23. The honor of primacy is less important than the useful details that

can be learned about these local corps. See "A Brief History of the Society of the War of 1812," in the August 12, 1894, *Philadelphia Inquirer.* See also "Original List of Members of the Baltimore Defenders Association," in Baltimore Defenders' Association Papers, Maryland Historical Society.

16. James B. Murray and Nicholas Haight to William H. Seward, Sept. 10, 1850, Seward Papers, University of Rochester. Murray was chairman of the group and Haight its secretary and dominant force in the 1850s; Nicholas Haight, *Argument and Appeal in Behalf of the Remains of the Revolutionary Patriots;* Peter J. Van Pelt, *A Discourse Delivered by Request of the Survivors of the Veteran Corps in the War of 1812.* See also the small collection of the Papers of the Veterans Corps of the City of New York, New-York Historical Society, and the *New York Times,* April 7, 1855, for details of its warrant brokerage operation.

17. *Proceedings of the National Convention of the Soldiers of the War of 1812,* p. 27. See also *Proceedings of a Meeting in the City of Philadelphia of the Soldiers of the War of 1812 Praying a Modification of the Bounty Land Law, Dec. 12, 1853,* in Accession Sen. 33A-H19. Proceedings or summaries of resolutions passed at these various local meetings are found in Accessions Sen. 33A-H19, and HR 33A-G20.5 and HR 33A-H.1.7.

18. *Proceedings of a Meeting of Officers and Soldiers Held at Poughkeepsie, Jan. 24, 1854,* Accession HR33A-G20.5.

19. See Land Patents File, Vassar Papers, Adriance Public Library, Poughkeepsie, New York, for the land warrant purchases and western land speculations of Matthew Vassar, Jr. The Vassar Papers at Thompson Memorial Library, Vassar College, contain details of Maison's dealings with the Vassar family. A lifelong Democrat, Maison abandoned his party and sought, along with other New York veterans' leaders, to boost William H. Seward for president in 1856. See Maison to Seward, May 19, 1856, Seward Papers.

20. *Proceedings of the Soldiers of the War of 1812, June 20–21, 1854,* p. 16. See James Bogert Papers, folders 1 and 2, New York State Archives. For the role of the New York Central in making the Syracuse convention possible, see Davies, *Patriotism on Parade,* p. 23.

21. *Proceedings of the National Convention, 1854,* pp. 10–11, 27. See also the newspaper reports throughout the convention period in mid-January in the *Philadelphia North American* and the *Public Ledger and Daily Transcript.*

22. *Proceedings of the Convention of the United Brethren of the War of 1812,* pp. 10–11. Most metropolitan newspapers covered the Washington convention, concentrating on the resolutions passed and the Pennsylvania Avenue march. Good accounts are in the *Washington National Intelligencer,* Jan. 9, 10, 1855; Thurlow Weed's *Albany Evening Journal,* Jan. 8, 9, 1855; and the *Baltimore Sun,* Jan. 10, 1855. One of the best sets of articles was published by the *Richmond Dispatch.* Its correspondent at the convention was so diligent that he compiled his own count of the Virginia delegates in attendance. The *Dispatch* tallied 158 delegates from the Old Dominion and listed the home city or county for each. The recording secretary for the convention counted only eighty-seven Virginians. Convention leaders at both the Philadelphia and Washington conventions claimed attendance of over one thousand delegates, yet the official proceedings list more modest numbers. For President Pierce's role in the convention and politics of the Old Soldiers bill, see Roy F. Nichols, *Franklin Pierce: Young Hickory of the Granite Hills,* p. 379.

23. *Proceedings of the United Brethren,* pp. 14–15, 20; *Richmond Dispatch,* Jan. 15, 1855; James M. Porter to William Darlington, Jan. 23, 1855, Connaroe Collection, Historical Society of Pennsylvania.

24. *Albany Evening Journal*, Jan. 9, 1855; General John McCalla to Samuel Williams, Jan. 12, 1855, McCalla Papers, Duke University. The active congressmen included four elected as Whigs in 1852: Middleswarth and Dick from Pennsylvania, Simmons of New York, and Farley of Maine. Six Democratic congressmen attended: Pratt of Connecticut, Straub of Pennsylvania, Bocock and Faulkner from Virginia, and Barry and Barksdale of Mississippi. See *Proceedings of the United Brethren*, pp. 1–9. Prominent among the retired congressmen was Pennsylvania's Andrew "Tariff Andy" Stewart. The three Pennsylvania delegates who served on the state Democratic Central Committee were John Horn of Philadelphia, Levi Reynolds of Delaware County, and John Clarke of Westmoreland County. See John F. Coleman, *Disruption of the Pennsylvania Democracy, 1848–1860*, App. C. See also Lawrence Taliaferro Papers, Minnesota Historical Society (microfilm), 1854 Correspondence with Joel Sutherland, reel 4.

25. Charles Sutherland, *A Memoir of the Life and Services of Joel Barlow Sutherland;* Joel Sutherland, *A Congressional Manual;* Clifford P. Reynolds, ed., *Biographical Directory of the American Congress, 1774–1961*, p. 1677; Dumas Malone, ed., *Dictionary of American Biography* (hereafter cited as *DAB*), s.v. "Sutherland, Joel"; "Memoirs of a Senator from Pennsylvania: Jonathan Roberts," *Pennsylvania Magazine of History and Biography* 62 (1938): 518; Henry Cohen, *Business and Politics in America from the Age of Jackson to the Civil War;* Robert Remini, *Andrew Jackson and the Course of American Democracy*, p. 177. See also Joel B. Sutherland file, University Archives, University of Pennsylvania. Sutherland also acted as a claims agent for Philadelphians having difficulty securing land warrants from the Pension Bureau. See Aaron Dayton to Sutherland, June 23, 1853, Aaron Dayton Collection, Historical Society of Pennsylvania. Charles Sutherland, the grandson of Colonel Sutherland, was himself surgeon-general of the army and later, in the 1890s, "historian" of the Society of the War of 1812. See the "Scrapbook" in the Papers of the Society of the War of 1812, Maryland Historical Society.

26. *DAB*, s.v. "Florence, Thomas." For Florence's interest in western land operations, see Miscellaneous Letters of the General Land Office, vol. 44, Nov. 21, 1855, in Record Group 49, Records of the Bureau of Land Management, National Archives. Mark Summers, *The Plundering Generation: Corruption and the Crisis of the Union, 1849–1861*, pp. 255–56, puts Florence squarely in the camp of the corrupt "Buchaneer" politicians by the end of the decade.

27. In addition to his other roles, Porter was president of the Lehigh Valley Railroad. *DAB*, s.v. "Porter, James M." James M. Porter, *Eulogium upon James Knox Polk;* Philip S. Klein, *President James Buchanan: A Biography;* Pamela Herr's *Jessie Benton Frémont*, pp. 79–81, discusses the feud between Porter and Thomas Hart Benton.

28. On Brodhead, see Coleman, *Disruption of the Pennsylvania Democracy*, pp. 41–43, 52; Uzal W. Condit, *History of Easton Pennsylvania from the Earliest Times to the Present;* Erwin S. Bradley, *Simon Cameron, Lincoln's Secretary of War*, pp. 85–87; *Portrait and Biographical Record of Lehigh, Northumberland and Carbon Counties, Pennsylvania;* Klein, *President James Buchanan*, p. 265; *Biographical Directory of the American Congress*, p. 601; and see the letters from Brodhead to lumber dealer and Democratic party official Lewis Coryell, of March 12, 1856, and Dec. 6, 1856, in Lewis Coryell Papers, Historical Society of Pennsylvania.

29. On Leslie Combs, *DAB*, s.v. "Combs, Leslie"; *Substance of an Address Made by General Leslie Combs to the Public Debt Committee of the Texas Legislature* (Austin: J. W. Hampton, 1854); also, see Leslie Combs to Daniel Ullman, Dec. 8, 12, 1854, Ullman Papers, New-York Historical Society; Hamilton, *Prologue to Conflict*, pp. 124–28;

Summers, *The Plundering Generation,* 219–21. On McCalla's role, see his letters to Sutherland Jan. 18, Feb. 6, 1854; to General John Van Renssalaer June 21, 1855; to William D. Bell, Dec. 20, 1854; to William Thomas, Nov. 20, 1854; and to Medard Couture, Jan. 6, 1854, in McCalla Papers, Duke University.

30. Joel Silbey in his *Partisan Imperative: The Dynamics of American Politics before the Civil War,* chap. 9, argues for a simultaneous sharpening of sectional, ethnocultural, and partisan conflict in the 1850s. Allan Bogue et al., "Members of the House of Representatives and the Processes of Modernization, 1789–1960," *Journal of American History* 63 (1976): 275–302 (esp. table 6) show that, although the median term in Congress decreased in the 1850s, one cause of that decline in the tenure of officeholding was electoral defeat, especially in 1854. See also Summers, *The Plundering Generation,* chap. 5, which argues that the public domain was a particular favorite for congressional logrolling.

31. *Proceedings of the United Brethren,* p. 17; *Proceedings of the National Convention, 1854,* p. 27; *Proceedings of the Soldiers, 1854,* pp. 6, 9.

32. *Proceedings of the United Brethren,* p. 20. The national convention also pressed for a monument in Independence Square to commemorate War of 1812 veterans; Mark L. Berger, *The Revolution in New York Party Systems, 1840–1860,* p. 95; General Nye's son later became a U.S. Senator from Nevada; see Eric Foner, *Reconstruction, 1863–1877,* p. 497; *Biographical Directory of the American Congress,* p. 1397.

33. *Proceedings of the Soldiers, 1854,* pp. 8–9.

34. The republicanism of the veterans reflects in part their motives and in part the more diffuse nature of republican ideology in the Jacksonian and Civil War eras. See Eric Foner, *Free Soil, Free Labor, Free Men: The Ideology of the Republican Party before the Civil War,* chaps. 1, 2; Holt, *The Political Crisis of the 1850s,* chap. 2; Robert Remini, *Andrew Jackson and the Course of American Freedom,* pp. 29–35; Gienapp, *Origins of the Republican Party,* pp. 353–65; William Barney, *The Passage of the Republic,* chaps. 4, 5.

35. *Congressional Globe,* 31st Cong., 1st sess., p. 2074; and 31st Cong., 2d sess., pp. 35–36, 299–303. James Seldon to John K. Martin, Dec. 20, 1850, John K. Martin Papers, Duke University. See also Petitions and Memorials, Accession Sen. 33A-H19.

36. Petitions and Memorials, Accession HR 33A-G20.1, *Congressional Globe,* 31st Cong., 1st sess., p. 2000.

37. Petitions and Memorials, Accession Sen. 33A-H19; Robbins, *Our Landed Heritage,* pp. 156–57; *Congressional Globe,* 31st Cong., 1st sess., p. 2000.

38. Petitions and Memorials, Accession Sen. 33A-H19.

39. *Congressional Globe,* 33d Cong., 2d sess., p. 151. James Young's *The Washington Community, 1800–1828,* chap. 5, argues that, until after 1828, congressmen rarely showed any great attachment to remaining in office. Expedience was less common in the early republic, in part because of the unpleasant setting of the new capital and in part because of the strength of the republican tradition of selfless public service.

40. *Proceedings of the United Brethren,* pp. 16–20.

41. James M. Porter to Stephen Brooks, Aug. 28, 1855, Connaroe Collection, Historical Society of Pennsylvania. See also the Constitution and Minute Book, 1857–61, of the Pittsburgh Association of the Soldiers of the War of 1812, Historical Society of Western Pennsylvania.

42. *Proceedings of the Soldiers, 1854,* p. 8.

43. Leslie Combs to John Van Renssalaer, July 4, 1855, in Benjamin Chew Howard Papers, Maryland Historical Society. See also *Proceedings of the Soldiers of the War of 1812* (1857) for Van Renssalaer's response.

44. Kirk H. Porter, ed., *National Party Platforms, 1840–1960,* pp. 16–18, 20–21; Richardson, ed., *Messages and Papers of the Presidents,* 5:216; Zahler, *Eastern Workingmen,* chap. 9.

45. Stephenson, *Political History of the Public Lands,* p. 118.

46. Robbins, *Our Landed Heritage,* chaps. 10, 11.

47. Roy F. Nichols, *The Disruption of the American Democracy;* for a recent example, see Gienapp, *Origins of the Republican Party.*

48. See App. C for an extended discussion of the method followed for scaling and analyzing the roll call votes on public lands questions in the 33d Congress.

49. For Butler's speech, see *Congressional Globe,* 33d Cong., 2d sess., p. 151; Robbins, *Our Landed Heritage,* chap. 11.

50. For the role of party in late antebellum America, see Holt, *The Political Crisis of the 1850s,* chap. 1; Gienapp, *Origins of the Republican Party,* Introduction; Gerald Wolff, "The Kansas-Nebraska Bill and Congressional Voting Behavior in the Thirty-third Congress"; Joel Silbey, *The Partisan Imperative;* and Thomas B. Alexander, *Sectional Stress and Party Strength: A Study of Roll-Call Voting Patterns in the United States House of Representatives.* The analysis offered here confirms the brief treatment of the issue given by Mark Stegmaier in his "U.S. Senate in the Sectional Crisis, 1848–1861: Roll-Call Voting Analysis," pp. 244–51, esp. table 7-3.

51. A simple bivariate regression, with the number of beneficiaries as the dependent variable and a state's position as either a public lands state or a nonpublic lands state as the independent variable, produces a Pearson correlation coefficient between nonpublic lands states and beneficiaries at .43, significant at the .05 level.

52. Gates, "The Homestead Law in an Incongruous Land System"; Allan Bogue, *The Earnest Men: Republicans in the Civil War Senate,* pp. 89–91; Dick, *The Lure of the Land,* pp. 350–66.

53. Gates, *Fifty Million Acres,* pp. 77–94; Robbins, *Our Landed Heritage,* pp. 169–82; Basler, *Collected Works of Abraham Lincoln,* 4:271.

54. Minutes of the April 22, 1861, meeting of the Pittsburgh Association of the Soldiers of the War of 1812, Association Papers, Western Pennsylvania Historical Society.

55. Gienapp, *Origins of the Republican Party,* pp. 190–92; Glyndon Van Deusen, *William Henry Seward,* pp. 151–52; Major L. Wilson, *Space, Time, and Freedom,* chap. 9; see also the speech of Seward on slavery in the territories in *Congressional Globe,* 33d Cong., 1st sess., App., pp. 150–55.

56. This, in brief, is the argument of Roy Nichols, first in his *Disruption of American Democracy* and more fully developed in his *Blueprints for Leviathan: American Style,* esp. chaps. 5–7. One historian argues that the Civil War itself brings forth a desire on the part of some for the Organizational Society. See Laura Censer Turner's Introduction to *The Papers of Frederick Law Olmstead,* vol. 4. Phillip Paludan's *"A People's Contest": The Union and Civil War* makes a similar argument. The irony here is that the Civil War in part weakened the old republican ideology despite the fact that both North and South believed they were engaged in its defense. Mark Summers argues that the political corruption and scandals of the 1850s helped contribute decisively to the general political crisis of the Republic. See his *Plundering Generation,* esp. chaps. 15–17.

CHAPTER 3

1. The U.S. free population amounted to about twenty million people in 1850, and, given a median household size of 5.55, the number of households nationwide

was about 3.6 million, hence the estimate of one in nine households receiving a warrant. Calculated from Commerce Department, *Historical Statistics of the United States, from Colonial Times to 1970*, pp. 8, 41; Peter McClelland and Richard Zeckhauser, *Demographic Dimensions of the Early Republic*, table A-2.

2. Pension Bureau, *Digest of Decisions and Opinions Relating to Pensions and Bounty Land*, pp. 60–89; George W. Raff, *Manual of Pensions, Bounty and Pay*, pp. 314–18, lists war service that qualified veterans for bounty land warrants. See also above, tables 4, 5, and 6.

3. Pension Bureau, *Digest of Decisions*, pp. 69–70. There is an irony here: several of the leaders and political supporters of the veterans' lobby later turned Confederate, notably Thomas Bocock of Virginia, who served fourteen years in Congress before becoming Speaker of the Confederate House from 1862 to 1865. *DAB*, s.v. "Bocock, Thomas."

4. In general, see Gustavus Weber, *The Bureau of Pensions: Its History, Activities, and Organization*; William Glasson, *Federal Military Pensions in the United States*; William P. Dillingham, *Federal Aid to Veterans, 1917–1941*; David R. B. Ross, *Preparing for Ulysses: Politics and Veterans during World War II*; Sar Levitan and Karen Cleary, *Old Wars Remain Unfinished: The Veterans' Benefits System*, chap. 1; Richard Severo and Lewis Milford, *The Wages of War.*

5. Letter from James L. Edwards, March 3, 1847, in "Pension Laws Now in Force, and Executive Regulations Touching the Subject, Applying as Laws on Bounty Lands," in *Senate Miscellaneous Document* 54, 30th Cong., 2d sess., Serial Set 533.

6. Cyrus Woodman to Sen. Henry Dodge, Dec. 20, 1850, Jan. 4, 1851, and Jan. 15, 1851, in Cyrus Woodman Papers; the Ten Regiments Act forbade sitting congressmen from receiving bounty land warrants, but an act of August 4, 1854, at 10 *Statutes at Large*, 576, repealed that prohibition.

7. Pension Bureau, *Instructions and Forms to Be Observed by Persons Applying to the Pension Office for Bounty Land under the Act of March 3, 1855*, p. 6; "Annual Report of the Commissioner of Pensions, 1855" in *Senate Executive Document* 1, 34th Cong., 1st sess., Serial Set 810, contains a long, detailed description of the mechanics of administering the application for and issue of 1855 series warrants; see also Cyrus Woodman to Enoch Chapman, April 5, 1851, in Cyrus Woodman Papers.

8. "Annual Report of the Commissioner of Pensions, 1853," in *Senate Executive Document* 1, 33d Cong., 1st sess., Serial Set 690, p. 492. Waldo referred to the masses of 1850 warrant applications suspended for insufficient proof (about 55,000 for that act alone) and singled out bounty land applications by Indian allies of the United States as especially troublesome. See also Raff, *Manual of Pensions, Bounty and Pay*, chap. 23.

9. The land warrant sample offers a good opportunity to study illiteracy before the first census, in 1840, directly asked Americans whether they could read or write. For a good discussion of the definitions of literacy and illiteracy, see Harvey Graff, *The Literacy Myth: Literacy and Social Structure in the Nineteenth Century City*, chap. 1, and his *Legacies of Literacy*; see also Lawrence Cremin, *American Education: The National Experience*; Lee Soltow and Edward Stevens, *The Rise of Literacy and the Common School in the United States.* I take up this issue in "Information Policy in an Era of Illiteracy: The U.S. Pension Bureau before the Civil War," pp. 287–94.

10. Pension Bureau, *Instructions and Forms to be Observed*, p. 6; John Dann, *The Revolution Remembered: Eyewitness Accounts of the American Revolution*; Constance B. Schulz, "Revolutionary War Pension Applications: An Overview," in Timothy Walch,

ed., *Our Family, Our Town: Essays on Family and Local History Sources in the National Archives*, pp. 36–45.

11. See Waldo's estimate in *Congressional Globe*, 31st Cong., 1st sess., p. 1280.

12. As part of a separate research project on the geographical mobility of the veteran population of the War of 1812, I have tracked most of the sample in state militia records. My interest was in those men who received warrants, that is, those who served at least fourteen days, but an impressionistic reading of the muster rolls indicates a vast number of units served less than two weeks. The researcher who wishes to track War of 1812 militiamen should consult the following publications: North Carolina Adjutant General, *Muster Rolls of the Soldiers of the War of 1812;* Chandler E. Potter, *The Military History of New Hampshire;* Pennsylvania Adjutant General, *Muster Rolls of the Pennsylvania Volunteers in the War of 1812–14;* Anderson C. Quisenberry, *Kentucky in the War of 1812;* Connecticut Adjutant General, *Record of Service of Connecticut Men in the War of the Revolution and War of 1812;* Gardner W. Pearson, *Records of the Massachusetts Volunteer Militia Called out by the Governor,* a volume that includes the Maine militia; William M. Marine, *The British Invasion of Maryland:* New Jersey Adjutant General, *Records of Officers and Men of New Jersey in Wars, 1791–1815;* Vermont Adjutant and Inspector General, *Roster of Soldiers in the War of 1812–14;* Ohio Adjutant General, *Roster of Ohio Soldiers in the War of 1812;* Hugh Hastings, *Military Minutes of the New York Council of Appointments;* and Virginia State Auditor, *Muster Rolls of those Entitled to Bounty Land under the Act of September 28, 1850.* For the militiamen of Tennessee, South Carolina, and Georgia, I consulted the manuscript muster rolls in those states' archives. For the few scattered militiamen in the sample from Rhode Island, Delaware, the District of Columbia, Mississippi, Louisiana, Indiana, Illinois, and other territories, I consulted the Pension Bureau's incomplete application files to determine the county of origin. A rough estimate would put sixty to sixty-five as the life expectancy of a twenty-year-old male in the early nineteenth century, and as 1791 was the median birth year for a subsample of War of 1812 warrantees, one would expect about half of the 1812 militiamen to be alive still by the time Congress voted bounty land benefits. See *Historical Statistics*, p. 56; McClelland and Zeckhauser, *Demographic Dimensions of the Early Republic*, pp. 54–68.

13. Interior Department circular, Oct. 3, 1850, in Galt Papers, folder 85, box 8, Manuscripts Division, College of William and Mary; on Stuart's career, see Alexander H. H. Stuart Faculty/Alumni File, College Archives, College of William and Mary; *Biographical Directory of the American Congress*, p. 1671.

14. It is difficult to calculate the number of warrant applicants who had agents aid them; many warrantees in all four samples used an agent's address as the return address for the warrant, while others entrusted the warrants' delivery to their congressmen.

15. *Trow's New York City Directory* for 1854 through 1856 identifies a dozen warrant dealers as notaries public. About another ten were bankers; the occupations of the rest are unidentified. See Gates, *History of Public Land Law Development*, pp. 275–77.

16. *New York Herald*, March 9, 1855. The last three words in the Pitkin & Dixey advertisement refer to the office at 75 Nassau Street, New York, not the Pension Bureau in Washington. See also the ads in the *New York Herald* and *New York Tribune* March 5, 9, 19, April 7, and May 20, 1855.

17. *Richmond Dispatch*, March 10, 1855. Among other cities featuring competing warrant brokers, as measured by newspaper ads, were Louisville and New Orleans.

See the March 1855 issues of the *Louisville Daily Democrat* and the *New Orleans Daily Picayune*.

18. Freeman Bradford and Zebulon Harmon ran a claims business in Portland, Maine, from the mid-1840s until the early 1890s. During the 1850s, the firm specialized in land warrants, especially the problems Aroostook War veterans had obtaining their bounties. The firm's business in the first half of 1853 shows some features of the application process. Bradford & Harmon helped forty individuals apply to Washington for warrants between February and May, and ultimately, thirty-two received their bounties. The median waiting time between the mailing of an application and the issuing of a warrant was forty-two days. Calculated from information in Zebulon Harmon Papers, vol. 53, Maine Historical Society.

19. "Pension Report, 1855," p. 582. A number of warrant counterfeiters, swindlers, and cheats managed to escape punishment in the 1850s because the basic 1823 statute on fraud was judged not to cover warrants. Finally, in 1859, Congress passed a law making warrant forgery or alteration a federal crime with a sentence of three to ten years' hard labor on conviction (Act of Feb. 5, 1859, 11 *Statutes*, 381).

20. The antebellum Treasury comprised the secretary, two comptrollers' offices, six auditors' offices, and auxiliary services such as the Coast Guard. The Third Auditor checked all War Department quartermaster and pension affairs, while the Fourth Auditor had similar responsibility for the navy. See Leonard D. White, *The Jacksonians: A Study in Administrative History,* pp. 166–69; see also Norman O. Forness, "The Origins and Early History of the United States Department of the Interior"; and "Report on Reorganization of the Treasury Department," *House Report* 81, 25th Cong., 2d sess., Serial Set 333.

21. The 1847 series warrant applicants rarely had to wait more than sixty days to receive their due. See "Annual Report of the Commissioner of Pensions, 1849," *Senate Executive Document* 1, 31st Cong., 1st sess., Serial Set 550, p. 1177; *Niles Weekly Register,* Dec. 18, 1847, p. 248.

22. "Annual Report of the Commissioner of Pensions, 1847," *Senate Executive Document* 1, 30th Cong., 1st sess., Serial Set 503, p. 725.

23. White, *The Jacksonians,* pp. 348, 507–8, 536; Forness, "Origins and Early History," pp. 134–35.

24. "Pension Report, 1850," p. 179; Cadwallader Washburn to Cyrus Woodman, July 9, 1850; Cadwallader Washburn to F. W. Risque, Oct. 3, 1850; and Cyrus Woodman to C. Rockwell, March 21, 1851, in the Cyrus Woodman Papers.

25. See "Annual Report of the Commissioner of Pensions, 1851," *Senate Executive Document* 1, 32d Cong., 1st sess., Serial Set 613; *Congressional Globe,* 32d Cong., 2d sess. Appendix, pp. 82–83.

26. Cyrus Woodman to Cadwallader Washburn, Dec. 15, 1850, and Feb. 14, 1851, in Cyrus Woodman Papers; *Congressional Globe,* 30th Cong., 2d sess., pp. 793–94.

27. *House Report* 4, 31st Cong., 2d sess., Serial Set 606, p. 27 (hereafter referred to as *Robinson Report*).

28. On Stuart's tenure as secretary of the interior, see Forness, "Origins and Early History," chap. 4; *DAB,* s.v. "Stuart, Alexander H. H."; Alexander Stuart to Fanny Stuart, items 69 and 70, Alexander H. H. Stuart Papers, Virginia Historical Society; *Thompson's,* Oct. 1, 1848.

29. On the subject of the clerks in the Pension Bureau, see *Congressional Globe,* 31st Cong., 2d sess., p. 280; *Robinson Report,* p. 7. Much of the trouble in the fall and winter of 1850 was the turnover among Interior Department officeholders caused by Millard Fillmore's patronage war on the Whigs allied with William H. Seward and

Thurlow Weed. The commissioner of pensions and his chief clerk were fired in the late fall of 1850, just as the volume of warrant applications and inquiries began to expand.

30. *Robinson Report*, pp. 4–5.

31. William E. Griffis, *Millard Fillmore: Constructive Statesman, Defender of the Constitution, President of the United States*, pp. 56–59; Glyndon G. Van Deusen, *William Henry Seward*, pp. 133–34, and his *Thurlow Weed, Wizard of the Lobby*, p. 184; *Congressional Globe*, 31st Cong., 2d sess., p. 175.

32. *Congressional Globe*, 31st Cong., 2d sess., pp. 281, 669; Oberly, "Information Policy in an Era of Illiteracy," pp. 287–94.

33. "Pension Report, 1855," p. 587; "Annual Report of the Commissioner of Pensions, 1856," *Senate Executive Document* 1, 34th Cong., 3d sess., Serial Set 875, p. 838; "Annual Report of the Commissioner of Pensions, 1857," *Senate Executive Document* no. 11, 35th Cong., 1st sess., Serial Set 919, p. 703; Circular of J. W. Clarke, Nov. 24, 1855 in James S. Easley Papers, Incoming Correspondence, box 61, reel 299, University of Virginia, microfilm copy at University of Iowa; *Congressional Globe*, 34th Cong., 1st sess., pp. 375, 924.

34. "Pension Report, 1856," p. 838; Act of 1856, 11 *Statutes at Large*, p. 1; *Congressional Globe*, 34th Cong., 1st sess., pp. 375, 921–28, 980–88; P. M. Henry to James S. Easley, Oct. 20, 1855, and Oct. 30, 1855, in the James S. Easley Papers, Incoming Correspondence, box 61, reel 299.

35. See the letter from the commissioner of pensions to Isaac Hodsdon, Jan. 11, 1853 on the question of civil posses, in the Isaac Hodsdon Papers, State Historical Society of Wisconsin, Madison; Raff, *Manual of Pensions, Bounty and Pay*, p. 316.

36. The Hodsdon Papers also contain Circulars A, K, N, 2, 4, 6, and 10 of the Pension Bureau between 1851 and 1858; Oberly, "Information Policy in an Era of Illiteracy," p. 290.

37. "Report of the Commissioner of the General Land Office, 1848," *House Executive Document* 12, 30th Cong., 2d sess., Serial 539, p. 257. The basic laws governing fees given to registers and receivers for land warrant work are set forth in Act of May 17, 1848, 9 *Statutes at Large*, p. 231; and Act of March 22, 1852, 10 *Statutes at Large*, pp. 3–4. See also GLO, *Forms and Regulations for the Assignment of Land Warrants and Locations*.

38. A separate sample of 600 settlers in Wisconsin and Minnesota who sought land under the 1841 Preemption Act shows that 10 percent encountered land claims conflicts, usually because of ineptitude on the part of GLO field personnel. A very common problem involved individuals filing claims on land in the sixteenth section of a township, which was reserved for education purposes. GLO employees frequently neglected to point this out to settlers. See chap. 6, n. 39, for details on the sample.

39. Cyrus Woodman to Richard S. Young, Sept. 15, 1847; act of Feb. 11, 1847, at 9 *Statutes at Large*, 124–25; and act of March 22, 1852, at 10 *Statutes at Large*, 3; GLO Commissioner Thomas Hendricks to James S. Easley, Nov. 28, 1855, in James S. Easley Papers, box 61, reel 299. Swierenga, *Pioneers and Profits*, pp. 138–41. See chap. 6 below for a fuller discussion of the uses of warrants by preemptors. Because of the changing GLO treatment, none of the act of 1850 sample warrants were used to pay for a "proved-up" preemption claim, but 22 percent of the sample of act of 1855 warrants were used for this purpose.

40. The warrant samples for the four acts show a modest number of cancellations, only some of them on account of fraud. Table 11 shows the rate of cancellations

per act. It should be noted that not all cancellations were due to fraud; frequently, the files of canceled warrants give no indication of wrongdoing. For the 1847 act alone, see Pension Bureau, *List of Military Bounty Land Warrants Cancelled and Suspended*.

41. Act of 1847, 61,656, 160 acres, Record Group 49, Records of the Bureau of Land Management, National Archives.

42. Act of 1847, 62,684, 160 acres.

43. Act of 1847, 72,457, 160 acres.

44. See act of 1850, 58,964, forty acres, for an example of a theft case.

45. The Alger case may be followed in warrant file act of 1855, 75, 199, 120 acres. Alger had distinguished himself in the Civil War at Gettysburg and later became governor of Michigan. See *National Cyclopedia of American Biography*, s.v. "Alger, R. A.," for details on his business career in Michigan land and timber.

46. Circular of Cyrus Woodman in Jason Easton Papers, Box 34, Minnesota Historical Society; Cyrus Woodman to George Woodman, July 26, 1852, Cyrus Woodman Papers. See also the comment on the costs of forged warrants to brokers in *Thompson's Bank Note and Commercial Reporter*, Jan. 3, 1857. For a discussion of the role of *Thompson's* and other banking periodicals, see William H. Dillistin, *Bank-Note Reporters and Counterfeit Detectors, 1826–1866*.

47. *Thompson's*, Aug. 21, 1854.

48. U.S. v. Bickford, Federal Cases, 29, Case 14,591; U.S. v. Myler, Federal Cases, 27, Case 15,849; U.S. v. Irwin, Federal Cases, 26, Case 15,445. See also n. 19 above. *House Executive Document* 95, 34th Cong., 1st sess., Serial Set 858.

49. One veteran who successfully appealed and received a full 160 acres has his story detailed in warrant file act of 1850, 56,201, forty acres.

50. *Instructions and Forms to be Observed*, p. 6.

CHAPTER 4

1. See "Annual Report of the Commissioner of the General Land Office, 1858," in *Senate Executive Document* 1, 35th Cong., 2d sess., p. 490, Serial Set 974 (hereafter, GLO Report).

2. Gates, *History of Public Land Law Development*, pp. 274–76. The estimates presented in table 13 may be compared with a different set of estimates done by Stephen W. Schoene, "The Economics of U.S. Public Land Policy Prior to 1860," tables 3–5. Schoene's work is based on regression analysis alone and is somewhat flawed by his assumption that the supply of warrants was constant rather than episodic as shown in tables 12 and 14. In addition, his equation does not account for the timing of General Land Office offerings within particular land districts of states and territories. See also Carstensen, *The Public Lands*, App. A, pp. 499–504, for a list of the opening dates of district land offices.

3. For a discussion of the workings of the warrants within the land system in Iowa, see Swierenga, *Pioneers and Profits*, chap. 6; for a different perspective on the land system in Minnesota, see Hildegard B. Johnson, *Order upon the Land*, chap. 6; R. Carlyle Buler, *The Old Northwest: Pioneer Period, 1815–1840*, chap. 3.

4. Lebergott, *The Americans*, chap. 19; Robbins, *Our Landed Heritage*, chap. 11; Lewis C. Gray, *History of Agriculture in the Southern United States to 1860*, 2:638–40.

5. Speech of George Julian in *Congressional Globe*, 40th Cong., 2d sess., pp. 2096–97. See also George Julian, *Political Recollections, 1840 to 1872*.

6. For the workings of the public lands system in Texas, see Thomas Miller, *The Public Lands of Texas, 1519–1970,* esp. part 2. Miller does not give a breakdown by decade of public lands disposition in Texas. Instead, he gives income receipts from the sale of Texas public lands. When grants and sales are included, Texas disposed of about 150 million acres of its public lands between 1836 and 1890. See chap. 15, App. 1.

7. Gates, *History of Public Land Law Development,* pp. 188, 194; 10 *Statutes at Large,* p. 574; for the pattern of sales under the first four years of the Graduation Act, see GLO Report, 1858, in *New American State Papers: Public Lands,* 8:487.

8. Paul David, "The Mechanization of Reaping in the Antebellum Midwest," in Robert W. Fogel and Stanley L. Engerman, *The Reinterpretation of American Economic History;* Atack and Bateman, *To Their Own Soil,* pp. 6–10. See also App. D below.

9. See Rohrbough, *The Trans-Appalachian Frontier,* chap. 8; Feller, *Public Lands in Jacksonian Politics,* chaps. 1, 2; Susan Gray, "Family, Land, and Credit: Yankee Communities on the Michigan Frontier, 1830–1860."

10. An χ^2 value was not statistically significant when the choice of locating or selling was measured against such variables as militia rank, literacy, or age. The test did prove statistically significant at the .05 level ($\chi^2 = 13.50$, df = 2) when widows and minor children were compared with surviving veterans. The biggest difference came in testing the choice to sell or locate on the basis of residence in a public lands state or a non–public lands state. Here the test showed statistically significant results at the .01 level ($\chi^2 = 31.18$, df = 1).

11. The breakdown by type of home state in the acts of 1847 and 1850s among sample sellers and locators is as follows: act of 1847—91 percent of public lands states warrantees sold, while 99 percent of non–public lands states warrantees sold; act of 1850—83 percent of public lands states warrantees sold their warrants, while 97 percent of non–public lands states warrantees did so; act of 1852—86 percent of public lands states warrantees sold, while all the sample from non–public lands states sold; act of 1855—95 percent of public lands states warrantees sold, 99 percent of non–public lands states warrant recipients also sold. The story of Peter McGlew may be followed in act of 1847, 73,373, 160 acres, Records of the Bureau of Land Management, Record Group 49, National Archives.

12. William Cook's land warrant is act of 1852, 1,484, forty acres.

13. In the sample 1847 series of Mexican War warrants, e.g., all sixteen Alabamians and both Floridians sold their warrants for cash.

14. Maury to Alfred Churchill, April 4, 1849, in Alfred Churchill Papers, file 1, Regional History Collection, Cornell University; Lewis Warner to John K. Martin, May 3, 1852, in John K. Martin Papers, Virginia State Library.

15. Swierenga, *Pioneers and Profits,* p. 112.

16. Cyrus Woodman to George Emery, March 16, 1851, in Cyrus Woodman Papers.

17. Cyrus Woodman to Rogers and Woodman, April 16, 1851; Cyrus Woodman to Henry Baretto, March 22, 1851; Cadwallader Washburn to Isaac Hodsdon, March 19, 1851, in Cyrus Woodman Papers.

18. John K. Martin was a Richmond Post Office employee until he was sacked by the Whigs in 1849 because of his Democratic loyalties. He then went into the claims business, sponsored by his patron, Judge (and Congressman) John Caskie of Richmond. The Martin Papers at the Virginia State Library are valuable both because they reveal the business details of warrant brokering and because they show the intimate political connections so useful in making a success of the business. Regret-

tably, the repository does not participate in the National Union Catalog of Manuscript Collections, so the Martin Papers are inaccessible to the unknowing. For calculations and quotes about warrants fees and prices, see boxes 27 and 28, which contain Martin's account books as well as those of Richmond dealer William Fulton between 1848 and 1853. Box 34 contains about five hundred empty envelopes from the Pension Bureau that once contained warrants or correspondence about warrant cases. Martin carefully wrote on each envelope the applicant's name and the price and fees charged if he bought the warrant.

19. William Fulton Land Warrant Account Book in box 28, Martin Papers. Chap. 5 below discusses in detail the market prices for legally assigned land warrants.

20. Martin to James Richardson, Jan. 2, 1852, box 34, Martin Papers.

21. Cyrus Woodman to George Paine, April 17, 1851; Cyrus Woodman to Cadwallader Washburn, April 5, 1852, in Cyrus Woodman Papers.

22. See *Opinion of Hon. Rufus Choate in Relation to Land Warrants;* Cyrus Woodman to Elihu B. Washburne, April 16, 1852; Cyrus Woodman to Cadwallader Washburn, April 5, 1852, Cyrus Woodman Papers; Gara, *Westernized Yankee*, p. 97.

23. Roy Basler, ed., *Collected Works of Abraham Lincoln*, 2:319. After March 1852, when Congress made assignment legal, power of attorney arrangements were made by only a few veterans. Half of the sample warrants issued under the act of 1850 were promptly sold within five months of the lifting of the ban, representing some six million acres worth of warrants.

24. See the Madison County Probate Court papers filed in act of 1847, 77,213, 160 acres.

25. The Swartwood family story is in act of 1850, 60,843, forty acres.

26. No one dismissed the officers of the United Brethren, as Herbert Hoover once did the Bonus Army leaders, as "professional money-hunting veterans . . . [who] drew large salaries for one major mission that was to bring home annually some 'bacon' from the Treasury." See Hoover, *Memoirs: The Cabinet and the Presidency, 1920–1933*, pp. 285–86. See also Davies, *Patriotism on Parade;* Glasson, *Federal Military Pensions*, pp. 10, 135.

27. The conversion of 1850 prices to 1990 ones rests on the Bureau of Labor Statistics' Consumer Price Index. With 1967 as the base year equal to 100, 1855 equals 28, while 1987 is at 340. See *Historical Statistics*, series 136; *Statistical Abstract for 1989*, p. 469. For the national average in 1850 of property holding of adult white males, see Lee Soltow, *Men and Wealth in the United States, 1850–1870*, pp. 88–91.

28. A statistical outlier or distortion explains why the mean real estate owned by veterans and widows was similar, $1,557 for men and $1,416 for women. The lone wealthy woman in the sample of widows skewed the sample so that the figure for widows was not far below that of men. A recent contribution to the literature on economic inequality between the sexes is Claudia Goldin and Kenneth Sokoloff, "Women, Children and Industrialization in the Early Republic," pp. 741–74.

29. For a discussion of the militia and the role it played in the early republic, see above, chap. 3, n. 12; Mahon, *History of the Militia and National Guard*, chaps. 3, 4; Marcus Cunliffe, *Soldiers and Civilians: the Martial Spirit in America, 1775–1860*, chap. 6; Lawrence Cress, *Citizens in Arms*, chap. 7. For the estimate of the white male population of military age, see *Historical Statistics*, p. 16. I take up the question of the representativeness of the sample and related issues in my "Westward Who? Estimates of Native White Migration after the War of 1812," pp. 431–40.

30. Speech of Richard Brodhead, *Congressional Globe*, 34th Cong., 1st sess., p. 924.

CHAPTER 5

1. *Congressional Globe*, 29th Cong., 2d sess., p. 173; Gates, *History of Public Land Law Development*, p. 271.

2. *Congressional Globe Appendix*, 30th Cong., 1st sess., p. 1687; Hibbard, *History of Public Land Policies*, pp. 273–74.

3. *Congressional Globe*, 33d Cong., 2d sess., p. 155.

4. Figure 9 and table 28 may be contrasted with the price series, compiled by Natalie Disbrow, summarized in Swierenga, *Pioneers and Profits*, table 6.1, and Gates, *History of Public Land Law Development*, p. 278. Sources used for calculating the price series summarized in figure 9 are more fully discussed in Appendix B. The prices discussed here represent those posted mainly for first-time sales. Warrant users in the West, particularly those buying on credit, tended to pay higher prices than those listed in market quotations. The turnover, or "velocity," of warrants is difficult to gauge. Most experienced warrant dealers did not enter a name on the assignment blank after a transaction, waiting instead until the warrant was finally ready for location at a land office. Nonetheless, some less knowledgeable traders attached as many as six warrant assignment sheets to the warrant, giving some indication of turnover. At some cash-scarce western land offices, the warrants served sometimes as a form of money, an American type of assignat. See Swierenga, *Pioneers and Profits*, chap. 6.

5. On the subject of the "reservation price," see Robert Jost, "An Entrepreneurial Study of a Frontier Financier," p. 9; Swierenga, *Pioneers and Profits*, p. 142.

6. Cyrus Woodman to Jacob B. Merrick, July 14, 1847, Aug. 12, 1847, and Sept. 22, 1847; Cyrus Woodman to John S. Hayward, Aug. 10, 1847, in Cyrus Woodman Papers; Gara, *Westernized Yankee*, pp. 79, 94–96.

7. *Congressional Globe*, 31st Cong., 1st sess., p. 1691.

8. See the editor's introduction in Paul W. Gates, *The Fruits of Land Speculation;* Swierenga, *Pioneers and Profits*, pp. 143–46.

9. Cyrus Woodman to Jacob B. Merrick, Aug. 18, 1847, in Cyrus Woodman Papers; circular of Clark & Co. (n.d. [1856]) in James S. Easley Papers, Incoming Correspondence, box 61, reel 299.

10. Original italics from *Thompson's Banknote and Commercial Reporter*, May 23, 1857; *Thompson's*, Oct. 10, 24, 1857.

11. Paul Gates, "Southern Investments in Northern Lands before the Civil War," p. 97; Gates, "The Struggle for Land and the Irrepressible Conflict," pp. 248–71; but see also *Thompson's*, Aug. 20, 1859, where the editor dismissed the effects of a homestead bill on warrant prices: "You, Mr. Speculator, have some money (and there may be more like you), and it makes but little difference whether you pay 90 or 100 cents per acre, for you are sure to get land that will, in less than ten years, be worth 1000 cents per acre."

12. *Congressional Globe*, 29th Cong., 2d sess., p. 295.

13. See *Thompson's*, Aug. 21, 1854; see also Arthur H. Cole, "Cyclical and Sectional Variations in the Sale of Public Lands, 1815–1860," pp. 41–53; Gates, "Charts of Public Land Sales and Entries," pp. 22–28.

14. Cyrus Woodman to Jacob B. Merrick, Oct. 4, 1847; Cyrus Woodman to Rogers & Woodman, Dec. 15, 1847, and Feb. 16, 1848; Cyrus Woodman to John Webb, Dec. 30, 1847, and Feb. 16, 1848, in Cyrus Woodman Papers.

15. Pitt Cooke to Jay Cooke, Nov. 15, 1855, in Jay Cooke Papers, Historical Society of Pennsylvania.

16. See General Land Office, *Laws and Regulations Respecting the Assignment, Location, and Use of Bounty-Land Warrants;* Gates, *History of Public Land Law Development,* pp. 244–45. Cyrus Woodman to GLO Commissioner Richard Young, Aug. 16, 1847; Cyrus Woodman to Elihu B. Washburne, Dec. 17, 1847, in Cyrus Woodman Papers; Gara, *Westernized Yankee,* p. 79.

17. Cyrus Woodman to Rogers & Woodman, Feb. 16, 1848; Cyrus Woodman to Jacob B. Merrick, Jan. 10, July 5, 1849; Cyrus Woodman to John S. Hayward, July 5, 1849; Cyrus Woodman to Cadwallader Washburn, Nov. 23, 1849; Cyrus Woodman to Elihu B. Washburne, March 19, 1850; Cyrus Woodman to J. H. Birch & Co., July 1, 1850; Cadwallader Washburn to Cyrus Woodman, July 9, 1850; and Cadwallader Washburn to Jacob B. Merrick, Nov. 2, 1850, all in Cyrus Woodman Papers.

18. Lebergott, *The Americans,* chap. 7; Circular of J. W. Clark & Co., Nov. 24, 1855; Circular of Sweeney, Rittenhouse & Fant, Nov. 27, 1855; Hamilton G. Fant to James S. Easley, Jan. 15, 1856, in Incoming Correspondence, James S. Easley Papers, box 61, reel 299. See also *Thompson's,* March 19, 1859.

19. Cyrus Woodman to John S. Hayward, Aug. 10, 1847, Cyrus Woodman Papers; *Congressional Globe,* 31st Cong., 1st sess., pp. 1999–2000.

20. The average used for the calculations on holding time is the median and is derived as follows: interval between General Land Office issue date and assignment date, minus four days for mailing. See also *Congressional Globe,* 29th Cong., 2d sess., p. 195.

21. Zebulon Harmon Papers, Maine Historical Society, Vol. 52, pp. 75–76.

22. Ibid., box 1, file 1.

23. Francis Dickins Papers, Virginia Historical Society, items 49–54, 96, Section A.

24. McCalla to Catherine Graham, Aug. 18, 1855 in Letterpress Copybooks, McCalla Papers, Duke University. Cyrus Woodman to Elihu B. Washburne, June 22, 1847, in Cyrus Woodman Papers.

25. McCalla to Jesse Griffith, June 2, 1855, McCalla Papers; P. M. Henry to H. C. Alexander, Sept. 11, 1860, in William E. Smith Papers, Duke University; for another broker's fee scales, see the December 1851 circular of the Boston agent Eber Smith in vol. 67, Harmon Papers.

26. Harmon Papers, vol. 52, pp. 75–76.

27. Ibid., file 12, box 15.

28. Ibid.

29. Folder 10A, box 1, Woodbridge Mercantile Company Papers, West Virginia University. Woodbridge issued circulars and placed ads in local Ohio Valley newspapers such as the November 1850 issues of the Parkersburg (Va.) *Gazette.* See also vol. 56 of the Woodbridge Papers.

30. Entry of July 23, 1853, in vol. 89, Woodbridge Papers.

31. Cyrus Woodman to John S. Hayward, Feb. 6, 1848, Cyrus Woodman Papers.

32. The revenue and expenditure calculations are derived from the sales information in file 12, box 15, and vols. 41, 52, and 73, Harmon Papers.

33. Vol. 67, Harmon Papers; and see *Thompson's,* 1857 and 1859 issues, passim.

34. Vol. 67, Harmon Papers.

35. Ibid.

36. Ibid.

37. Harmon to Green & Sewell Co., Nov. 9, 1856, file 12, box 15; see also the list of warrant buyers in vol. 71, Harmon Papers. For a short history of Green & Sewell, one of Bradford & Harmon's largest customers, see *Thompson's,* Oct. 15, 1859.

38. Speech of Richard Brodhead in *Congressional Globe,* 34th Cong., 1st sess., p. 928.

CHAPTER 6

1. *New York Herald,* March 30, 1855. The standard summary of the National Reformers' view on land monopoly remains Zahler, *Eastern Workingmen and National Land Policy;* see also Ray Allen Billington, "The Origin of the Land Speculator as a Frontier Type." Reginald Horsman has restated this view, or at least called for a fuller restatement, in his "Changing Images of the Public Domain." Edward Rastatter forcefully defends the speculator in his appropriately titled "The Case for the Speculator," in Klingaman and Vedder, eds., *Essays on Nineteenth Century Economic History.* See also Stanley Lebergott, "The Demand for Land"; Robert W. Fogel and Jack Ruttner, "The Efficiency Effects of Federal Land Policy, 1850–1900: A Report of Some Provisional Findings"; R. Taylor Dennen, "Some Efficiency Aspects of Nineteenth Century Federal Land Policy: A Dynamic Analysis"; Peter Passell, "Essays in the Economics of Nineteenth Century American Land Policy"; Robert Swierenga, "Land Speculation and Its Impact on American Economic Growth and Welfare."

2. Young, "Congress Looks West," pp. 77–96; Swierenga, *Pioneers and Profits,* pp. 217–20; Bogue, *From Prairie to Cornbelt,* pp. 42–46.

3. The researcher interested in tracing public lands locators by land district should consult the Abstracts of Cash Entry and the Abstracts of Military Bounty Land Warrant Entry, both in Record Group 49, Records of the Bureau of Land Management, National Archives.

4. Two of the Washburn brothers' land warrant purchases appear in the sample: act of 1847, 52,700 for 160 acres (Elihu, who spelled his last name "Washburne"), and act of 1847 6,305 for forty acres (Israel). See also John Wentworth, *Congressional Reminiscences,* p. 52; Larry Gara, *Westernized Yankee,* chaps. 2–4; in general, see Paul Gates, "Frontier Land Business in Wisconsin."

5. Cyrus Woodman to A. C. Lombard, Aug. 11, 1847; Cyrus Woodman to John S. Hayward, Nov. 13, 1847, in Cyrus Woodman Papers; Gara, *Westernized Yankee,* p. 77; Robert F. Dalzell, Jr., *Enterprising Elite: The Boston Associates and the World They Made,* chap. 4; Lawrence M. Friedman, "The Usury Laws of Wisconsin: A Study in Legal and Social History."

6. Cyrus Woodman to John S. Hayward, Feb. 15, 1848; Cyrus Woodman to Woodward & Dusenberry, Dec. 31, 1847; Cyrus Woodman to Jacob B. Merrick, Jan. 18, 1848, in Cyrus Woodman Papers.

7. Ibid., Cyrus Woodman to Aziel Chandler, Aug. 29, 1847; Gara, *Westernized Yankee,* pp. 93–95.

8. Cyrus Woodman to Jacob B. Merrick, Jan. 18, 1848; Cyrus Woodman to Henry Hubbard, Jan. 3, 1849; Cyrus Woodman to John S. Hayward, July 5, 1849, in Cyrus Woodman Papers.

9. Ibid., Cyrus Woodman to G. W. Washburn, July 18, 1849; Cyrus Woodman to Henry Hubbard, March 7, 1849; Cyrus Woodman to Cadwallader Washburn, Dec. 5, 1849, and April 19, 1852; Friedman, "The Usury Laws of Wisconsin," pp. 544–46.

10. Cyrus Woodman to John Burt, Dec. 6, 1847, in Cyrus Woodman Papers.

11. Ibid., Cyrus Woodman to Woodward & Dusenberry, May 1, 1849; Cyrus Woodman to Jacob B. Merrick, Nov. 23, 1849; Gara, *Westernized Yankee,* pp. 103–7.

12. Cyrus Woodman to Cadwallader Washburn, Nov. 10, 1849; Cyrus Woodman to Warren Brewster, June 25, 1849, in Cyrus Woodman Papers.

13. Ibid., Cyrus Woodman to Rogers & Woodman, April 2, April 16, and April 30, 1851; Cyrus Woodman to John L. Redman, March 11, 1852; Cyrus Woodman to William Turbell, Feb. 15, 1852; Cyrus Woodman to Thomas Douglas, Jr., April 2,

1852; Cyrus Woodman to Alexander Ostrander, April 28, 1852; Cyrus Woodman to Ole Knudsen, April 28, 1852.

14. Paul Gates, *The Illinois Central and its Colonization Work,* p. 113; Gates, "Research in the History of the Public Lands," p. 38; Bogue, *From Prairie to Cornbelt,* pp. 39–46.

15. Cook & Sargent circular, Oct. 15, 1850, in W. W. Corcoran Papers, Library of Congress (photocopy supplied courtesy of Robert Swierenga, Kent State University); and see Swierenga, *Pioneers and Profits,* pp. 110–12.

16. *Portrait and Biographical Record of Jefferson and Van Buren Counties, Iowa,* p. 656. Again, Professor Swierenga kindly provided a photocopy of this reference; see also *Pioneers and Profits,* pp. 112–13, App. 5.

17. See Preston's advertisement in the March 19, 1855, *New York Times;* Lucille Kane, "Federal Protection of Public Timber in the Upper Great Lakes States," in Carstensen, ed., *The Public Lands,* pp. 439–47; for warrants used in postwar timber speculations, see below, n. 49.

18. James B. Hedges, *The Browns of Providence Plantation: The Nineteenth Century,* chap. 12.

19. Gates, "Southern Investments in Northern Lands."

20. Swierenga, *Pioneers and Profits,* chap. 7; Casady & Test to James S. Easley, Dec. 2, 1855, box 61, reel 299, in James S. Easley Papers.

21. Calculated from land warrant ledgers, journals, and daybooks in the James S. Easley Papers, box 60, reel 298.

22. Swierenga, *Pioneers and Profits,* pp. 149–51; Allan Bogue, "Land Credit for Northern Farmers, 1789–1940"; Friedman, "The History of Usury Laws in Wisconsin," pp. 522–26.

23. Cook, Downey & Sargent to James S. Easley, Aug. 16, 1853; William J. Barney to Easley & Willingham, Feb. 15, 1854; in James S. Easley Papers, Incoming Correspondence, box 61, reel 299; see also the warrant ledgers in box 60, reel 298.

24. W. T. Smithson to James S. Easley, Sept. 17, 1857; Rider & White to James S. Easley, Jan. 22, 1858; Circular of J. Orr (Greene Co., Iowa), Nov. 1, 1859; all in James S. Easley Papers, box 61, reel 299.

25. For Sherman, see act of 1847, 4,766, 160 acres; for Brodhead, see act of 1850, 51,175, forty acres; for Dix, see act of 1852, 7,683, forty acres; and for Slidell, see act of 1855, 66,785, 120 acres, and 53,306 for 160 acres. For Stokes, see Gates, "Southern Investments in Northern Lands," p. 170. See also Gates, "The Struggle for Land and the Irrepressible Conflict," pp. 250–51; Henry Cohen, *Business and Politics in America from the Age of Jackson to the Civil War,* p. 209; on Belmont and Slidell, see Irving Katz, *August Belmont: A Political Biography;* Summers, *The Plundering Generation,* p. 240.

26. See the ads the Fants, Jr. and Sr., placed in the Aug. 13, 1859, issue of *Thompson's Bank Note and Commercial Reporter;* Ellis P. Oberholtzer, *Jay Cooke, Financier of the Civil War,* 1:91, briefly discusses the Cookes' real estate ventures in western land before the war. See also Henrietta Larson, *Jay Cooke, Private Banker,* pp. 75–77.

27. Pitt Cooke to Jay Cooke, Oct. 22, 1855; and Pitt Cooke to Jay Cooke, April 13, 1856, in Jay Cooke Papers, Historical Society of Pennsylvania. On warrant prices in the summer of 1855, see Horatio Woodman to Cyrus Woodman, July 25, 1855, and George Woodman to Cyrus Woodman, July 17 and November 6, 1855, in Cyrus Woodman Papers, State Historical Society of Wisconsin.

28. Pitt Cooke to Jay Cooke, Nov. 5, 11, 1855, Jay Cooke Papers.

29. Pitt Cooke to Jay Cooke, Dec. 12, 1855, March 29, 1856; on the maneuverings in Chickasaw County, see circular to "People of Chickasaw County, Iowa," April 7,

1856, in Jay Cooke Papers; see also Pitt Cooke to Jay Cooke, July 20, 1856, Jay Cooke Papers.

30. Pitt Cooke to Jay Cooke, August 13, 1856, Jay Cooke Papers.

31. Pitt Cooke to Jay Cooke, May 4, 1855, Jay Cooke Papers.

32. Pitt Cooke to Jay Cooke, May 4, 1855, Jay Cooke Papers; another perspective on the time-entry business is found in the Papers of Easley & Willingham, University of Virginia, especially Series E ledgers for 1852–57.

33. Jason Easton to Le Huray & Co., May 12, Oct. 6, 1857, in Jason Easton Papers, Minnesota Historical Society. See also Jost, "An Entrepreneurial Study of a Frontier Financier," chap. 1. The interest rates cited in this passage and the following paragraphs sound very high to the modern reader, but in the imperfect capital market of the nineteenth century, high-risk borrowers paid a correspondingly high premium. Similar rates, e.g., were charged the freedmen in the postbellum South. See Roger Ransom and Richard Sutch, *One Kind of Freedom*, pp. 128–31.

34. Easton as cited in Jost, "An Entrepreneurial Study," p. 11. See also Easton to Taylor, Bennet & Co., Jan. 30, 1857; Easton to F. S. Nichols, April 28, 1857; calculations about Easton's land warrant business are based on a study of his warrant business journals; see esp. vol. 518, Easton Papers.

35. *Thompson's*, April 9, 1859; Gates, *Fifty Million Acres: Conflicts over Land Allotments in Kansas*, pp. 74–77; for the land policy of the Buchanan years, see Roy Nichols, *Disruption of the American Democracy*, p. 323; Richard Current, *The History of Wisconsin: The Civil War Era, 1848–1873*, pp. 108–10; Johnson, *Order upon the Land*, pp. 127–140; Robbins, *Our Landed Heritage*, chap. 5. For the 1855 act, 287 warrants out of the total of 1,315 were used by preemptors. Multiplied by the sample size of one in two hundred, this projects out to over 57,000 preemptors.

36. Gates, "The Struggle for Land and the Irrepressible Conflict," pp. 248–71; Dick, *The Lure of the Land*, chaps. 5, 7; *Thompson's Bank Note and Commercial Reporter*, May 2, Aug. 20, Oct. 22, 1859.

37. The Registers of Declaratory Statements are arranged by land office in RG 49, Records of the Bureau of Land Management, National Archives. See also Jason Easton to F. S. Nichols, April 28, 1857, Easton Papers, Minnesota Historical Society.

38. Gates, *History of Public Land Law Development*, pp. 238–40; Robbins, *Our Landed Heritage*, pp. 89–91. Act of September 4, 1841, 5 *Statutes*, pp. 453–58.

39. I drew a 1 percent sample of the 60,000 squatters from the eight land office Registers of Declaratory Statements listed in table 26. I next took the sample and checked each squatter's parcel against the original entrant listed in the "tract books" compiled by the General Land Office for Wisconsin and Minnesota. The one hundred plus tract books for each state are organized by range, township, section, and within each section, down to the forty-acre level. The tract books (of which there is a set at the National Archives and at each state archive for public lands states) list the original entrant, extent of acreage, method of entry (i.e., cash or warrant), date of entry, and date of patent issue. The Wisconsin tract books are part of Record Series 1673, Wisconsin Local Office Tract Books, 1835–1909, State Historical Society of Wisconsin; for the comparable series of land office tract books in Minnesota, see Microfilm Series U.S. 46, Minnesota Historical Society.

40. The warrant files contain the proof statements of squatters demonstrating the extent of improvements made to the preempted parcels. The proof statements, although not uniform for all land offices, do give some biographical details about squatters. Each land office devised its own forms and contracted the printing out to a local business. In Minnesota, the most detailed proof forms were the ones required

at the Minneapolis office, while the Chatfield forms asked for the least amount of evidence on improvements to the land, housing characteristics, and family background of the squatter.

41. For the story of Jonas Brown, see Register of Declaratory Statements 217, Eau Claire Land District, and warrant file under act of 1855, 32,744, 160 acres, and Census of 1860, Population Schedule, Eau Claire County, Wisconsin, Bridge Creek Township, p. 85; for Rathburn, who ultimately failed to gain title to his parcel, see Register of Declaratory Statements 6,992, La Crosse Land District, and Census of 1860, Population Schedule, Monroe County, Wisconsin, Leon Township, p. 70.

42. See Current, *History of Wisconsin*, pp. 42–48; Joseph Schafer, "The Yankee and the Teuton in Wisconsin"; John Gjerde, *From Peasants to Farmers: the Migration from Balestrand, Norway, to the Upper Midwest.*

43. Peno's story may be followed in warrant file under act of 1855, 42,918, 160 acres.

44. The Wage family proof statement is in act of 1855, 45,804, 160 acres.

45. The rate of homesteaders remaining on their land long enough to fulfill the requirements of the law to gain title was about 50 percent in the 1880s. See *Historical Statistics*, p. 429; Gates, *History of Public Land Law Development*, pp. 401–17.

46. Minnesota took a territorial census in 1857 in anticipation of statehood. I am at work at tracing the Minnesota preemptors in this earlier census as part of another study.

47. The persisting preemptors found in the 1860 Census numbered 176 out of the original 600. The figures discussed in this paragraph are based on an analysis of the 176 preemptors and their families.

48. I used the statistical technique of discriminant analysis to further study the differences between persisting preemptors who gained title and persisting preemptors who did not. The results, displayed in part below, show a weak ability of the function to separate the two groups but point to significant differences in wealth and age:

Indendent	*Group Means*		*Understandardized*	
Variable	*Title—Yes*	*Title—No*	*Coefficient*	*(F)*
Total estate ($)	2,073	992	.0002	(5.03)*
Squatters' age	39.43	35.98	.0271	(3.13)*
Marital status	1.01	1.05	−1.896	(2.20)
Children in 1860	2.96	2.39	.1559	(2.07)

*significant at the .05 level.
NOTE: Marital status was coded as 0 = married, 1 = single.

49. Paul W. Gates, *The Wisconsin Pine Lands of Cornell University;* Thomas LeDuc, "State Disposal of Agricultural College Land Scrip"; Gates, *History of Public Land Law Development*, pp. 417–18; Gara, *Westernized Yankee*, p. 165; Robert Fries, *Empire in Pine: The Story of Lumbering in Wisconsin;* Duane Fischer, "The Disposal of Federal Lands in the Eau Claire Land District of Wisconsin, 1848–1925"; Dale Peterson, "Lumbering on the Chippewa."

CHAPTER 7

1. Hibbard, *History of Public Land Policies*, p. 125; Gates, *History of Public Land Law Development*, p. 281, echoes Hibbard's condemnation.

2. See *House Executive Document* 95, 33d Cong., 2d sess., Serial Set 790.

3. Historians now believe that an "agricultural ladder" existed in the mid-nineteenth century where young men started their work lives as tenants and saved to buy a farm in mid-life. This gives tenancy a much different and less offensive character than that portrayed by Gates and others. See Seddie Cogswell, "Tenure, Nativity and Age as Factors in Iowa Agriculture, 1850–1880"; Donald Winters, *Farmers without Farms: Agricultural Tenancy in Nineteenth Century Iowa*.

4. See Gates, "Charts of Public Land Sales and Entries"; and Gates, "The Struggle for Land"; see also *Thompson's*, Aug. 6, 20, and Oct. 8, 1859.

5. See the petition of Cornelius Coffey for testimony on the power of land warrants as recruiting device in Accession 33A-H19, RG 46, Records of the Senate, National Archives.

6. The sample of warrants shows, when analyzed by war service of the veteran, that about 35 million acres were granted to War of 1812 veterans and heirs; 0.6 million acres to veterans and the heirs of veterans of conflicts before 1812 (e.g., Wayne's War); 0.4 million acres to militiamen in the Canadian border controversies of 1837–39; 16.4 million acres on the basis of Mexican War service; and 7.7 million acres to veterans of various Indian wars after 1815. Because of GLO cancellations, the war service of some veterans is not included in the above distribution.

7. *Historical Statistics*, p. 165. Horace Greeley estimated that about $150 could keep a family of four alive in New York for half a year; cited in Norman Ware, *The Industrial Worker, 1820–1860*, pp. 31–34.

8. *Historical Statistics*, p. 433, and the data from tables 1 and 15, above.

9. Arthur H. Cole, "Cyclical and Sectional Variations in the Sale of Public Lands, 1815–1860"; Gates, "Charts and Entries of Public Land Sales and Entries," pp. 22–28.

10. Schoene, "The Economics of U.S. Public Land Policy Prior to 1860," p. 174.

11. Schoene found that the price of public land was very inelastic, but he measured only up from the minimum price of $1.25. That is, he looked only for evidence of elasticity in land prices at public auction. Studying land prices by way of warrant prices introduces an element of elasticity below the minimum price.

12. Appendix D takes up in greater detail the calculations surrounding table 27.

13. See Richard Steckel, "Economic Foundations of East-West Migration during the Nineteenth Century"; his "Census Matching and Migration: A Research Strategy"; John Hudson, "Migration to an American Frontier"; McClelland and Zeckhauser, *Demographic Dimensions of the Early Republic*, chap. 4; and my "Westward Who?"

Sources Cited

PRIMARY SOURCES

Manuscript Collections

Association of Soldiers of the War of 1812 Papers, Western Pennsylvania Historical Society.
Baltimore Defenders' Association Papers, Maryland Historical Society.
James Bogert Papers, New York State Archives.
Kit Carson Papers, University of California-Berkeley.
Alfred Churchill Papers, Cornell University.
Connaroe Collection, Historical Society of Pennsylvania.
Jay Cooke Papers, Historical Society of Pennsylvania.
William W. Corcoran Papers, Library of Congress.
Ezra Cornell Papers, Cornell University.
Lewis Coryell Papers, Historical Society of Pennsylvania.
Aaron Dayton Papers, Historical Society of Pennsylvania.
Francis Dickins Papers, Virginia Historical Society.
James S. Easley Papers, University of Virginia.
Jason Easton Papers, Minnesota Historical Society.
Galt Papers, College of William and Mary.
Zebulon Harmon Papers, Maine Historical Society.
Isaac Hodsdon Papers, State Historical Society of Wisconsin.
Benjamin Chew Howard Papers, Maryland Historical Society.
John McCalla Papers, Duke University.
John K. Martin Papers, Duke University.
John K. Martin Papers, Virginia State Library.
William H. Seward Papers, University of Rochester.
William E. Smith Papers, Duke University.
Society of the War of 1812 Papers, Maryland Historical Society.
Alexander H. H. Stuart Papers, Virginia Historical Society.
Joel B. Sutherland File, University Archives, University of Pennsylvania.

Lawrence Taliaferro Papers, Minnesota Historical Society.
John B. Tweedy Papers, State Historical Society of Wisconsin.
Daniel Ullman Papers, New-York Historical Society.
Matthew Vassar, Jr., Papers, Adriance Public Library, Poughkeepsie, New York.
Matthew Vassar Papers, Vassar College.
Veteran Corps of the City of New York Papers, New-York Historical Society.
Woodbridge Mercantile Company Papers, West Virginia University.
Cyrus Woodman Papers, State Historical Society of Wisconsin.

United States Public Records

Commerce Department. *Historical Statistics of the United States, from Colonial Times to 1970.* Washington, D.C.: Government Printing Office, 1975.
———. *Statistical Abstract of the United States for 1989.* Washington, D.C.: Government Printing Office, 1989.

Federal Cases

General Land Office. Abstracts of Cash Entry. Record Group 49. Records of the Bureau of Land Management. National Archives.
———. Abstracts of Military Bounty Land Warrants Entry. Record Group 49. Records of the Bureau of Land Management. National Archives.
———. *Annual Report of the Commissioner.* Washington, D.C., 1848–1907. Printed in *Senate Executive Documents.*
———. *Forms and Regulations for the Assignment of Land Warrants and Locations.* Washington, D.C., 1852.
———. *Laws and Regulations respecting the Assignment, Location and Use of Bounty-Land Warrants.* Washington, D.C.: Government Printing Office, 1912.
———. Military Bounty Land Warrant Files. Acts of 1847, 1850, 1852, and 1855. Record Group 49. Records of the Bureau of Land Management. National Archives.
———. Miscellaneous Letters, Record Group 49. Records of the Bureau of Land Management, National Archives.
———. Register of Declaratory Statements. Record Group 49. Records of the Bureau of Land Management. National Archives.
———. Tract Books. Record Group 49. Records of the Bureau of Land Management. National Archives.
New American State Papers: Public Lands. Wilmington, Del.: Scholarly Resources, 1968.
Pension Bureau. *Annual Report of the Commissioner.* Washington, D.C., 1847–1870. Printed in *Senate Executive Documents.*
———. Applications for Bounty Land. Acts of 1847, 1850, 1852, and 1855. Record Group 15. Records of the Veterans' Administration. National Archives.

———. *Digest of Decisions and Opinions Relating to Pensions and Bounty Lands.* Washington, D.C.: Government Printing Office, 1897.

———. *Instructions and Forms to Be Observed by Persons Applying to the Pension Office for Bounty Land under the Act of March 3, 1855.* Washington, D.C., 1855.

———. *List of Military Bounty Land Warrants Cancelled and Suspended.* Washington, D.C., 1850.

Peters, Richard, ed. *Statutes at Large of the United States of America.* Boston, 1855–1873.

Richardson, James, ed. *Messages and Papers of the Presidents.* New York: Bureau of National Literature, 1912.

U.S. Congress. *Congressional Globe.* 29th–44th Congress. Washington, D.C., 1846–69.

U.S. House of Representatives. *House Executive Documents.*

———. *House Journal.*

———. *House Miscellaneous Documents.*

———. *House Reports.*

———. Petitions to the 33d Congress. Record Group 233. Records of the House of Representatives. National Archives.

U.S. Senate. Petitions to the 33d Congress. Record Group 46. Records of the Senate. National Archives.

———. *Senate Executive Documents.*

———. *Senate Journal.*

———. *Senate Miscellaneous Documents.*

———. *Senate Reports.*

State Public Records

Connecticut Adjutant General. *Record of Service of Connecticut Men in the War of the Revolution and War of 1812.* Hartford: Case, Lockwood & Brainard, 1889.

Hastings, Hugh. *Military Minutes of the New York Council of Appointments.* Albany: J. B. Lyon, 1902.

Marine, William M. *The British Invasion of Maryland.* Baltimore: Society of the War of 1812, 1913.

New Jersey Adjutant General. *Records of Officers and Men of New Jersey in Wars, 1791–1815.* Trenton: State Gazette Publishing, 1907.

North Carolina Adjutant General. *Muster Rolls of the Soldiers of the War of 1812.* Raleigh: Charles C. Raboteau, 1851.

Ohio Adjutant General. *Roster of Ohio Soldiers in the War of 1812.* Columbus: Edward T. Miller, 1916.

Pearson, Gardner W. *Records of the Massachusetts Volunteer Militia Called out by the Governor.* Boston: Wright & Potter, 1913.

Pennsylvania Adjutant General. *Muster Rolls of the Pennsylvania Volunteers in the War of 1812–14.* Baltimore: Genealogical Publishers, 1967.

Potter, Chandler E. *The Military History of New Hampshire.* Concord: McFarland & Jenks, 1869.

Quisenberry, Anderson C. *Kentucky in the War of 1812*. Frankfort: Kentucky State Historical Society, 1915.

Vermont Adjutant and Inspector General. *Roster of Soldiers in the War of 1812–14*. St. Albans: Messenger Press, 1933.

Virginia State Auditor. *Muster Rolls of the Virginia Militia in the War of 1812 Being a Supplement to the Pay Rolls Printed and Distributed in 1851*. Richmond: W. F. Ritchie, 1852.

———. *Pay Rolls of Militia Entitled to Land Bounty under the Act of Sept. 28, 1850*. Richmond: W. F. Ritchie, 1851.

Newspapers

Albany Evening Journal
Baltimore Sun
Louisville Daily Democrat
New Orleans Daily Picayune
New York Herald
New York Times
New York Tribune
Philadelphia Inquirer
Philadelphia North American
Philadelphia Public Ledger and Daily Transcript
Richmond Dispatch
Thompson's Bank Note and Commercial Reporter
Washington National Intelligencer

Printed Works

Basler, Roy, ed. *Collected Works of Abraham Lincoln*. New Brunswick, N.J.: Rutgers University Press, 1953.

Benton, Thomas Hart. *Thirty Years' View.* 2 vols. New York: D. Appleton, 1854–56.

Choate, Rufus. *Opinion of Hon. Rufus Choate in Relation to Land Warrants.* Boston, 1852.

Combs, Leslie, *Substance of an Address Made by General Leslie Combs to the Public Debt Committee of the Texas Legislature.* Austin: J. W. Hampton, 1854.

Committee of New York Association of Officers of the War of 1812. *To Officers of the Late War.* New York: W. A. Mercein, 1833.

Committee of the Officers of the War of 1812. *Bounty Lands to the Surviving Officers of the Late War of Second Independence.* New York: W. Grattan, 1826.

Haight, Nicholas. *Argument and Appeal in Behalf of the Remains of the Revolutionary Patriots.* New York: A. Baptist, 1854.

Ingersoll, Charles Jared. *History of the War of 1812*. 2 vols. Philadelphia, 1845–51.

Julian, George Washington. *Political Recollections, 1840 to 1872*. Chicago: Jansen, McClurg, 1889.

"Memoirs of Jonathan Roberts." In *Pennsylvania Magazine of History and Biography* 62 (1938): 502–51.
Peterson, Charles J. *Military Heroes of the War of 1812*. Philadelphia, 1852.
Porter, James Madison. *Eulogium on J. K. Polk*. Easton, Pa.: Sentinel, 1849.
Portrait and Biographical Album of Jefferson and Van Buren Counties, Iowa. Chicago: Lake City, 1890.
Portrait and Biographical Record of Lehigh, Northumberland and Carbon Counties, Pennsylvania. Chicago, 1894.
Proceedings of a Meeting in the City of Philadelphia of the Soldiers of the War of 1812 Praying a Modification of the Bounty Land Law. Philadelphia, 1853.
Proceedings of a Meeting of Officers and Soldiers Held at Poughkeepsie. Poughkeepsie, N.Y., 1854.
Proceedings of the Convention of the Soldiers of the War of 1812. Albany, N.Y., 1857.
Proceedings of the Convention of the United Brethren of the War of 1812. Washington, D.C., 1855.
Proceedings of the National Convention of the Soldiers of the War of 1812. Philadelphia, 1854.
Proceedings of the Soldiers of the War of 1812. Syracuse, N.Y., 1854.
Proceedings of the Soldiers of the War of 1812. Albany, N.Y., 1857.
Raff, George W. *Manual of Pensions, Bounty and Pay*. Cincinnati: Robert Clarke and Co., 1862.
Sutherland, Joel Barlow. *A Congressional Manual*, rev. ed. Philadelphia: P. Hay, 1841.
Van Pelt, Peter J. *A Discourse Delivered by Request of the Survivors of the Veteran Corps in the War of 1812*. New York: C. C. Childs, 1851.
Weed, Thurlow. *Memoirs of Thurlow Weed*. 2 vols. Boston: Houghton Mifflin, 1884.
Wentworth, John. *Congressional Reminiscences*. Chicago: Fergus, 1882.
Wilson, H. *Trow's New York City Directory*. New York, 1854, 1855, 1856.

SECONDARY SOURCES

Books, Articles, and Theses

Alexander, Thomas B. *Sectional Stress and Party Strength: A Study of Roll-Call Voting Patterns in the United States House of Representatives*. Knoxville: University of Tennessee Press, 1967.
Appleby, Joyce O. "Commercial Farming and the 'Agrarian Myth' in the Early Republic." *Journal of American History* 68 (1982): 833–49.
Atack, Jeremy, and Fred Bateman. *To Their Own Soil: Agriculture in the Antebellum North*. Ames: Iowa State University Press, 1987.
Barney, William. *The Passage of The Republic*. Lexington, Mass.: D. C. Heath, 1987.
Berger, Mark L. *The Revolution in New York Party Systems, 1840–1860*. Port Washington, N.Y.: Kennikat, 1973.

Billington, Ray Allen. "The Origin of the Land Speculator as a Frontier Type." *Agricultural History* 19 (1945): 204–12.

Bogue, Allan. *The Earnest Men: The Republicans of the Civil War Senate*. Ithaca, N.Y.: Cornell University Press, 1981.

———. *From Prairie to Cornbelt: Farming on the Illinois and Iowa Prairies in the Nineteenth Century*. Chicago: University of Chicago Press, 1963.

———. "Land Credit for Northern Farmers, 1789–1940." *Agricultural History* 50 (1976): 68–100.

———. "Members of the House of Representatives and the Processes of Modernization, 1789–1960." *Journal of American History* 63 (1976): 275–302.

Bogue, Allan, and Margaret B. Bogue. "'Profits' and Frontier Land Speculations." *Journal of Economic History* 17 (1957): 1–24.

Bradley, Erwin S. *Simon Cameron, Lincoln's Secretary of War: A Political Biography*. Philadelphia: University of Pennsylvania Press, 1966.

Buler, R. Carlyle. *The Old Northwest: Pioneer Period, 1815–1840*. Indianapolis: Indiana Historical Society, 1950.

Carlson, Theodore. *The Illinois Military Tract: A Study of Land Occupation, Utilization and Tenure*. Urbana: University of Illinois Press, 1951.

Carstensen, Vernon, ed. *The Public Lands*. Madison: University of Wisconsin Press, 1963.

Chambers, William N. *Old Bullion Benton*. Boston: Little, Brown, 1956.

Clawson, Marion, and Burnett Held. *The Federal Lands: Their Use and Management*. Baltimore: Johns Hopkins University Press, 1957.

Coffman, Edward. *The Old Army*. New York: Oxford University Press, 1987.

Cogswell, Seddie. "Tenure, Nativity and Age as Factors in Iowa Agriculture, 1850–1880." Ph.D. dissertation. University of Iowa, 1972.

Cohen, Henry. *Business and Politics in America from the Age of Jackson to the Civil War*. Westport, Conn.: Greenwood, 1971.

Cole, Arthur H. "Cyclical and Sectional Variations in the Sale of Public Lands, 1815–1860." *Review of Economic Statistics* 9 (1927): 41–53.

Coleman, John F. *The Disruption of the Pennsylvania Democracy, 1848–1868*. Harrisburg: Pennsylvania Historical and Museum Commission, 1975.

Condit, Uzal W. *The History of Easton Pennsylvania from the Earliest Times to the Present*. Easton, Pa.: G. W. West, 1887.

Cremin, Lawrence. *American Education: The National Experience*. New York: Harper & Row, 1980.

Cress, Lawrence. *Citizens in Arms: The Army and the Militia in American Society to the War of 1812*. Chapel Hill: University of North Carolina Press, 1982.

Cunliffe, Marcus. *Soldiers and Citizens: The Martial Spirit in America, 1775–1860*. Boston: Little, Brown, 1968.

Current, Richard. *History of Wisconsin: The Civil War Era, 1848–1873*. Madison: State Historical Society of Wisconsin, 1976.

Dalzell, Robert F., Jr. *Enterprising Elite: The Boston Associates and the World They Made*. Cambridge: Harvard University Press, 1987.

Danhof, Clarence. *Change in Northern Agriculture, 1820–1870*. Cambridge: Harvard University Press, 1970.

Dann, John. *The Revolution Remembered: Eyewitness Accounts of the American Revolution*. Chicago: University of Chicago Press, 1980.

Davies, Wallace E. *Patriotism on Parade: The Story of Veterans and Hereditary Organizations in America, 1783–1900*. Cambridge: Harvard University Press, 1955.

Dennen, R. Taylor. "Some Efficiency Effects of Nineteenth-Century Federal Land Policy: A Dynamic Analysis." *Agricultural History* 51 (1977): 718–36.

Dick, Everett. *The Lure of the Land: A Social History of the Public Lands from the Articles of Confederation to the New Deal*. Lincoln: University of Nebraska Press, 1970.

Dillingham, William P. *Federal Aid to Veterans, 1917–1941*. Gainesville: University of Florida Press, 1952.

Dillistin, William H. *Bank-Note Reporters and Counterfeit Detectors, 1826–1866*. New York: American Numismatic Society, 1949.

Donaldson, Thomas C. *The Public Domain: Its History with Statistics*. Washington, D.C.: Government Printing Office, 1884.

DuBois, James, and Gertrude Mathews. *Galusha Grow: Father of the Homestead Act*. Boston: Houghton Mifflin, 1917.

Feller, Daniel. *The Public Lands in Jacksonian Politics*. Madison: University of Wisconsin Press, 1984.

Fischer, Duane. "The Disposal of Federal Lands in the Eau Claire Land District of Wisconsin, 1848–1925." M. A. thesis. University of Wisconsin, 1961.

Fogel, Robert W., and Stanley L. Engerman. *The Reinterpretation of American Economic History*. New York: Harper & Row, 1971.

Fogel, Robert W., and Jack I. Ruttner. "The Efficiency Effects of Federal Land Policy, 1850–1900: A Report of Some Provisional Findings." In *The Dimensions of Quantitative Research in History*, ed. William O. Aydelotte et al. Princeton, N.J.: Princeton University Press, 1972.

Foner, Eric. *Free Soil, Free Labor, Free Men: The Ideology of the Republican Party before the Civil War*. New York: Oxford University Press, 1970.

———. *Reconstruction, 1863–1877*. New York: Harper & Row, 1988.

Forness, Norman O. "The Origins and Early History of the United States Department of the Interior." Ph.D. dissertation. Pennsylvania State University, 1964.

Freund, Rudolph. "Military Bounty Lands and the Origins of the Public Domain." *Agricultural History* 20 (1946): 8–18.

Friedman, Laurence M. "The Usury Laws of Wisconsin: A Study in Legal and Social History." *Wisconsin Law Review* 1963 (1963): 515–65.

Fries, Robert. *Empire in Pine: The Story of Lumbering in Wisconsin, 1830–1900*. Madison: State Historical Society of Wisconsin, 1951.

Gara, Larry. *Westernized Yankee: The Story of Cyrus Woodman*. Madison: State Historical Society of Wisconsin, 1956.

Gates, Paul W. "Charts of Public Land Sales and Entries." *Journal of Economic History* 24 (1964): 22–28.

———. *The Farmer's Age, 1815–1860*. New York: Harper & Row, 1960.
———. *Fifty Million Acres: Conflicts over Land Allotments in Kansas*. Ithaca, N.Y.: Cornell University Press, 1954.
———. "Frontier Land Business in Wisconsin." *Wisconsin Magazine of History* 53 (1969): 306–27.
———. *The Fruits of Land Speculation*. New York: Arno Press, 1979.
———. *History of Public Land Law Development*. Washington, D.C.: Government Printing Office, 1968.
———. "The Homestead Act in an Incongruous Land System." *American Historical Review* 41 (1936): 652–81.
———. *The Illinois Central and Its Colonization Work*. Cambridge: Harvard University Press, 1934.
———. "Research in the History of the Public Lands." *Agricultural History* 48 (1974): 31–50.
———. "The Role of the Land Speculator in Western Development." *Pennsylvania Magazine of History and Biography* 66 (1942): 314–33.
———. "Southern Investments in Northern Lands before the Civil War." *Journal of Southern History* 5 (1939): 155–85.
———. "The Struggle for Land and the Irrepressible Conflict." *Political Science Quarterly* 66 (1951): 248–71.
———. *The Wisconsin Pine Lands of Cornell University*. Ithaca, N.Y.: Cornell University Press, 1942.
Gienapp, William. *The Origins of the Republican Party*. New York: Oxford University Press, 1987.
Gjerde, Jon. *From Peasants to Farmers: The Migration from Balestrand, Norway, to the Upper Midwest*. New York: Cambridge University Press, 1985.
Glasson, William H. *Federal Military Pensions in the United States*. New York: Oxford University Press, 1918.
Goldin, Claudia, and Kenneth Sokoloff. "Women, Children and Industrialization in the Early Republic." *Journal of Economic History* 42 (1982): 741–74.
Graff, Harvey. *The Legacies of Literacy*. Bloomington: Indiana University Press, 1986.
———. *The Literacy Myth: Literacy and Social Structure in the Nineteenth Century City*. New York: Academic, 1979.
Gray, Lewis C. *History of Agriculture in the Southern United States to 1860*. 2 vols. Washington, D.C.: Carnegie Institution, 1932.
Gray, Susan. "Family, Land, and Credit: Yankee Communities on the Michigan Frontier, 1830–1860." Ph.D. dissertation. University of Chicago, 1985.
Griffis, William E. *Millard Fillmore: Constructive Statesman, Defender of the Constitution, President of the United States*. Ithaca, N.Y.: Cornell University Press, 1915.
Hahn, Steven, and Jonathan Prude, eds. *The Countryside in the Age of Capitalist Transformation*. Chapel Hill: University of North Carolina Press, 1985.

Hamilton, Holman. *Prologue to Conflict: The Crisis and Compromise of 1850.* Lexington: University of Kentucky Press, 1964.

Hammond, Bray. *Banks and Politics from the Revolution to the Civil War.* Princeton, N.J.: Princeton University Press, 1957.

Haney, Lewis. *Congressional History of Railroads.* 2 vols. Madison: University of Wisconsin Press, 1910.

Hedges, James B. *The Browns of Providence Plantation: The Nineteenth Century.* Providence: Brown University Press, 1968.

Herr, Pamela. *Jessie Benton Frémont.* New York: Franklin Watts, 1987.

Hibbard, Benjamin H. *History of the Public Land Policies.* New York: Macmillan, 1924.

Holt, Michael F. *The Political Crisis of the 1850s.* New York: John Wiley, 1978.

Hoover, Herbert. *Memoirs: The Cabinet and the Presidency, 1920–1933.* New York: Macmillan, 1952.

Horsman, Reginald. "Changing Images of the Public Domain: Historians and the Shaping of Midwest Frontiers." In *This Land of Ours: The Acquisition and Disposition of the Public Domain.* Bloomington: Indiana University Press, 1978.

———. *The Frontier in the Formative Era.* New York: John Wiley, 1970.

Howe, Daniel Walker. *The Political Culture of the American Whigs.* Chicago: University of Chicago Press, 1979.

Hudson, John. "Migration to an American Frontier." *Annals of the Association of American Geographers* 66 (1976): 242–65.

Hutchinson, William. "The Bounty Lands of the American Revolution." Ph.D. dissertation. University of Chicago, 1927.

Johanssen, Robert. *To the Halls of Montezuma: The Mexican War in the American Imagination.* New York: Oxford University Press, 1985.

Johnson, Hildegard B. *Order upon the Land: The U.S. Rectangular Land Survey and the Upper Mississippi Country.* New York: Oxford University Press, 1976.

Jones, Alice Hanson. *Wealth of a Nation to Be.* New York: Columbia University Press, 1978.

Jost, Robert R. "An Entrepreneurial Study of a Frontier Financier." Ph.D. dissertation. University of Minnesota, 1957.

Katz, Irving. *August Belmont: A Political Biography.* New York: Columbia University Press, 1968.

Klein, Phillip S. *President James Buchanan: A Biography.* State College: Pennsylvania State University Press, 1962.

Klingaman, David, and Richard Vedder, eds. *Essays on Nineteenth Century Economic History.* Athens: Ohio University Press, 1975.

Kreidberg, Marvin A., and Merton G. Henry. *History of Military Mobilization in the United States Army, 1775–1945.* Washington, D.C.: Government Printing Office, 1955.

Larson, Henrietta. *Jay Cooke, Private Banker.* Cambridge: Harvard University Press, 1936.

Lebergott, Stanley. *The Americans: An Economic Record*. New York: W. W. Norton, 1984.

———. "The Demand for Land: The United States, 1820–1860." *Journal of Economic History* 45 (1985): 181–212.

LeDuc, Thomas. "State Disposal of Agricultural College Land Scrip." *Agricultural History* 28 (1954): 99–107.

Lee, Lawrence B. "American Public Land History: A Review Essay." *Agricultural History* 55 (1981): 284–99.

Levitan, Sar, and Karen Cleary. *Old Wars Remain Unfinished: The Veterans' Benefits System*. Baltimore: Johns Hopkins University Press, 1973.

McClelland, Peter, and Richard Zeckhauser. *Demographic Dimensions of the Early Republic*. New York: Cambridge University Press, 1982.

McCusker, John, and Russell Menard. *The Economy of British America, 1607–1789*. Chapel Hill: University of North Carolina Press, 1985.

McPherson, James. *Battle Cry of Freedom: The Era of the Civil War.* New York: Oxford University Press, 1988.

Mahon, John K. *History of the Militia and National Guard*. New York: Macmillan, 1983.

———. *The War of 1812*. New York: Macmillan, 1971.

Malone, Dumas, ed. *Dictionary of American Biography.*

Maxwell, Richard S. "The Public Land Records of the Federal Government, 1850–1900 and their Statistical Significance." *National Archives Reference Information Paper no. 57*, 1963.

Meyers, Marvin. *The Jacksonian Persuasion*. Stanford, Calif.: Stanford University Press, 1959.

Miller, Thomas. *National Cyclopedia of American Biography.* New York: James T. White, 1891.

Miller, Thomas L. *The Public Lands of Texas, 1519–1970*. Norman: University of Oklahoma Press, 1972.

Nichols, Roy Franklin. *Blueprints for Leviathan: American Style*. New York: Atheneum, 1963.

———. *The Disruption of the American Democracy.* New York: Macmillan, 1948.

———. *Franklin Pierce: Young Hickory of the Granite Hills*. Philadelphia: University of Pennsylvania Press, 1931.

Oberholtzer, Ellis P. *Jay Cooke, Financier of the Civil War.* 2 vols. Philadelphia: George W. Jacobs, 1907.

Oberly, James W. "Information Policy in an Era of Illiteracy: The U.S. Pension Bureau before the Civil War." *Government Publications Review* 14 (1987): 287–94.

———. "Westward Who? Estimates of Native White Migration after the War of 1812." *Journal of Economic History* 46 (1986): 431–40.

O'Callaghan, Jerry. "The War Veteran and the Public Lands." *Agricultural History* 28 (1954): 163–68.

Opie, John. *The Law of the Land*. Lincoln: University of Nebraska Press, 1987.

Paludan, Phillip. *"A People's Contest": The Union and Civil War.* New York: Harper & Row, 1988.

Passell, Peter. "Essays in the Economics of Nineteenth Century American Land Policy." Ph.D. dissertation. Yale University, 1970.

Perkins, Edwin. *The Economy of Colonial America.* New York: Columbia University Press, 1980.

Peterson, Clarence S. *Known Military Dead during the Mexican War.* Baltimore, 1957.

Peterson, Dale. "Lumbering on the Chippewa." Ph.D. dissertation. University of Minnesota, 1970.

Porter, Kirk H., ed. *National Party Platforms, 1840–1960.* Urbana: University of Illinois Press, 1961.

Potter, David. *The Impending Crisis.* New York: Harper & Row, 1976.

Poulson, Barry. *Economic History of the United States.* New York: Macmillan, 1981.

Ransom, Roger, and Richard Sutch. *One Kind of Freedom.* New York: Cambridge University Press, 1977.

Remini, Robert V. *Andrew Jackson and the Course of American Freedom.* New York: Harper & Row, 1981.

———. *Andrew Jackson and the Course of American Democracy.* New York: Harper & Row, 1984.

Reynolds, Clifford P., ed. *Biographical Directory of the American Congress, 1774–1961.* Washington, D.C.: Government Printing Office, 1961.

Richardson, James, ed. *Messages and Papers of the Presidents.* Vol. 5. New York: Bureau of National Literature, 1912.

Risjord, Norman. *Chesapeake Politics, 1781–1800.* New York: Columbia University Press, 1978.

Robbins, Roy M. *Our Landed Heritage: The Public Domain, 1776–1936.* Princeton, N.J.: Princeton University Press, 1942.

Rohrbough, Malcolm. *The Land Office Business.* New York: Oxford University Press, 1968.

———. *The Trans-Appalachian Frontier.* New York: Oxford University Press, 1978.

Ross, David R. B. *Preparing for Ulysses: Politics and Veterans during World War II.* New York: Columbia University Press, 1968.

Schafer, Joseph. "The Yankee and the Teuton in Wisconsin." *Wisconsin Magazine of History* 6 (1923): 125–45.

Schoene, Stephen W. "The Economics of U.S. Public Land Policy Prior to 1860." Ph.D. dissertation. University of North Carolina, 1981.

Schultz, Constance B. "Revolutionary War Pension Applications: An Overview." In Timothy Walch, ed. *Our Family, Our Town: Essays on Family and Local History Sources in the National Archives.* Washington, D.C.: National Archives, 1987.

Severo, Richard, and Lewis Milford. *The Wages of War: When America's Soldiers Came Home—From Valley Forge to Vietnam.* New York: Simon and Schuster, 1989.

Shanks, Bernard. *This Land Is Your Land*. San Francisco: Sierra Club, 1984.

Silbey, Joel H. *The Partisan Imperative: The Dynamics of American Politics before the Civil War.* New York: Oxford University Press, 1985.

Singletary, Otis A. *The Mexican War.* Chicago: University of Chicago Press, 1960.

Soltow, Lee. *Men and Wealth in the United States, 1850–1870*. New Haven, Conn: Yale University Press, 1975.

Soltow, Lee, and Edward Stevens. *The Rise of Literacy and the Common School in the United States*. Chicago: University of Chicago Press, 1981.

Stagg, J. C. A. "Enlisted Men in the United States Army, 1812–1815: A Preliminary Survey." *William and Mary Quarterly,* 3d ser. 43 (1986): 615–45.

Steckel, Richard. "Census Matching and Migration: A Research Strategy." *Historical Methods* 21 (1988): 52–60.

———. "Economic Foundations of East-West Migration during the Nineteenth Century." *Explorations in Economic History* 20 (1983): 14–36.

Stegmaier, Mark. "The U.S. Senate in the Sectional Crisis, 1848–1861: Roll-Call Voting Analysis." Ph.D. dissertation. University of California, Santa Barbara, 1973.

Stephenson, George. *Political History of the Public Lands, 1840–1862*. Boston: Houghton Mifflin, 1917.

Summers, Mark. *The Plundering Generation: Corruption and the Crisis of the Union, 1849–1861*. New York: Oxford University Press, 1987.

Sutherland, Charles. *A Memoir of the Life and Services of Joel Barlow Sutherland, First President of the Society of the War of 1812*. Washington, D.C., 1894.

Swierenga, Robert. "Land Speculation and Its Impact on American Economic Growth and Welfare." *Western Historical Quarterly* 8 (1977): 283–302.

———. *Pioneers and Profits: Land Speculation on the Iowa Frontier.* Ames: Iowa State University Press, 1968.

Turner, Frederick Jackson. *The Frontier in American History.* New York: Henry Holt, 1920.

———. *The United States, 1830–1850. The Nation and Its Sections*. New York: Henry Holt, 1935.

Turner, Laura Censer, ed. *The Papers of Frederick Law Olmstead*. vol. 4. Baltimore: Johns Hopkins University Press, 1986.

Van Atta, Jerry. "Securing the West: Public Lands and Political Economy in America, 1784 to 1841." Ph.D. dissertation. University of Virginia, 1982.

Van Deusen, Glyndon G. *Thurlow Weed, Wizard of the Lobby.* Boston: Little, Brown, 1947.

———. *William Henry Seward*. New York: Oxford University Press, 1967.

Walch, Timothy. *Our Family, Our Town: Essays on Family and Local History Sources in the National Archives*. Washington, D.C.: National Archives, 1987.

Ware, Norman. *The Industrial Worker, 1820–1860*. 2d ed. Chicago: University of Chicago Press, 1964.

Weber, Gustavus A. *The Bureau of Pensions: Its History, Activities, and Organization*. Baltimore: Johns Hopkins University Press, 1923.

Weigley, Russell F. *History of the United States Army*. New York: Macmillan, 1967.

Wellington, Raynor G. *The Political and Sectional Influence of the Public Lands*. Cambridge, Mass.: Riverside, 1914.

Wesley, Edgar B. *Guarding the Frontier: A Study of Frontier Defense from 1815 to 1825*. Minneapolis: University of Minnesota Press, 1935.

White, Leonard D. *The Jacksonians: A Study in Administrative History*. New York: Macmillan, 1954.

Wilburn, Jean. *Biddle's Bank*. New York: Columbia University Press, 1966.

Wilson, Dorothy Clarke. *Stranger and Traveler: The Story of Dorothea Dix, American Reformer*. Boston: Little, Brown, 1975.

Wilson, Major L. *Space, Time, and Freedom: The Quest for Nationality and the Irrepressible Conflict 1815–1861*. Westport, Conn.: Greenwood, 1974.

Winters, Donald. *Farmers without Farms: Agricultural Tenancy in Nineteenth Century Iowa*. Westport, Conn.: Greenwood, 1978.

Wolff, Gerald. "The Kansas-Nebraska Bill and Congressional Voting Behavior in the Thirty-third Congress." Ph.D. dissertation. University of Iowa, 1969.

Woloch, Isser. *The French Veteran from the Revolution to the Restoration*. Chapel Hill: University of North Carolina Press, 1979.

Yoshpe, Harry, and Philip Brower. *Preliminary Inventory of the Land-Entry Papers of the General Land Office*. Washington, D.C.: National Archives Publication no. 49–30, 1949.

Young, James. *The Washington Community, 1800–1828*. New York: Columbia University Press, 1968.

Young, Mary. "Congress Looks West: Liberal Ideology and Public Land Policy in the Nineteenth Century." In David Ellis, ed. *The Frontier in American Development: Essays in Honor of Paul W. Gates*. Ithaca, N.Y.: Cornell University Press, 1969.

Zahler, Helene S. *Eastern Workingmen and National Land Policy, 1829–1862*. New York: Columbia University Press, 1941.

Zaslowsky, Dyan. *These American Lands: Parks, Wilderness and the Public Lands*. New York: H. Holt, 1986.

Index